REVERSE OF A BRONZE AS OF THE EM-
PEROR NERO SHOWING THE TEMPLE OF
JANUS WITH A CLOSED DOOR ON THE
RIGHT — COMMEMORATING NERO'S
SYMBOLIC GESTURE TO SIGNIFY PEACE
THROUGHOUT THE EMPIRE.

REVERSE OF A TETRADRACHON ISSUED
DURING THE REIGN OF THE EMPEROR
PROBUS — DEPICTING THE GODDESS OF
PEACE, EIRENE, OR PAX, WHO HOLDS AN
OLIVE BRANCH IN HER RIGHT HAND AND A
SCEPTRE IN HER LEFT.

REVERSE OF BRONZE AS OF THE EM-
PEROR NERO SHOWING THE ARA PACUS
(THE ALTAR OF PEACE).

Peace
in the Ancient World

Matthew Melko and *Richard D. Weigel*

with the collaboration of
Sally L.D. Katary and *Michael McKenny*

Maps by *Richard Ward*

Jefferson, N.C..
McFarland & Company, Inc., Publishers
1981

Library of Congress Cataloging in Publication Data

Melko, Matthew.
Peace in the ancient world.

Bibliography: p.
Includes index.
1. History, Ancient. 2. Peace.
I. Weigel, Richard, 1945- joint author.
II. Title.
D62.M44   930   80-20434

ISBN 0-89950-020-X

Manufactured in the United States of America

McFarland & Company, Inc., Publishers
Box 611, Jefferson, North Carolina 28640

Acknowledgments

Thanks to all the people we should have remembered but neglected to mention, who were willing along the way to discuss a point in the hallway, to suggest a possible reference for a problem, who raised an eyebrow at the criteria, who asked how the manuscript was going, who didn't put us down.

To Betty Snow, who did most of the typing, who suffered constant meddling and interference with a manuscript that seemed forever to be in "progress" and who made the contacts that ultimately led to publication; to Bev Wright, Kathy Kear, Lottie Carroll and Shirley Mullins, who assigned the work study students who made countless trips to the library to check references; to the students themselves: Chris Smith, Cathy Mills, and Connie Smith.

To Steve Haas and Rich Tyce for their valuable aid in helping us at various times to find references and sources and to Freda Kinyon and Kathy Gallagher for their help with the index; to Wright State colleagues like Jan Gabbert, Cynthia King, Vic Sutch, Elisa Cambria, Reed Smith, Bill King, Martin Arbagi and others who helped with various kinds of advice along the way; to members of the International Society for the Comparative Study of Civilizations like the late Benjamin Nelson, Vytautas Kavolis, Edmund Leites, Robert Wesson and others who helped us get together for a conference presentation and gave advice on preparation and marketing along the way; to Nell Melko, who listened and sympathized.

To Professor Ronald J. Williams of the University of Toronto for his comments and advice concerning the Egyptological content; to Narasim Katary for his comments, criticisms and patience in reading portions of the manuscript; and to Leslie Anne Weigel for reading proof and making helpful suggestions.

Table of Contents

Acknowledgments   iii
List of Maps   v

I. Finding Peace

1. The Criteria for Peace   1
2. The Definition of Periods of Peace   8

II. Ten Cases of Peace

3. The Middle Kingdom Peace (1991-1720 B.C.)   13
4. The New Kingdom Peace (c1560-1231 B.C.)   29
5. The Phoenician Peace (1150-722 B.C.)   47
6. The Athenian Peace (683-513 B.C.)   55
7. The Corinthian Peace (655-427 B.C.)   66
8. The Achaemenid Peace (520-331 B.C.)   72
9. The Ptolemaic Peace (332-216 B.C.)   83
10. The Roman Republican Peace (203-90 B.C.)   93
11. The Pax Romana (31 B.C.-A.D. 161)   107
12. The Hispanic-Roman Peace (19 B.C.-A.D. 409)   122

III. A Provisional Analysis

13. Settings   131
14. Leaders   134
15. Polities   142

16. Economies   148
17. Societies   153
18. Religion and Civilization   158
19. Creativity and Outlook   163
20. Foreign Relations   170
21. The Termination of Peace   175
22. Recapitulation   183

Notes
  to Part I   189
  to Part II   191
  to Part III   196

Selected Bibliography   198

Index   205

List of Maps

Ancient Egypt   14
The Phoenician Peace   48
Ancient Greece   56
The Achaemenid Peace   74
The Ptolemaic Peace   84
The Roman Republic   94
Pax Romana   108
Hispanic-Roman Peace   124

Let me have war, say I; it exceeds peace as far as day does night; it's spritely, waking audible, and full of vent. Peace is a very apoplexy, lethargy, mull'd, deaf, sleepy, insensible; a getter of more bastard children than war's a destroyer of men.
                                    Coriolanus, IV, v

1

The Criteria for Peace

The servant's observations in *Coriolanus* ring true. War does exceed peace as far as day does night. A servant living in the early days of the city of Rome would have thought so and a groundling in Stuart England would have agreed, especially when the war was fought elsewhere. And so we think today, apparently, at least as far as we are concerned with war and peace in the safely distant Ancient World.

For war seems spritely and waking audible. We are fascinated by the siege of Troy, by the Hyksos charging in their chariots, the philosophers turned hoplites in a moment, the gallant Greeks resisting volleys of Persian arrows, the irresistible Macedonian phalanx, the relentless Roman Legions, the elephant tanks charging each other at Raphia or crossing the Alps, the total destruction of Carthage, the crossing of the Rubicon, the board-and-grapple sea battles, the victory against odds at Salamis or the flight of Cleopatra from Actium.[1]

Against that we have a single, lethargic, sleepy peace, the *Pax Romana*, with a declining art, a nostalgia for the past, and the assurance of such authorities as Arnold Toynbee, Carroll Quigley and Robert Wesson that such periods mark the end of growth, creativity and vitality.[2]

But surely, amidst the vent of ancient warfare, there were times of peace when trade could be carried out, when crops could be harvested, when games could be held, poets could write and philosophers could convene at the *agora*? Surely the people of the Ancient World were not eternally preoccupied with war, or even the fear of war? Surely the Roman Empire does not represent the sole instance of peace in the Ancient World?

Richard Coudenhove-Kalergi observes that we tend to focus our attention and concern on war. It provides the action, the events of history. Peace, by contast, has seemed to be the firmament upon which events occur. Few languages even have a plural for the word peace. War appears to be created by man; peace has seemed to be what existed when man was not creating. Does it not seem likely, however, that peace also may be created, that it does not just occur, but is likewise the work of man? And could it be that it is, in fact, a more impressive creation than war?[3]

When you study war, you do not have to worry overmuch about criteria. There is considerable agreement about the wars of the Ancient World, except, perhaps, for some that have been obscured by absence of information. But among students of the Ancient World, debates about war mostly concern causes and consequences.

With peace, there are few agreed upon criteria. If it is necessary to begin establishing them before the subject can be addressed, this must be done in expectation of disagreement. The criteria are set down here as clearly as possible, the reasons for choosing them are explained and the reader is left free to judge their efficacy.

1. Peace is defined as an absence of physical conflict.

2. The area in which peace occurs may be any definable region, whether it is a political unit, a group of such units, or a clearly discernible region within a larger political entity.

3. The period in which peace occurs must last a century or more.

4. If after a century of peace conflict brings that peace to an end, but then peace resumes for another century in the same area, these shall be considered as two phases of the same peace period.

5. If two contiguous areas have peace and neither is a full century earlier or later than the other, this shall be considered a single peace period.

6. If peace begins in one area, and later expands to a contiguous area, the whole shall be considered as existing in one period, provided that the contiguous area experiences at least a full century of peace.

7. Minor interruptions of peace are discounted.

8. If the government of the area of peace is fighting somewhere else, that does not negate the peace of the area.[4]

Some further explanation of each of these points may be desirable.

1. The Absence of Physical Conflict. This may seem to be a conservative definition but it is difficult to go further. We usually begin our consideration of war with physical conflict. Measures short of physical war are considered part of peace. Angry words, threats, even an atmosphere of prevailing fear are considered on the peaceful side of the continuum. It could be that such situations are harmful but that is a problem to be examined after the existence of peace has been established.

This definition of peace has been criticized because it is negative. Peace should include much more than an absence of physical conflict; it should include such positive relationships as tolerance, justice, equality, good will and love. This criticism echoes the conflict between the "realists" and the "rationalists" as Martin Wight called them, or "realists" and "utopians" (a more loaded phrase), as Hans Morgenthau described the philosophical disagreement of the 1940's and 1950's. The World Federalists of that period were rationalists, articulating a normative model. The realists tended to gravitate toward government or toward university political science departments where they articulated descriptive models like Morgenthau's *Politics Among Nations*. If they did produce normative models, such as Henry Kissinger's *Nuclear Weapons and Foreign Policy*, they did not presume that men were likely to become wiser or acquire higher morals.[5]

So in the 1970's and 1980's, the realists still control the centers of power in politics and education, and the rationalists form peripheral networks tied together by "centers" that are usually peripheral within their institutions.[6]

The study of peace seems to the realists as if it is a proper sphere for the rationalists, a subject for hypothetical models, for futurist conferences, and, not to put too fine a point on it, for dreaming. The study of peace, especially imperfect peace, seems to the rationalists a perversion, a cheapening of a high moral enterprise, a settling for a reality that would undercut the search for the ideal and inevitably lower standards.

2. Areas of Peace. The area of peace had to be definable in some way. Size did not seem very useful since the two most obvious cases in world history, the Pax Romana and the peacefulness of Switzerland, were of very different sizes, but each remarkable in its own way. So all that was required was that some area be defined, whether as city, region, or territories of an empire. The area did not have to have political unity or social continuity. If evidence was lacking about the extension of peace to an area, that area was left out. Thus the peace of an empire would not need to include all the territory of that empire, nor would it need to coincide with the time periods assigned to the empire by historians.

3. Duration. The use of a century as the minimum period to be considered was arbitrary but has proved to have utility. It soon became apparent that if the period was set at the traditional human life expectancy, three score and ten, there would be far too many societies to handle. But if that figure were doubled, there might be too few. A century seemed about right for the minimum and it has the advantages of being longer than the life of most people and a familiar division already in historical use.

Arthur Iberall has illustrated the dilemma on a hypothetical frequency curve:

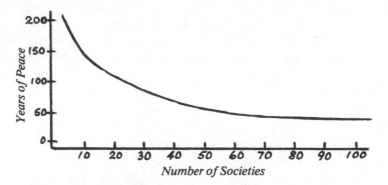

At a century there were about fifteen possible cases. At two centuries the number fell to four. At even two decades under a century the number rose amazingly.

4. Interrupted Peace. It seemed that if two clear centuries of peace should follow one another after a brief interruption (say a few decades at most), they might be connected by

related factors and the two periods should be treated as one. There was no overriding principle involved here. Such interrupted periods could well have been treated separately.

5. Peace in Contiguous Areas. As with periods of peace contiguous in time, it was presumed that peace in neighboring areas was connected and could be more usefully studied as one. This idea has not proven to be controversial so far, though the objection has been raised that peace in contiguous areas could be fortuitous. If this was the case, however, it should become apparent in subsequent study and a decision to separate would then be made. It may be that, for certain purposes, either time or space separations would be appropriate.

6. Expanding Peace. The idea was that peace in one area might spread to other parts of the same society. This phenomenon is likely to be characteristic of situations in which one people moved into an area inhabited by another and established peace by force or compromise while conflict arose or continued in the hinterlands. Eventually this too was resolved by force or compromise and the area of peace expanded. Such additional areas were included in a peace period, however, only if they too were at peace for at least a century.

If a hinterland was added to the original peace and then the original peace ended while the hinterland continued in peace for another century or more, the hinterland was regarded as a separate peace. In an interrupted peace there is continuity in space while in a contiguous peace there is continuity in time. But when peace is transferred to a hinterland and maintained for more than a century after the original peace has been lost, there has been a transfer in both space and time, and that would seem to be reason for considering the new area of peace separately.

7. Minor Interruptions to Peace Are Discounted. Quantitative measurements here were difficult to delineate. Battle casualty figures were often not available. If they were, population figures may not have been available. Lacking either of these, it was necessary to guess at probabilities, at a general consensus of the physical disruption to society, and to assess this against the size and estimated population of the peace area.

8. The idea that the government of a peaceful society might be fighting somewhere else came from the Roman Empire.

This was perceived as *the* peace period in the Ancient World, but Roman Legions were often fighting in Dacia, or Britain or Parthia. Therefore it appeared that fighting somewhere was not necessarily inconsistent with peace somewhere else.

This proved to be even more controversial than the definition of peace. Martin Wight has observed that it seemed to him unreal to contend that a state organized for war, its economy involved in the production of armaments, its politics dominated by the issue of extending or ending the war, is at peace simply because its citizens have not suffered foreign action on its own soil.[7] Several Americans have pointed out that if this criterion is applied to modern times, the United States was at peace between 1964 and 1974 while prosecuting the war in Vietnam. In fact, Milton Leitenberg calls this criterion "obscene."[8]

The problem here is one of distinguishing the situation from the motive. First we perceive an area in which no physical conflict is taking place, then we ascertain why the peace exists. We perceive a peaceful Roman Empire. We observe that one reason it is peaceful is that, under Hadrian, walls have been set up that may have served to keep out invaders. That seems reasonable and prudent. And the empire is perceived to be at peace even though the walls, from time to time, are defended against attackers by Legions.

But what, then, if the Legions follow the enemy into the wilderness to preempt future attacks? The empire is still at peace. What if, as in the earlier period under Trajan, the empire is expansive, and conducts offensive attacks into new territories? The empire is still at peace. In Rome men may carry on their business without carrying swords. What if, as in the case of the Roman Republic, a Scipio Africanus brings peace to his country by attacking an enemy in its own territory, winning a victory and utterly destroying the enemy capital? Peace has been maintained for the Republic. Motives for the United States involvement in Vietnam are mixed and require study. But during that involvement, Hanoi and Saigon were embattled, people were being killed, it was dangerous to live there. In Washington, however, while people were killed and there was danger, they were not being killed in warfare. They carried on their business without the wearing of swords. In studying the intervention in Vietnam we may decide that as with Scipio's intervention peace at home was a consequence. We may also decide to the contrary, that as in the case of Trajan the intervention was aggressive and unnecessary to peace at home.

The first task is to discover areas of peace and the next is to find out how peace was created and maintained. Then we may examine the motives of the peacemakers. Questions of cause and consequence can be approached better after the peace periods have been established. It may turn out that peace was preserved in some cases because a government prudently defended itself at its borders and in other cases because it fought in someone else's homeland.

Once we have isolated our areas of peace, we may study them. We may examine whether external conflict is often or sometimes a factor in maintaining internal peace by providing a focus for unity. So Shakespeare's Henry IV advises the future Henry V:

> Therefore, my Harry,
> Be it thy course to busy giddy minds
> With foreign quarrels ... [*Henry IV, Pt. II,* IV, v].

Was that wise advice? It did not prove to be for the peace of fifteenth-century England. But from studying cases of peace accompanied by foreign quarrels, we may be able to ascertain whether there are circumstances in which such strategy is successful.

2

The Definition
of Periods of Peace

The idea that there could be a long period of peace anywhere may have had its origins, for those of us who live in the West, with the Roman Empire. This was the political climax of the Ancient World. There was no question, from the beginning, that peace and war were early human achievements.

One reason we study the Ancient World is to better sort out what in our own world is a characteristic common to civilized man as differentiated from a characteristic of Western civilization, European society or industrial society. We can, therefore, hope to distinguish what is universal about peace from what is unique to modern civilization.

The Ancient World is roughly defined as existing in time from the origins of civilization along the Tigris and Euphrates as well as the Nile rivers until the demise of the Roman Empire, during the A.D. 400's. Geographically it surrounded the Mediterranean, extending to the western borders of India, south into Africa, north toward the Baltic and east to the Atlantic.

The periods of peace were found by the authors' general reading of history during this period, followed by a closer investigation of those areas in which peace looked possible. Fifteen areas were given a more intensive investigation, and eventually ten cases of peace were chosen for description.[1]

Tables have the advantage of clarity, the disadvantage of exaggerated precision. It would be splendid if each of the dates presented represented a specific event that led to the beginning or end of a peace. Sometimes they do but often they approximate the ambiguous end or beginning of a period of conflict.

Ten Ancient World Periods of Peace

Middle Kingdom	1991-1720 B.C.	Nile Valley
New Kingdom	1565-1231 B.C.	Nile Valley and Syria
Phoenician	1150-722 B.C.	Eastern Mediterranean Coast
Athenian	683-513 B.C.	Attica
Corinthian	655-427 B.C.	Corinth
Achaemenid	520-331 B.C.	Iran, Mesopotamia and Syria
Ptolemaic	332-216 B.C.	Egypt and Cyprus
Roman Republican	203-90 B.C.	Italy
Pax Romana	31 B.C.-A.D. 161	Southern Europe, Asia Minor, Levant, North Africa
Hispanic-Roman	19 B.C.-A.D. 409	Iberian Penninsula

One great problem in the study of the Ancient World is that caused by gaps in information. Much is inferred by researchers and as this information is passed on and reused it sometimes becomes difficult to sort out what has been clearly demonstrated from documentary or archaeological evidence and what is merely the undemonstrated hypothesis of an earlier researcher. The absence of data could indicate a probability of peace, since the presence of war would likely be noted by someone or other. But in the Ancient World, where we rely on ambivalent inscriptions and chance preservations, this is less likely to be so, especially if the losers are the record keepers. For instance, the Exodus of Moses is not to be found anywhere in Egyptian annals. And if the kingdom of David and Solomon subsequently had been obliterated by the Assyrians, comparatively little of the course of Israelite civilization would be known to us today. We would have to rely upon the bare bones of Palestinian archaeology and the occasional and brief mentions of the Israelites in contemporary Egyptian and Assyrian annals. Therefore we have tended, with reservations and exceptions, to regard an absence of information as an absence of validation.[2]

The cases chosen exhibit considerable variety. They range in size from the Roman Empire to individual city-states like Athens and Corinth. They differ widely in governments, economies, quality of life, cultural styles, foreign policies, and basic problems. Their variety indicates that long periods of peace are possible under many different conditions.

But all of them had beginnings and endings and each is characterizable. We have, therefore, arranged each in the same pattern, describing origins first, then characterizing the society during its peace period, then describing the circumstances of termination. A fourth section, entitled *Reflections,* provides a preliminary reconsideration of some of the salient features of each period. Within this outline, however, each case is written differently, following the contours of its own development.

It may be useful, before describing the cases, to review the established criteria as they affect the cases actually chosen.

1. *Absence of physical conflict*: In all cases this criterion was met, allowing for modifications described in 7 and 8 below.

2. *The area experiencing peace*: As it turned out eight of the peaceful societies were under a single government. The Roman Republic and the Phoenician Peace included a number of sovereign governments while the Hispanic-Roman Peace was a discernible region within a larger political entity. The Achaemenid and Roman Empires included formerly sovereign states, some of which were to regain their sovereignty after the peace period had ended. All ten cases did appear to have some measure of social continuity.

3. *A century or more duration*: This was true in every case, with the Middle Kingdom exceeding two centruies, the New Kingdom three and the Phoenician and Hispanic-Roman four.

4. *Interrupted peace treated as continuous*: This applies to two periods: the New Kingdom and the Hispanic-Roman. Each could have been divided into two separate peace periods of more than a century. A third case, an ironic one, suffered an interruption just short of a century of peace, which was followed by another peaceful period of more than nine decades. By this criterion, therefore, it did not qualify and should have been withdrawn. But this was a very special case: the *Pax Romana* itself! After 99 years of peace there was a violent interruption lasting less than two years (as compared to two or three decades in the other double peace periods), followed by 92 years (perhaps a few more) of resumed peace. We allowed a small variance because the territory involved was so immense, because the in-

terruption was brief compared to that of the other two interrupted peace periods, and above all because the *Pax Romana* had been *the* classic period of peace, the one that had suggested many of the criteria in the first place.

5. *Peace in contiguous areas treated as being in a single period*: This rule lumps all Phoenician states and the two imperial entities into one period each. It also allowed Syria to be included for part of the total period in both the New Kingdom and Achaemenid Peace periods.

6. *A long hinterland peace regarded as separate:* The Hispanic-Roman Peace fits this criterion, extending into the A.D. 400's, whereas its parent *Pax Romana* had ended in the second century.

7. *Minor interruptions discounted*: We were not able to evolve any quantitative measurement for the Ancient World. We considered whether the Roman struggles of A.D. 68-70 could be called minor, and decided they were too extensive and too violent. We considered whether any of the dynastic battles for the Persian throne could be called minor, and decided they could, as they were local, one-battle conflicts at worst, often virtually bloodless coups, in a very large and populous empire. And a brief invasion by the Franks in 310 was discounted in the Hispanic case. We decided against including a Saite case that was interrupted by a coup d'état, though the extent of that conflict is difficult to determine.

8. *War outside an area does not negate the peace within*: All ten cases seem to have been involved in at least some fighting outside the peaceful territory during the peace period.

We have no expectation that the presentation of these cases will prove to be definitive. We hope they will provide a base from which other researchers—and perhaps we—will be able to pursue further research on a new set of problems in the Ancient World. What patterns of international relations produced peace and harmony? What approaches to government and economy produced favorable environments for the people of the Ancient World? We know they had many troubles, but did they often live peacefully, were they often free from alienation? Did they enjoy the warm and sunny climate that gives us pleasure still today?

3

The Middle Kingdom Peace
(1991-1720 B.C.)

Egypt is an unusual land. Since it has little rainfall, farming can only be carried out on land made fertile by the flooding of the Nile. For this reason the country has a two-dimensional aspect, with people living along the river in a 750 mile line from the first cataract to the mouth of the Nile Delta. South of the Delta the cultivable land is never greater than 13 miles wide. The Delta itself forms an equilateral triangle more than 100 miles wide near the Mediterranean Sea and almost 100 miles in a straight line from the sea to the ancient capital of Memphis. Beyond the land made fertile by flooding is desert and the line between soil and desert is so definite it is often possible to put one foot in each.

The cultivable area within this span is some 12,500 square miles. In this land now live 40 million persons, and even in the ancient days of Egypt there were probably several million inhabitants.

The land is relatively isolated. The first of several cataracts in the river provides a natural southern frontier. The Nubian population to the south is not great; today the river in this tropical region supports barely 200,000 inhabitants. The desert flanks the river both east and west. On the north is the Mediterranean, which became a source of vulnerability when seafaring came of age in the first millennium B.C. Otherwise the area was vulnerable to external invasion only from the northeast across 90 miles of Sinai Peninsula desert.

Around 3100 B.C. a central authority emerged in Egypt

13

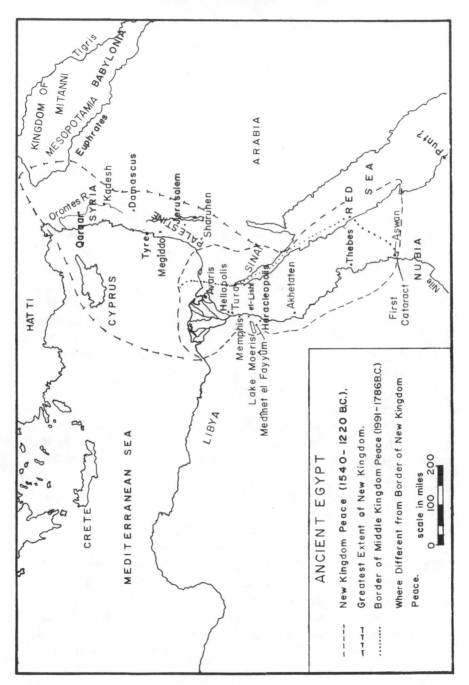

ANCIENT EGYPT

New Kingdom Peace (1540-1220 B.C.).

Greatest Extent of New Kingdom.

Border of Middle Kingdom Peace (1991-1786B.C.)

Where Different from Border of New Kingdom
Peace.

scale in miles

0   100   200

capable of controlling both the Nile Delta and the Nile Valley, formerly two separate kingdoms. Absolute power was vested in the divine king (much later referred to as "Pharaoh," *i.e.* "Great House") who ruled Egypt much as a medieval lord ruled his private manor. Under a series of vigorous and astute absolute monarchs, Egypt grew into a strongly united, self-confident and prosperous nation despite the changes in dynasty which reflect the changes in the political ascendancy of the different ruling elites, apparently without serious consequences to the domestic peace.

As the period of consolidation progressed, the Old Kingdom (the Third through Sixth Dynasties), as it is called by Egyptologists, produced monumental art and architecture, a promising library tradition and superb craftsmanship in the material industries. The raw materials and minerals of the Sinai and Nubia poured into the country via commercial expeditions and stimulated native industries. Egypt traded with cities on the Syrian coast and probably farther to the east as well.

The decline of the Old Kingdom came with the gradual erosion of pharaonic absolute authority beginning as early as the end of the Fourth Dynasty when the provincial governorships became more or less hereditary. The provincial governors, or *nomarchs* as they are customarily called, waxed in power and wealth proportionately as the central authority waned with the depletion of national treasuries and loss of ever greater revenues to the maintenance of the costly funerary cults of earlier kings. The final undoing of Old Kingdom society, however, seems to have been the gradual extension of the prerogative of divine immortality to an ever-increasing elite or privileged class. At the dawn of Egyptian recorded history, immortality and its trappings seem to have belonged to the king alone. Gradually they were extended to the royal family and their descendants and later to an ever-widening circle of lords and ladies, poets and artists, sages and master craftsmen as a means of assuring their unquestioned loyalty to the Memphite government. This gradual "democratization" of the hereafter and its accompanying prestige cost the kings dearly since it blurred the distinction between the god-king and the rest of the Old Kingdom aristocracy. Despite the outwardly peaceful and prosperous reigns of Fifth and Sixth

Dynasty Memphite kings, the infrastructure of the society was disintegrating and with it the political system of absolute monarchy.

Origins

By the twenty-second century B.C., the Old Kingdom was dissolving into a state of anarchy. The next two centuries constitute a period of severe social and political upset known as the First Intermediate Period. Eventually rival dynasties emerged at Heracleopolis, not far south of the Old Kingdom capital of Memphis, and at Thebes, many days' journey south of the Delta. A civil war between these two powers ended with the victory of the Theban Eleventh Dynasty under Mentuhotpe II (2060-2010), who succeeded in reunifying the country and in so doing prepared the way for the establishment of the Middle Kingdom Peace.

The latter part of Mentuhotpe II's reign appears to have been peaceful but his successors were evidently less forceful than he. They were soon superseded by an Upper Egyptian not of royal birth who took the throne after several years of civil war as Amenemhet I (1991-1962). Perhaps he used the prestige of Mentuhotpe II to consolidate his position, since he continued to honor his former sovereign's monuments in Thebes even while moving his capital north to el-Lisht, a more central location. He did think of himself as inaugurating a new epoch, however, as is evident in his choice of the epithet "Repeater of Births" (*i.e.,* of the moon) in his royal titulary. His Twelfth Dynasty was to rule over an essentially peaceful society for more than two centuries.

Characterization

Amenemhet I had to contend with various *nomarchs* who controlled hereditary principalities or administrative districts (*nomes*) along the Nile. Both Mentuhotpe II and Amenemhet I seem to have come to an agreement with these *nomarchs*, allowing them to retain their domestic authority in exchange for their loyalty. Amenemhet I evidently had to rely heavily upon the support of this landed nobility in his bid for the kingship. To reward the nobles for their support against Heracleopolis, he restored to them ancient privileges and titles lost during the social upset of the preceding years. It may be that Thebes prevailed over Heracleopolis because the *nomarchs* felt that the remote Theban rulers would be content to be first among equals, while the rulers at Heracleopolis would seek to reassert the centralized rule characteristic of the Old Kingdom. The Twelfth Dynasty rulers were careful, however, to protect themselves from nomarchal uprisings and possible rebellion by carefully defining and maintaining *nome* boundaries, lest one *nomarch* impinge on another's domain and in so doing become more powerful.

As a method of securing his reign, Amenemhet I (Greek form *Ammenemes*) raised his eldest son, Senwosret I (1971-1928 B.C.; Greek form: *Sesostris*), to the kingship during his own lifetime. Father and son reigned as joint kings. This practice, known as co-regency, was followed throughout the dynasty when the heir to the throne reached an age at which he was judged capable of ruling. This may have helped in securing successsion for when Amenemhet I was assassinated ten years later in a palace conspiracy, peace was maintained without a dynastic struggle. The son and heir to the throne, away on a military campaign in Libya, returned posthaste to take full command. Under this loosely gathered system the provincial *nomarchs* had authority over irrigation, planting, the local militia, justice and tax collection. Judges, however, were appointed by the king and *nomarchs* were required to make available to the king supplies, ships and men for royal enterprises both within Egypt and abroad.[1]

Later, during the years of Senwosret III, from 1878 to 1843, there seems to have been considerable centralization of power in response to increasing power among the *nomarchs* of Middle Egypt. Senwosret III successfully reduced the landed nobility to little more than political figureheads and reorganized the administration of Egypt into three departments, each headed by an official directly responsible to the chief administrative officer of the state, the *vizier*.

Senwosret III is well remembered for having built up a strong military consisting of professionals, Nubians and provincial militia. In abolishing the system of local armies (*i.e.,* infantry) at the disposal of the *nomarchs*, Senwosret III reversed the trend toward decentralization and so strengthened his own hand. He also instituted a system of conscription of native Egyptians and augmented these forces with Nubian volunteers. These forces were well armed with simple bows and arrows or axes. The Egyptian infantry wore no armor and were protected only by huge shields covered with hide. Under Senwosret III, Egyptian military control expanded both north and south. Egyptian rule was extended to Lower Nubia and was maintained by a series of massive brick fortresses. Senwosret III also led forces into western Asia to overthrow nomadic tribes threatening trade routes to the Levant and beyond. During the Middle Kingdom, Egypt maintained close ties with the Syrian principality of Byblos, which continued to be ruled by a native prince under Egyptian influence. The net result was an "Egyptianization" of Syria, counterbalanced by a simultaneous influx into Egypt of western Asiatic styles, motifs, products and even household servants. Thus an aggressive defense along the borders helped to preserve peace and stability. On the whole, however, contacts with western Asia during the time of the Middle Kingdom were a matter of peaceful and genial diplomacy and economically advantageous trade relations.

The major powers of western Asia posed no threat to Egypt's well-being and security during the halcyon days of the Twelfth Dynasty and probably throughout the Thirteenth Dynasty as well. The ease with which Egypt succeeded in influencing the political and economic life of the principalities of Syria and Palestine over the span of the Middle Kingdom Peace was in large measure the result of the absence of interference in those areas on the part of any government in Mesopotamia. With the fall of the Isin-Larsa Dynasty in about 1850, Mesopotamia had entered a period of political eclipse during which rival Amorite nation-states fought continuously among themselves for the control of the Tigris-Euphrates River Valley. Mesopotamia remained in political disarray until it was reconsolidated under Hammurabi in the 18th century.

The Twelfth Dynasty, especially during the reign of Amenemhet III, was particularly concerned with the construction of public works to support and expand agricultural productivity. Land was reclaimed and farmed by the use of drainage, dikes, dams, canals, and embankments. The major accomplishment in this regard was the reclamation of approximately 17,000 acres of arable land to the north and west of modern-day Medînet el-Fayyûm by the careful regulation of the inflow of Nile waters into the area. The ancient Mi-wér or Lake Moeris as it was known to the classical geographers, survives today as the much reduced Birket Kârûn connected to the Nile by the channel Bahr Yûsuf. Canals were dug near the island of Sehêl at the First Cataract to aid both commercial shipping and military transport in Nubia. The economic expansion of Egypt was further assured by the development of mines and quarries in the Sinai, at Tura, Aswan and in Nubia as well. Extensive trade was carried on with Syria, Cyprus, Crete, Nubia and the Somali Coast.

Although Egypt was rich in building stone (granite, limestone, sandstone, diorite), had access to a wealth of semi-precious stones and above all received vast quantities of gold from Nubia, she was greatly lacking in timber and metals. To obtain the former, she traded with the coastal states of Syria and Palestine. From the Lebanon came the prized cedars and from Anatolia oak, ash, beech, and birch. In regard to Egyptian metal needs, while the mines of the Sinai provided malachite ore from which copper could be extracted, other sources of ore were as far south as the Wâdi 'Allâki in Nubia and thus not readily accessible. Egypt therefore came to import copper from Cyprus possibly as early as the time of the Middle Kingdom. Silver was imported in large quantities as was the tin required for the alloying of bronze. Also imported were wines and oils (cedar and olive) from Syria and incense from Punt on the Somali Coast. Trade with Crete may have commenced as early as the Middle Kingdom era since typical Minoan pottery appears in the Twelfth Dynasty towns at el-Lâhûn and el-Haraga. In addition to gold, Egypt exported surplus grain, rolls of papyrus and fine linen fabric.

It appears as though the Egyptians of the Middle Kingdom were more realistic and less arrogant than their Old Kingdom forebears. Indeed, the entire nation appears to have turned inward in a display of community- and nation-mindedness. The Middle Kingdom pharaohs perceived themselves as the guardians of their people and the conscience of the nation as a result of the psychological trauma suffered by all Egyptians during the social and political upheaval of the First Intermediate Period. The turmoils of that time, together with the severe upset of the social order and general political and economic chaos, had sparked the desire for stability of nationhood through the bringing of social justice to all. This justice or quality call *ma'at* was conceived of as emanating from the king to the humblest of subjects. John Wilson has pointed out the importance of *ma'at* in government by defining it, in its most basic meaning of evenness, straightness or correctness, as the "moral control which must accompany intelligence and authority." The concept of *ma'at* as a guiding principle essential to the effective functioning of government is vividly described in *P. Sallier* on the occasion of the accession of a 13th-century monarch: "The happy time has come ... order has gone down in its [proper] place. *Ma'at* has banished falsehood. Days are long, nights have [the correct number of] hours, and the moon comes regularly...." Thus the pharaohs of the Twelfth Dynasty became truly conscientious rulers, occupying themselves with the righting of social wrongs, the economic development of the country, the safeguarding of the nation's borders and the politics of *détente*.[2]

With the increased prosperity and security of good times, however, came complacency and the tendency to forget the guiding principles of equality and social justice handed down as a legacy from the trouble-scarred years of the First Intermediate Period. Therefore, although Egypt approached a true humanitarianism during the Middle Kingdom era, that ethos with its spirit of individual worth and dignity was never fully realized. What did survive was the energy of the age, with its emphasis on national pride and national purpose and the obligation of each individual to contribute to the welfare of the state.

It is implied in the literature of the period that the government, as represented by the king, his counselors, administrators and magistrates, was an institution sensitive to the needs of the populace. The popular Middle Kingdom literary text, *The Tale of the Eloquent Peasant* tells of the trials endured by a poor man in his search for redress of injustices committed against him by one richer and more powerful than he. It conveys the idea that justice (*ma'at*) was available to the common person — but alas not to just any, only to the one who could plead a case most eloquently! The combination of the plea for justice with the hard-hitting demonstration that fine rhetoric is the means to that end was evidently not unacceptable to Egyptian readers since the story was relished for many generations. Another revealing text, this one from the repertoire of didactic literature, is a brief treatise on kingship in the form of a royal testament, which provides a glimpse into the contemporary conception of ideal government. *The Instruction for Merikare*, as it is called, provides a host of recommendations for the new king at his accession including the financial reward of government officials lest they be tempted to show partiality, the respect for the property of the individual, the appointment to office of men on the basis of skill and accomplishment rather than mere accident of birth, the avoidance of inappropriate punishments for wrongdoers and the comfort of the afflicted in society (especially widows). How far the new king succeeded in following his father's advice is something that history unfortunately does not reveal.[3]

The greater egalitarianism of secular life was reflected in religion. As gods the pharaohs had long enjoyed the prospect of life after death. Obedience and service to the king might procure this benefit for those around him as well. By the time of the Middle Kingdom, immortality was within the grasp of those rich enough to afford the necessary equipment, texts, rituals, and the services of a mortuary priest. Thus the king could no longer command loyalty simply by promising immortality to those around him. The afterlife and all it entailed was in the process of democratization. The replacement of the solar deity Re by Osiris as the principle god of the afterlife reflects a shift in emhasis from the King ("the son of Re") as the central figure in the funerary cult to a deity, hitherto obscure, with whom everyone could hope to be identified.

The troubled years of the First Intermediate Period had witnessed the disintegration of the state religion centered about the cult of the god-king and dominated by the Heliopolitan priesthood. Political fragmentation led to an upsurge in the popularity of local cults, especially that of Mont of Hermonthis

and later that of Amun of Thebes in association with strong
political factions within the country. With the establishment of
the Theban Twelfth Dynasty came the ascendancy of the god
Amun over Mont, the latter having been the special deity of the
Eleventh Dynasty.

In order to ensure Amun's superior position as the
supreme deity of the state, theologians combined Amun with the
Heliopolitan sun god Re as the composite deity Amun-Re and
gave him the epithet, "King of the Gods." In order to justify their
kingship, the Twelfth Dynasty pharaohs (and those Theban
monarchs of later dynasties as well) proclaimed themselves to be
literally sons of Amun-Re, that is, begotten by the great god
upon the queen. This development in the doctrine of divine
kingship not merely gave authority to a new royal house but also
served to reconcile two major cults and their adherents, thus
avoiding future conflict.

The Middle Kingdom saw a reassertion of artistic virtuosity and creativity with a change in emphasis to a vital and
forceful realism. The Middle Kingdom was a period of
naturalism in style in which there was delicacy and balance in
execution. This style arose out of the tradition of Theban artists
conversant with the best of Old Kingdom art while possessed of a
new virtuosity and dynamism that gave special character to their
work. Whereas royal sculpture in the Old Kingdom conveyed the
ideal of god-like majesty with a trend toward ever greater formalism and precision in geometrical balance, sculpture in the
Middle Kingdom was more realistic and less grandiose, the royal
statues portraying the kings as serious, even brooding in aspect.
The humanity of the kings was reinforced by a certain melancholy in demeanor in contrast to the self-control which went
hand in hand with Old Kingdom confidence that the god-king
was all powerful. Painting and painted relief work in the Middle
Kingdom exhibit great technique and control of the medium
while carrying on the Old Kingdom tradition of depicting scenes
of everyday life. Jewelry and other minor arts reached a peak
never to be surpassed in the history of Egyptian art.

The literature of the Middle Kingdom was written in a
form of the Egyptian language known as Middle Egyptian, inscribed on monuments in hieroglyphic characters and written on

papyrus in a cursive form of writing known as hieratic. The ancient Egyptian language has striking affinities with the Hamitic languages, especially the Berber dialects. In addition, many Semitic loan words appear that evince early and continuing close contacts with Mesopotamia. The Egyptian language in use in the Middle Kingdom was already an admixture of African and west Asiatic elements.

The corpus of Middle Kingdom literature available to us today is a vast potpourri consisting of entertaining and well written short stories, pithy satires, didactic treatises and political propaganda with the prime intention of justifying the rule of the Theban Twelfth Dynasty. Wisdom literature in the form of maxims and precepts, mythological epics, pessimistic philosophical musings, prayers and hymns round out the picture and revel the depth of emotion and height of intellect to which the Middle Kingdom Egyptian aspired. Many of the literary works of the age were based upon historical events of the more recent past, including the fall and eventual dissolution of the Old Kingdom, the political and economic disturbances of the First Intermediate Period, and the emergence of the Theban royal house. The lamentation known to us as *The Admonitions of Ipuwer,* for example, must be read against the background of anarchy and conflict during the First Intermediate Period as also should the already noted didactic discourse on kingship, *Instruction for Merikare.* The popular, autobiographical *Story of Sinuhe* takes place at the accession of Senwosret I and does double duty as both an adventure filled narrative and a powerful piece of political propaganda. In the latter function, the story fosters the image of Egypt as the best of all possible countries and the Egyptian king as a beneficent and just monarch beloved by his subjects. As for literature in the humorous vein, the *Satire on the Trades* reveals the keen wit and sparkling humor of the day in its exaggerated derisive characterizations of all professions, with the exception of that of the scribe. The ever popular fantasy romance *The Story of the Shipwrecked Sailor* is a simple unadorned narrative told by a sailor cast ashore on an island inhabited by a frightful but good-natured sea serpent. The great quantity and variety of literature preserved from the Middle Kingdom was the happy result of the use of classic Middle Kingdom texts during the New Kingdom as model compositions in the training of scribes.₄

During the era of the Middle Kingdom a number of scientific treatises were in general use, the concepts of which probably date back well into the Old Kingdom. Among these various technical works are several medical treatises the extant copies of which date from the Hyksos period and the early years of the New Kingdom but which indisputably reflect the corpus of scientific knowledge in use during and probably prior to the time of the Middle Kingdom. In the field of mathematics, the primary source is the great Rhind Papyrus, which is preserved in a copy dating to the reign of the Hyksos king Apophis I but which reflects a text going back in date to the reign of Amenemhet III. The Rhind Papyrus, together with a number of shorter mathematical documents of the Middle Kingdom, supplies valuable insights into the decimal notation, practical geometry and even algebra in use during and prior to the Middle Kingdom era. The calendrical system, perhaps the greatest single achievement of the Egyptians in the realm of science, was well established long before the advent of the Middle Kingdom.⁵

Termination

The royal statuary of the Middle Kingdom conveys a grim forcefulness if not severity of expression, interpreted by many scholars as reflective of tense dynamism in character together with the awareness of the awesome responsibilities of kingship. This is especially evident in the portraits of Senwosret III, perhaps the most remarkable king of the dynasty. After the death of Amenemhet III early in the 18th century B.C., however, central control began to break down. Very little is known about the reign of Amenemhet IV (1798-1790), who was succeeded by Queen Sobeknefru (1789-1786), possibly his sister or half-sister with whom there was probably no co-regency. The succeeding Thirteenth Dynasty witnessed the increased weakness and instability of the monarchy as a series of insignificant kings was dominated by a line of powerful *viziers*. Although the central government was seriously deteriorating throughout this dynasty, Egypt continued to be a respected political power abroad until later in the 18th century B.C. Then came what is commonly termed the Second Intermediate Period, a poorly documented epoch that experienced enough political breakdown and fragmentation of power to give historians considerable difficulty in sorting out the next couple of centuries.

The causes of the breakup of the seemingly stable Middle Kingdom are many. Perhaps the policies of centralization of Senwosret III aroused the anger and opposition of the *nomarchs*, causing them to break away from the overlordship of the government at el-Lisht. Perhaps the relative incompetence of the rulers who succeeded Amenemhet III provided the opportunity for defection. The Middle Kingdom government, with its delicate nomarchal structure, required astute leadership.

The stellar rise to power of the Babylonian dynast Hammurabi in about 1792 marks a turning point in the history of western Asia at which emerged a strong west Semitic empire, with Babylon as its center, capable of effectively dominating the political life of neighboring west Asiatic nation-states.

The consolidation of Hammurabi's empire coincides with the rapid decline of the Thirteenth Dynasty as nomadic west Asiatic tribes pressed ever westward in their search for new territory. The resulting disruption of normal trade relations with neighboring Mediterranean and Asiatic countries undoubtedly contributed to the weakening of the Middle Kingdom. The so-called *Execration Texts*, imprecations inscribed on a series of pots and statuettes, directed against the enemies of Egypt, real or imaginary, and dating onward from the reign of Senwosret III, bespeak the growing paranoia with which Egypt regarded the nomadic movements from the north and east, possibly from as far as the Caucasus Mountains. These peoples included the Kassites, who in cooperation with the Hittites overturned Babylon, and the Hyksos, who began to infiltrate the eastern Delta during the declining years of the Middle Kingdom and eventually came to dominate Egypt.[6]

The Middle Kingdom Peace was preserved more or less intact through the first half of the Thirteenth Dynasty (1786-1633).

Unfortunately, our all too sketchy knowledge of that dynasty and its politics precludes a more confident assessment of the longevity of the peace. The evidence of a relief found at Byblos would appear to indicate that as late as the reign of Neferhotpe I (*c.* 1740-1730) Egypt's primacy in Syria and Palestine was undisputed, despite her loss of prestige at the disaffection and secession of the district of Xois in the central Delta. The reign of Neferhotpe I and those of his immediate predecessors (especially Sobekhopte IV) seem to have enjoyed "business as usual" in the kingdom, with building projects progressing as far south as Aswan despite the fact that the Hyksos were already firmly entrenched in their capital of Avaris in the eastern Delta. While it is likely that the political authority of the legitimate Egyptian government at el-Lisht was increasingly diminished with the growth of Hyksos power, there is no evidence that the domestic peace was broken in the period from 1786 to 1720. Alliances between and among local dynasts and Hyksos appear to have preserved the peace.[7]

After 1720, however, the plight of the central government at el-Lisht degenerated increasingly. In the reign of Neferhotpe III (*c.* 1715) there is some evidence from royal inscriptions for the breakdown of peaceful conditions, though even this is subject to more than one interpretation. The fall of Memphis (*c.* 1674) appears to be the first conclusive evidence of military action. It seems reasonable to conclude that the peace lasted until 1720 and that it may have lasted some years or even decades longer.[8]

Reflections

One factor conducive to peace in Egypt was the geographical isolation of the land. During the greater part of the Middle Kingdom, there does not seem to have been much indication of threat from outside, aside from sporadic raids requiring the construction of defensive fortifications, though the foreign policy of the Twelfth Dynasty may also have contributed to discouraging external threats before they could develop.

It is probable that the Old Kingdom state provided a model for the establishment of the Middle Kingdom state. There had been a period in the past, perhaps after two centuries somewhat idealized, in which the people of Egypt had lived at peace. Once that model had been reestablished, the supporters of the new government were able to resurrect and revitalize most of the institutions (among them, kingship, vizierate, military, judiciary) operative in the Old Kingdom, modifying them where necessary to suit new conditions. Once again there was a strong king who symbolized the religious virtues of the nation, but the king of the Middle Kingdom was a feudal king—a ruler *primus inter pares*. The institution of absolute monarchy as it existed in the Old Kingdom, where the king faced virtually no opposition from within the country, was not reestablished in the Middle Kingdom.

Loyalty to the crown, once established, was also reinforced by economic prosperity in which the government played a forceful role. That most people were living acceptable or even reasonably happy lives is indicated by the sculpture, painting and written documents of the era. By associating himself with his son while he was still in power, Amenemhet I established a tradition of co-regency. It may be significant that evidence of succession struggle emerges with the first monarch who did not come to power through previous association.

The political structure of the Middle Kingdom, feudalism, provided an alternative political model to the unquestioned absolute monarchy of the Old Kingdom. During the early part of the Old Kingdom, regional authority was delegated and a landed nobility created that owed its very existence to the king; in the late Old Kingdom and throughout the Middle Kingdom the prerogatives of the landed gentry came to be inherited. In the Old Kingdom, regional authority was directly obligated to the central authority that had created it; by the time of the Middle Kingdom, it was loyal so long as central authority respected inherent rights. When Senwosret III began to curb drastically the power of the feudal lords, the seeds for the collapse of the peace may have been planted.

We have a clearer view of the founding of the Middle Kingdom than we have of the Old Kingdom. Mentuhotpe II seems to have been a warrior-diplomat capable of both defeating his opponenets and gaining their loyalty. Amenemhet I, who completed the consolidation of the kingdom, may have relied in part upon the reputation of Mentuhotpe II in reestablishing control over the nomarchs. The successful unifiers came from a relatively obscure area of Upper Egypt. Their success may have been attributable in part to this fact since, as such, they may have seemed less of a threat to the petty princes of Lower Egypt. Once secure, however, Amenemhet I saw that Egypt could not be governed effectively from so far south and astutely moved his capital to el-Lisht where it was closer to the center of the land.

On balance, it may be said that many of the basic components of life in the Old Kingdom were re-established with the commencement of the Middle Kingdom. These componenets include the institutions of monarchy, landed nobility, the vizierate, priesthoods, the judiciary and military as well as patterns of economic stability and prosperity, nation-mindedness and self-determinism. The institutional and also attitudinal components of the Middle Kingdom were, however, in some respects markedly different from those of the Old Kingdom as a result of the redefinition and adaptation necessitated by the trouble-scarred years of the First Intermediate Period. Among the components of Old Kingdom life which appear to persist into the Middle Kingdom are the patterns of a nationwide peace.[9]

4

The New Kingdom Peace
(*c*. 1560-1231 B.C.)

Origins

After two centuries of political chaos attended by a severe disruption of the social order, a new Egyptian epoch began. It is commonly referred to as the New Kingdom or the Empire.

The period of chaos, known as the Second Intermediate Period, ended after a protracted struggle between native Egyptian monarchs and Hyksos kings who had claimed the leadership of those Hyksos tribes that had begun to infiltrate the Nile Delta in the 18th century B.C. during the last years of the Middle Kingdom. The struggle was concluded by a Theban general whose accession to the throne as Ahmose I (1570-1546; Greek form: *Amosis*) marked the beginning of the Eighteenth Dynasty. His victory over the Hyksos was concluded after a lengthy siege of the Hyksos capital, Avaris, in the eastern Delta. He followed this victory with the reputedly three-year siege of Sharuhen in southwest Palestine and thereby reasserted Egypt's primacy in the geographical area. He also conducted three campaigns in Nubia, finally establishing a viceroy there and in so doing laid the foundation for peace in that area.[1]

The reign of Amenhotpe I (1546-1526; Greek form: *Amenophis*), son and successor of Ahmose I, further consolidated the Egyptian state and colonized Nubia. Military activity was undertaken against the Nubian *iwntyw*, possibly raiding desert dwellers who threatened the settled Nubian populace. Relations between Egypt and Libya were peaceful throughout the greater part of the dynasty, suggesting that the first kings of the dynasty

29

had successfully impressed upon the Libyans the greater military superiority of Egypt and the mutual advantage of a peaceful political relationship.

The New Kingdom Peace may be said to have commenced with the expulsion of the Hyksos (*c.* 1565) in the first decade of the reign of Ahmose I. The peace was to last, with one interruption, until a 1231 B.C. invasion of Libyans and Sea Peoples.

Characterization

When Amenemhet I (1991-1962) had attained the throne of a reunified Egypt, he had to contend with a powerful landed aristocracy. Under Senwosret III (1878-1843) the power of this hereditary nobility was sharply curtailed. With the reunification of Egypt by Ahmose I, the complex civil administration born during the Middle Kingdom was reestablished, modified to some degree by the new political scene and by the political attitudes and conceptions of effective government of the Eighteenth Dynasty pharaohs. Although the civil service was theoretically within the reach of any competent and enterprising Egyptian dedicated to the interests of state and pharaoh, its most important offices tended to be monopolized by a very few especially dynamic families. Also dominant throughout the New Kingdom was the ecclesiastical bureaucracy, especially that of the House of Amun-Re of Thebes.

Rounding out the picture of political forces and influences was the military, which by the time of the New Kingdom had become a completely professional, tightly organized body capable of playing a decisive role in politics. The preeminence of the military in political affairs during the New Kingdom was the natural consequence of a dynasty whose kings were themselves astute and eminently competent generals. So important was the military at this time that the king would reward those exhibiting great bravery, loyalty and service with grants of agriculturally productive land. From the ranks of the civil bureaucracy, priesthoods and military, there arose what was, in effect, a new aristocracy, for which loyalty to the king was the preeminent qualification.

The Egyptian army became a truly effective professional corps under the military leaders of the Seventeenth Dynasty, having absorbed the superior Asiatic tactics and weapons. The horse and chariot, bronze weaponry, body armor and composite bow were all introduced into Egypt by the time of the Hyksos occupation. The Egyptian generals increased the effectiveness of these importations and combined them successfully with their own superior organizational talents and the use of volleys of concentrated, long-distance archery fire. This efficient and effective army served Egypt well during her years of empire building and contributed to the preservation of the peace.

During the Eighteenth Dynasty the Egyptian state had developed to a point where it was necessary to divide the direction of the adminstration between two *viziers*, one for the north and one for the south. The primary function of the vizierate was to govern Egypt and direct her internal affairs in accordance with the wishes of the pharaoh. The *viziers* coordinated the various departments of the central government including the treasury, which had been the center of government accounts since the Old Kingdom. The *vizier* also appointed numerous government officials, including judges and priests, saw to the construction and maintenance of canals and public buildings, performed a judicial role as chief justice, served as chief of police and security for the country and communicated to the king all matters of importance to the well-being and financial stability of the Egyptian state.

Although tax revenues in gold, silver, cattle and textiles seem to have been handled directly by the office of the *vizier*, as in the Middle Kingdom, payments in grain were apparently collected by local functionaries. The *vizier* was kept informed of the latest details of tax collection by the overseer of the treasury and thus was able to keep an up-to-date account of the receipts and expenses of the state.

The first serious threat to the stability and domestic peace of the Eighteenth Dynasty came with Hatshepsut's (1503-1482) vigorous opposition to the designation of her stepson Thutmose (Greek form: *Tuthmosis*) as successor to his father, her husband and brother Thutmose II (*c.* 1512-1504). In year two of the reign of the new king Thutmose III (1504-1450), Hatshepsut took control of political affairs and made herself *de facto* king, allowing

Thutmose III only the outward display of kingship. Realizing the weakness of her position, she sought to legitimize her rule by emphasizing the mystery of her divine parentage and her rights as Great Royal Daughter. This she achieved by courting the Amun priesthood, but a heavy price was paid for this support. Her reliance upon the priesthood of Amun resulted in an astronomical rise in its political power and influence. The queen was probably too absorbed in her own struggle to maintain rule to have grasped the ramifications of this politically portentous situation either for the kingship or for the country-at-large.

Although the cause of Hatshepsut's death in year 22 of her reign is not known, there is no reason to suppose that she died of anything but natural causes. What is certain, however, is that Thutmose resented his stepmother so greatly that after her death he systematically expunged her name from all public monuments. He failed, however, to destroy the memory of this remarkable woman, the third and most dynamic queen to reign as " 'King' of Upper and Lower Egypt."

Thutmose III greatly expanded Egyptian control in Syria, commencing with great victories in both Syria and Palestine in regnal years 22 and 23, including the great Battle of Megiddo against the "vile enemy of Kadesh." He then consolidated his gains with 14 separate military campaigns. This expansion in turn brought an increase of tribute from defeated rulers in Syria and Palestine together with flattery and wives from more distant states in western Asia, the benefits of which his successors continued to reap for many years. Also significant, though perhaps less interesting, were Thutmose III's Nubian campaigns, which brought Egypt even greater prosperity and prestige among nations.

The military campaigns were also accompanied by an extension of trade. The timber trade, previously conducted with Syria and Palestine, now expanded as far as Asia Minor while copper was imported from Cyprus and the Kingdom of Mitanni, which flourished northeast of Syria.

After the death of Thutmose III, with the country well into a second century of domestic peace, there were signs of impending trouble. A new power, Hatti, had arisen in Anatolia, becoming an immediate concern for Egypt's neighbor, Mitanni.

Thutmose IV (1425-1417) made an alliance with Mitanni against the Hittites, but refrained from any confrontation. After a relatively brief and undistinguished reign, his son Amenhotpe III (1417-1379) acceded to the throne. Amenhotpe III was apparently uninterested in politics, content to reap the rewards of the many years of military victory of his more enterprising predecessors. Preoccupied with grandiose building projects (temples, palaces, pleasure lakes) and the "sporting tradition" of elephant and lion hunts, he apparently conducted no military campaigns in Syria and Palestine. Although he did keep in touch with various western Asiatic rulers, he did so largely for reasons of personal prestige and the desire for valuable imports. It could be said that Amenhotpe III allowed Egypt's primacy to slip by reducing her relationships with her neighbors, great and small, to a matter of luxury merchandising.[2]

Amenhotpe IV (1379-1362), who succeeded his father, faced a political situation in which reform was both needed and overdue. The bureaucracy had become top-heavy, the priesthoods, especially that of Amun, too rich and too politically powerful. The new monarch realized that political reform was essential to the preservation of the traditional monarchy and he had the courage of conviction to carry it out. In keeping with his philosophical turn of mind and sharp intellect, Amenhotpe IV found the means to the end in the establishment of the cult of the Aten or "sun disk" to replace the state religion of Amun-Re. The new religion, in which the Aten was worshipped to the exclusion of all other deities, was designed as much to curtail the enormous power of the Amun priesthood and assert the primacy of the kingship as it was to provide a departure from traditional Egyptian theology. Changing his name to Akhenaten (meaning "The Effective Spirit of Aten") the king ordered the closing of temples and chapels of all other deities and publicly forbade the continued worship of other gods. Then, in regnal year six, in a stunning break with tradition, he moved his capital from Thebes to a new city he had built called Akhetaten ("Horizon of the Aten"), situated at modern-day Tell el-Amarna.

While Akhenaten was preoccupied with internal affairs, the Hittites, under the great warrior king Suppililiumas, succeeded in dominating the entire region west of the Euphrates unchecked. Egypt's failure to block the growth of the Hittite state and its absorption of Mitanni and eventual domination of the Syrian political scene is often incorrectly attributed to Akhenaten's supposed "pacifism" in external affairs and preoccupation with the Aten cult. The disruption of the Syrian political scene actually has its roots in the uneventful reign of Amenhotpe III, who preferred to reap the benefits of prosperity achieved by his predecessors rather than actively assert Egypt's presence abroad. Akhenaten had the ill fortune to have inherited a politically fluid Asian scene upon which, admittedly, he failed to exert any meaningful control.

Atenism as practiced by Akhenaten and his immediate family did not long survive his death. It was probably early in Tutankhamun's reign (1361-1352) that the orthodox religion was reestablished and the city of Akhetaten and Atenism was itself abandoned. The famous Karnak Restoration Stela describes the return to the "old religion" and the *status quo* before the "aberrations" of Akhenaten.[3]

The reforms of Akhenaten may have seriously disturbed the peace. It is not known how deeply the rift affected the general populace, but it is clear that Akhenaten forcibly closed temples of the other gods, forbade their worship and obliterated their names on monuments and reliefs. Such disruption in the country would not have been accepted without a great deal of opposition, not only from the priests whose temples were shut and whose revenues were suspended, but from the people themselves, who suddenly found their traditions overturned and their gods the subjects of execration.

Because such a vital thing as the integrity and primacy of the kingship was at stake in the so-called "Amarna Revolution," it was inevitable that all important segments of the Egyptian citizenry would be forced to take sides and render their allegiance. The army and the *nouveaux riches* aligned themselves with the king, while the priests and clerical bureaucracy allied themselves with the old established families intent upon preserving the *status quo*. By involving the military in the power plays, Akhenaten, perhaps unwittingly, strengthened its hand just as Hatshepsut before him had increased the power of the Amun priesthood. The increased importance of the military under Akhenaten paved the way for the eventual and apparently peaceful usurpation of the throne by the general Haremhab at the close of the dynasty. Haremhab (1343-1320) is credited with restoring order in Egypt and initiating the Ramessid phase of the New Kingdom Peace. As an important member of the coterie directing the country during young Tutankhamun's years as pharaoh, he was a logical candidate for the kingship at the death of his aged father-in-law, Ay. Haremhab appears to have been a thoroughly capable and energetic military administrator, laboring behind the scenes throughout the stormy Amarna years, who came to the fore and seized the kingship when the time was ripe.

The two preoccupations of Haremhab were domestic reform and an ambitious building program. In his 28 years of essentially peaceful rule, he attempted to reestablish law and order throughout the country by means of a series of strict prohibitions designed to eliminate corruption within the administration and ensure the upright behavior of the soldiery. Haremhab was particularly concerned with the integrity of the court system throughout the country. To ensure excellence in the operations of the judicial system, he promised rewards to those personnel who performed their responsibilities justly and efficiently.

Haremhab's restoration of nationwide peace and prosperity was effective enough that his people comfortably survived his death without heir. The new king, Ramesses I (1320-1318), had been a military commander under Haremhab. His brief reign ushered in the new Nineteenth or first Ramessid Dynasty. Sety I (1318-1304; Greek form: *Sethos*) and Ramesses II (1304-1237), his son and grandson respectively, each embarked upon a policy of domestic reconstruction and reassertion of Egyptian power against the challenge of the Hittites. Under Sety I, a series of campaigns were undertaken to crush local rebellion in Palestine and Syria. Sety I confronted the Hittite army and attacked the town of Kadesh on the Orontes River, where he later set up a great stela of victory. The final confrontation of Hittites and Egyptians for control of western Asia occurred during the reign of Ramesses II. The height of the conflict was the great Battle of Kadesh. Despite both Hittite and Egyptian propaganda to the contrary, the battle held no victory for either side: Egypt found that she could not hold northern Syria, while Hatti found she could not keep Egypt out of Syria. The treaty that was agreed upon 16 years later appears to formalize what was in essence a "draw" between the two great but declining powers.[4]

Termination

By the end of Ramesses II's long life, the stability of the New Kingdom government was visibly eroding. Merenptah (1236-1223) succeeded his father when an elderly man, having outlived 12 older brothers who died in the course of their father's long reign. He showed considerable energy, despite his age, in quelling rebellion in Syria and then in defending Egypt against a major invasion of Libyans and Mediterranean Sea Peoples in year five of his reign. This invasion was the first of a series of invasions that marked the end of the New Kingdom Peace.[5]

Merenptah was succeeded on the throne by his son Sety II (1216-1210?), who ruled during some uneventful and poorly documented years. After Sety II's death, the political stability of the dynasty was threatened when rival parties within the royal family contested for the control of the government. The course of events from the death of Sety II to the inception of the Twentieth Dynasty (1200) is extremely difficult to reconstruct on the basis of present evidence. There is little doubt, however, that these were troubled times for the Egyptian state and her people. Evidence from Thebes points to possible open hostilities and overall disturbance at least in Upper Egypt. A government document of the time describes conditions prior to the inception of the Twentieth Dynasty in the most gloomy terms imaginable. Modern scholars, however, agree that the document is a skillful piece of political propaganda designed to glorify the deeds of Ramesses III (1198-1166), the founder of the Twentieth Dynasty. It is, therefore, unwise to accept the portrait of conditions throughout the land on face value. What can be said, however, is that political conditions within the country were serious enough to require an interruption of the Peace.[6]

With the advent of the Twentieth Dynasty, internal order was restored, inaugurating what could be interpreted as a "Later Ramessid" phase of the peace, lasting possibly another century.

Ramesses III reigned for 36 relatively prosperous years marked by intermittent warfare against Sea Peoples and Libyans on Egypt's northernmost borders, east and west respectively. All this was something of a "last hurrah," however, since the military victories of Ramesses III were costly and revealed that Egypt could not hope to regain the glories of the early Ramessid Period. The paucity of historical documentation after the death of Ramesses III makes it difficult to fairly assess the reigns of his undistinguished successors. Although none of the later Ramessids made much of a mark on history, there is no hard evidence to indicate that Egypt was not substantially "at peace" internally during much of the Twentieth Dynasty.

It was not until the end of the dynasty that an event took place which constitutes a serious rupture of this Indian Summer reprise to the New Kingdom Peace. This is the so-called "Suppression of Amenhotpe," a sort of civil war lasting perhaps nine months during which the High Priest of Amun, Amenhotpe, was censured and driven from office by forces loyal to the king. The event left the Theban *nome* in a tumult and brought Nubian troops north to pursue the fallen pontiff and restore order. The date of the Suppression is not certain, but is likely to have been sometime after year 17 of Ramesses IX and before year 19 of Ramesses XI (*i.e.*, between 1123 and 1094 B.C.). Undoubtedly the Suppression would never have happened had the later Ramessids had a firmer grasp on the country and its affairs. If the central government did eventually succeed in overcoming the disruptive forces exemplified in the outbreak of hostilities at Thebes, it surely failed to follow up its victory with the sort of "hard line" policies that serve to discourage further insurrection. Shortly thereafter the General and High Priest of Amun Herihor challenged the government by his assumption of royal titles and prerogatives. This time, the government did not rally and the days of the New Kingdom were over.[7]

Reflections

In order to attain any meaningful comprehension of the great events and personalities marking the pages of New

Kingdom Egyptian history, it is essential to consider the collective mind of New Kingdom civilization and its perception of the world around it. The areas of religion, philosophy, art and literature each provide valuable insights into the psyche of the civilization, which made such an impact upon the course of human history.

The religious attitudes and ideas prevailing during the period of New Kingdom peace were an outgrowth of the increased solemnity and introspection of Middle Kingdom religious thought. The painful experiences of two periods of political and social upheaval accompanied by economic instability served to change drastically the basic Old Kingdom Egyptian attitudes toward life in general, the world at large, and man's relationship with the gods.

During the time of the Old Kingdom Egyptians had been supremely confident of their place in the world as children of the gods and in their country as the land most blessed and favored by the gods. This self-centered spirit of selection and uniqueness was in large part the result of both the geographic isolation of the country and the fact that Egypt was a rich and bounteous country in contrast to its neighbors.

By the time of the Middle Kingdom, the humilation and sufferings of the First Intermediate Period had left an indelible mark on the Egyptian psyche: once so carefree and arrogant, they had come to realize that Egypt was not invulnerable, that peace and prosperity could not be presumed and that disaster, however unlikely, could occur to their beloved homeland. With the disintegration of the social order and collapse of the economy in the First Intermediate Period, the Egyptian turned introspective and for the first time contemplated the role of the individual in society. The social consciousness of the Middle Kingdom, born of years of humiliation and defeat, was still based, however, upon a fundamentally optimistic belief that man is the creation of a benevolent and solicitous godhead. Though life during the Middle Kingdom began to take on a somber hue, it was still a life to be enjoyed: the living of a good life in this world would still assure a good life in the next.

The legacy of the next and perhaps even more disastrous period of social and political upset, the Second Intermediate

Period, was a nationwide fear neurosis, a near mania for physical security above all else. Egypt had been physically violated, infiltrated by foreign peoples, among them the Hyksos who went so far as to assume the kingship in defiance of the legitimate heirs at el-Lisht. The new awareness of the potential dangers of an "outside world" had been painfully achieved. The concept of Egypt as the nucleus of a stable and orderly universe was dashed forever. Egyptians now rallied to the call of imperialism believing that the only way to defend themselves from violent attack or takeover was to strike first and conquer all possible antagonists. The state cult of Amun-Re was pressed into service as the justification for the "manifest destiny" of a new line of military kings: Amun ordered military conquest and Egypt, with the god-king at her head, heeded the call. This then was the collective state of mind that prevailed during the time of the New Kingdom Peace. As the fear of foreign attack or takeover increased over the years, so did the collective neurosis. It may perhaps be asked if fear of a common enemy may not, in providing a rallying point for a people, actually contribute to internal peace and solidarity. There would, of course, be a point beyond which neurosis becomes psychosis and a real danger to the mental health of a nation. Egypt may have reached this point after the reign of Ramesses III and, indeed, the case could be made that this stage had been attained much earlier.[8]

The gradual transformation of Egypt from a nation confident of its place in the world to one fearful for its security and doubtful of its future is reflected most poignantly in the funerary traditions of art and literature. Middle Kingdom Egyptians, although more sober in their attiudes toward life and death than their supremely confident Old Kingdom forebears, continued to perceive the afterlife as a happy continuation of an essentially worthwhile life on earth. Life on earth, they reasoned, was good and meant to be enjoyed. In affirmation of this view, they continued to decorate their funerary monuments with happy scenes of daily life, though adding burial and other religious scenes to the standard repertoire.

As time went on and Egypt was badly shaken by the Hyksos interregnum, its people, uncertain, perplexed, and no longer able to rationalize themselves out of this state, began to look toward the afterlife as an escape from the ills of earthly existence. Tomb paintings mirror the changing attitude: no longer do carefree scenes of hunting and drinking and vignettes of family life dominate the walls of the tomb. Now scenes of the solemn judgment of the dead fill the tomb with the sense of foreboding, gloom and desperation. The present life was to be endured until the blessings of the afterlife could be obtained. The afterlife was, moreover, no longer the happy assumption as one's due reward. It was a goal to be reached not merely through a good life but by utter submission to the will of the gods, sincere and unceasing veneration and supplication. Life was, to turn a phrase, "in deadly earnest." To pass the great test of the "weighing of the heart" after death was the goal to which men and women now aspired. Certainly, the communal spirit and nation-mindedness engendered by such a retreat from the self-centered individualism of earlier times contributed something to the maintenance of peace.

The full-flowering of nationalism and the communal spirit over the course of the New Kingdom undoubtedly served to provide a united front through the suppression of individual or local ambitions that might threaten the common welfare. Only when the suppression of individualism over and against the communal well-being reached a point where innovation was no longer tolerated and personal freedom was denied did stagnation overcome the culture. Such stagnation of philosophy, art and literature is apparent toward the end of the New Kingdom and continues through to the end of pharaonic Egypt.[9]

The art and architecture of New Kingdom Egypt may be said to reflect to some degree the changes in the political and economic conditions experienced over the course of the New Kingdom Peace. Three major periods may be identified: Thutmosid, Amarna and Ramessid, the last of which consists of two phases, the Early and Late Ramessid, corresponding to the Nineteenth and Twentieth Dynasties respectively. The building and plastic arts flourished during the Thutmosid Period (Eighteenth Dynasty through Amenhotpe III), the architecture epitomized in the majestic funerary temple of Hatshepsut at Deir el Bahri on the west bank of Thebes. In one sense, Thutmosid art seems to be a continuation of Middle Kingdom classicism, but with an emphasis on elegance, vitality and harmony of proportion lacking in the austerity of Middle Kingdom art.

With Akhenaten came a remarkable revolution in art, deliberately initiated by the king himself, a style that arose out of a new naturalism dating back perhaps as early as the reign of Thutmose IV. Amarna art is characterized by a deliberate distortion of proportion and exaggerated liveliness indicative of an intense desire to break away from traditional forms.

Following the distortion of Amarna art came the period of Ramessid art in the early part of which artists succeeded in portraying realism and beauty in a style that still looks fresh and free. The temple of Sety I at Abydus is an excellent example of Ramessid grace and craftsmanship. In the later Ramessid Period, however, the emphasis was on colossalism rather than quality, a legacy of Ramesses II's all-pervasive megalomania. While some of the later Ramessid art is remarkable for grace and beauty of design and technical virtuosity (as for example, the tomb of Queen Nefertari), the overwhelming impression is one of sheer weight or massiveness of form and material and unending stereotyping of subject matter. The inscriptions of later Ramessid years are often heavy handed as well, the signs ill formed and coarse in general effect.[10]

During the better part of the Eighteenth Dynasty, the creative literary genres drew heavily upon the triumphs of the Middle Kingdom or Classical Period in Egyptian literature. The language and style of the earlier period were rigidly emulated regardless of the fact that by the time Middle Egyptian was no longer a living language understandable to all. The chasm between the so-called classical or literary language and the spoken language grew wider and wider until the reign of Akhenaten, when a break was made with the literary fashions of the past, coincidental, it would appear, with the social and religious (not to mention political) revolutions of that epoch. During the Ramessid Period a new literary school writing in the New Egyptian vernacular produced an outpouring of creativity in the form of short compositions (*The Story of Wenamun, The Capture of Joppa, The Quarrel of Apophis and Seqenenre*); bawdy tales (*The Contendings of Horus and Seth*); allegories (*The Blinding of Truth*); love poetry (*P. Harris 500, P. Chester Beatty I*); satire

(*P, Anastasi I*); and historical works (*The Kadesh Battle Inscriptions of Ramesses II*). Although in its desire to appeal to the masses, the new literary school broke with many of the classical literary conventions, it eventually incorporated the most characteristically Egyptian of these and called them its own. Thus the best of the new joined with the best of the old and in so doing acquired the hallmark of public approval.[11]

Ahmose and Amenhotpe I in some respects resemble the two founders of the Middle Kingdom, Mentuhotpe II and Amenemhet I. In each case the leaders came from Thebes in Upper Egypt. In each case a pair of leaders was required to bring order out of chaos. Was this pairing a coincidence? Or is it that the founding and early consolidating of a kingdom requires a set of qualities not commonly found in one man? Would the man who has the charismatic qualities needed to gather supporters around him also be likely to possess the subtlety and diplomacy necessary to conciliate and satisfy his warlike followers and their successors in a peaceful society?

In periods of consolidation, we meet a monarch of a different kind, the monument builder, the enjoyer of power and prestige presiding over a fulfilled empire. Amenhotpe III throughout his reign and Ramesses II and Ramesses III in their later years of monument building are examples of this type of monarch, although both Ramesses in their early years were also aggressive military leaders. These kings, tiresomely glorified and magnified, may have been superb monarchs, but in their enjoyment of power and stability they allowed the seed of internal discord to take root and grow until, at their passing, the fruit of discord burst upon the country. So the indolent years of Amenhotpe III were followed by the ill-starred reign of a reformer king, a true noncomformist who worked to reassert the primacy of the monarchy by crossing a political constituency whose power had never been questioned before. So too the reign of the megalomaniac king Ramesses II who left to his son and heirs a country financially overburdened, a populace overtaxed and underpaid, and a government unprepared to meet political pressures at home and abroad.

The reigns of such kings as Thutmose III, Sety I and Ramesses II represent yet another historical phenomenon. All four kings presided over a country at peace within, with relatively few internal problems. All four kings, with domestic problems well in hand, preferred the enlargement of the kingdom to the aggrandizement of the capital and similar displays of "success," though in later years they sought these as well. Territorial expansion, it would seem, is rather like the building of temples, a luxury that can be borne in times of strength without disturbing inner peace and prosperity. As with public works, such expansion may increase prosperity and make possible further building or expanding but it also increases the size and complexity of the structure that must be maintained.

During the New Kingdom there was a marked tendency toward both greater proliferation of government and increased decentralization. The clerical and civil bureaucracy gained in power and wealth with both material enrichment and self-perpetuation as major objectives. Such trends worked to the detriment of the central government and most specifically to the kingship. The result was a state whose financial resources were found to lie largely in the hands of the priesthood of Amun, which continued to enrich itself at the expense of the state. While the reign of the magnificent monarch Amenhotpe III was a prosperous period for Egypt, it was also a critical time for the institution of the monarchy, threatened as it was by the tendency of the state to drift from monarchy toward theocracy with wealth and power in the hands of a few priestly oligarchs. Although Akhenaten was astute enough to appreciate the dangers inherent in such a *mise en scène* and in response tried to trim the sails of the over-rich, over-powerful priesthood, his reforms only served to increase the power of the priesthood in the reactionary backlash which followed his death. By precipitating a political crisis, Akhenaten also advanced the perhaps untimely termination of what had been a true "golden age" in the history of Egypt. The Thutmosid phase of the New Kingdom Peace was successful despite the increased proliferation of government and decentralization of authority because the kings of this period were very strong personalities and as such gave authority to the monarchy. The Hatshepsut-Thutmose III feud had, to our knowledge, no deleterious effect upon the country at large since both persons were dynamic individuals able to keep their power struggle on a level that did not affect the lives of the general citizenry. Only when Akhenaten began his reformation did the country at large suffer disruption. Akhenaten's reform was not restricted to the upper echelons of politics but, rather, since the reform was carried out through the medium of religion, came to involve the general populace.

After Haremhab had restored law and order and the old religion was reinstalled, the peace was once again upheld by strong personalities who gave their personal authority to the throne they occupied. Only when a series of *rois fainéants* came to the throne after the death of Merenptah and again after Ramesses III did the peace collapse once again. The element of reform was not a factor in the termination of peace in these cases; rather, lack of dynamic leadership, absence of a reliable power base and exhaustion of resources as a result of war and excessive building projects were the key factors. In addition to drastic religious reform touching everyday life, the factor of economic overextension may have played a part in the collapse during Akhenaten's reign as well as in the subsequent terminations.

With the expansion and elaboration of the state during the New Kingdom, the role of the armed forces (army, navy, and police) became increasingly important. The New Kingdom army, unlike the armies of earlier periods, was a well-trained, well-disciplined professional fighting corps that owed much of its effectiveness to the absorption of Asian arms and tactics inherited from the Hyksos experience. The military was made up primarily of native Egyptians but also, from the reign of Amenhotpe III onwards, of foreign troops whose members had been taken as prisoners of war. The presence of a strong military was undoubtedly a positive factor in maintaining the peace.

In the Thutmosid Period, Egypt was confident in her military superiority over other nations. In the Ramessid Period, Egypt had lost much of her arrogance and confidence, but was still assured that at least she could not be invaded or overcome by any other nation—the Hittite-Egyptian confrontation had proved that much. Internally there was law and order throughout the period with the day to day peacekeeping placed in the hands of the eminently competent Medjay people, who served as scouts and police.

There was, however, one component of the situation that had a significant impact on Egyptian political history: the practice of rewarding military leaders with retirement posts in the civil administration. Such an infiltration, as it were, of the military into Egyptian political affairs allowed for the formation of a military pressure group. These retired military officers stood in a unique and critical position between the king, as commander-in-chief, and the active armed forces. It was probably inevitable that when the opportunity arose, this political faction would exert itself to dictate the politics of the government. The strong military may have helped to maintain peace at home by quelling disturbances before they became unmanageable, but it also carried the seeds of war by providing a political faction capable of asserting and accomplishing its will by sheer force. In the case of Haremhab, this military intervention helped restore peace.

In foreign affairs we have an example of the preservation of peace by means of a treaty between two well-matched powers. The Hittite-Egyptian treaty, concluded in year 21 by Ramesses II, was probably successful because both powers were on the decline in their military effectiveness. If one had been growing stronger, the treaty probably would have been broken once its generals felt able to expand.

Another factor which may have contributed to the success of the treaty was the superiority of the defense over the offense at this point in Egypt's history. Offense involved moving armies a long way from home. In such a situation, armies would grow weaker as their lines of supply grew longer. The treaty line accepted was undoubtedly drawn through an area in which an attack from either side could probably be effectively repelled by the other.

The period of military effectiveness that ended with the campaigns of Ramesses III seems to have been something of an exception in Egyptian history. There has not been a native Egyptian dynasty since the Ramessid Period that has been capable of successful and long-lasting international expansion. Egypt's failure to meaningfully participate in the affairs of western Asia subsequent to the Ramessid Period was, however, certainly no reflection of her lack of interest in imperialist pursuits or her aversion to military conflict.

The Libyan frontier posed a different sort of problem for both the Middle and New Kingdoms. It was typical of Egyptian military strategy during both these periods to try to keep the Libyans continually off-balance, since they repeatedly encroached upon the western Delta. Senwosret I was on such a campaign in Libya against the Tjehnyu peoples when he was called home upon the assassination of his father.

With the conquest of Egypt by Alexander in 332 B.C., the native Egyptians ceased to be the directing force in the nation's business and politics and the pharaonic heritage became more and more diluted. What happened to Egypt subsequent to Alexander happened to a hybrid civilization becoming increasingly distant from the pharaonic civilization from which it was descended until comparisons between the two cease to be meaningful.

Taking pharaonic Egypt as a whole, with roughly 3000 years of relative homogeneity in its civilization, it is possible to conclude that the pharaonic peace periods indicate the strength and durability of the nation and its monarchy. Egypt's ability to overcome two major crisis periods attests to the resilience of the culture in recovering from both foreign domination and internal discord. That Egypt was not merely able to recover, but go on to achieve new heights in her civilization is remarkable. It would appear that the crises of the First and Second Intermediate Periods left the Egyptians with the awareness that peace within the nation was a vital prerequisite to national survival.[12]

5

The Phoenician Peace
(1150-722 B.C.)

Origins

Since the area between Egypt and Mesopotamia was so often a battleground in the politics of the second millennium, it would not seem to be a very promising area in which to look for peace. On the whole it is not, with one interesting exception.

The Phoenicians were a Canaanitic (west Semitic) people whose ancestors may have lived along the Mediterranean coast since the fourth millennium. The Egyptians seem to have traded for their timber as early as the time of the Old Kingdom. They began to appear in historical records when the New Kingdom Egyptians expanded into Syria. The area may have been subject to uprisings when Akhenaten lost his control. After Sety I and Ramesses II reestablished themselves in Syria, under the 13th-century treaty with the Hittites, the Canaanite areas were retained by Egypt. In the centuries that followed, the southern Canaanite areas were regained by Israelites and Philistines, but those living in cities along the Mediterranean maintained their independence.

Those coastal Canaanites were very likely known as Phoenicians by Mycenaean Greeks with whom they traded. The name may be connected with the Greek word for "purple" and would seem to refer to the famous reddish-purple dye used by the Phoenicians. The strip they occupied was less than 200 miles long and extended only a few miles inland. All the Phoenician towns of any consequence were built on the Mediterranean coast; several were based on promontories or nearby islands, thus increasing their independence and security.

47

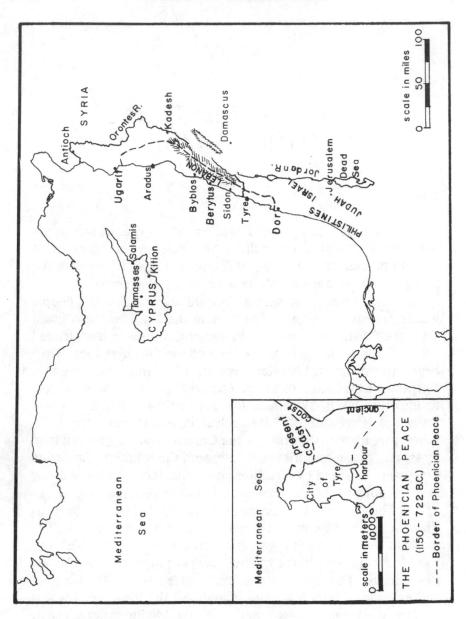

THE PHOENICIAN PEACE
(1150 - 722 B.C.)
--- Border of Phoenician Peace

The five chief Phoenician cities were Aradus, Berytus, Byblos, Sidon, and Tyre. The land around them was fertile but not extensive enough to support an expanding population. The Lebanon mountain chain, which formed the eastern border of Phoenicia and at several points lay within ten miles of the coast, restricted the available farm land, isolated cities from the east and often from each other, and forced the inhabitants of the region to make their livelihood from the sea.

The Phoenician peace begins following the invasion of the "Sea Peoples." The invaders apparently destroyed Aradus and Sidon around 1200 B.C. and did considerable damage to other cities in the region. However, the Sea Peoples and the Canaanites seem to have amalgamated rapidly and commenced a long period of peace soon after the invasions, some time around 1150 B.C.[1]

It should be noted that the sources for Phoenician history are not extensive. Most references exist in inscriptions or in records kept by other peoples. Although the Phoenician peace appears to have been stable, individual battles or wars could easily have escaped notice.

Characterization

Throughout the period, the cities of Phoenicia remained independent of one another. The territory around them was ordinarily small, with just enough land to provide food for the inhabitants. Major cities sometimes enjoyed hegemony over others nearby, but there was never a Phoenician confederacy. During most of this period Tyre was the richest and most vital of all the Phoenician cities. It may have provided some leadership in commercial and diplomatic relationships, and it may have been thought of by aliens as something like the capital of Phoenicia, but the independence of the other cities does not appear to have been challenged.

The cities were ruled by hereditary kings throughout most of the period of peace. Oligarchy replaced kings later, but perhaps not until after eighth-century Assyrian sieges had ended the peace. Certainly councils of elders, comprised of merchants, served as advisors to the kings and wielded considerable influence.

Succession did not always flow smoothly. In Tyre, during the tenth and ninth centuries, at least three monarchs were assassinated.

The Phoenicians gained their reputation as traders during the period of peace, though it continued long afterward. They did not become active outside their own waters before the 12th century, while trading posts and colonies were probably not established much before the 10th. Then they were extended across the length of the sea, with particular centers of commerce and strength established at Kition and Tamasses in Cyprus, Motya in Sicily, Utica and Carthage on the North African coast, and Gades in Spain.

The establishment of widening trade stimulated industry at home, which was at first based on local materials, later on imported raw materials. Their major products were timber, especially the famed "cedars of Lebanon," and textiles, customarily dyed with the purple secretion of murex shells. They were renowned for their accomplished stone masons. Their pottery, however, was utilitarian, apparently produced for a mass market. They accumulated considerable wealth through a complicated barter system—coins were not introduced until the seventh century. Though they had a reputation for honesty, in that they produced goods of consistent quality and did not cheat in quantity, they also had a penchant for increasing their income by piracy and kidnapping.

The citizens of the various Phoenician cities held similar religious beliefs. Although the names and some attributes might differ from one city to the next, they all generally revered a triad including a god of the city, an earth mother goddess, and a youth whose death and resurrection parallel the agricultural cycle. At Byblos these were called El, Baalat, and Adonis respectively. Sidon named than Baal, Astarte, and Eshmun. Tyre chiefly worshipped Melquart, Astarte, and Eshmun. Various other gods entered the pantheon to fulfill specific functions. The Phoenician temples and shrines were often closely connected with nature and located near mountains, sacred groves of trees, and water. Many of their religious practices seem to have been related to those of other Semitic peoples, including the practice of infant sacrifice.[2]

Not surprisingly, much of their art was pragmatic and

utilitarian. It tended to be greatly mixed with other styles, especially Egyptian and Syrian, and was usually decorative, and narrative. Their finest work is found on small items such as ivory reliefs and decorated metal bowls. The Phoenician craftsmen were competent in handling their materials, but were perhaps a bit commercial in their ideals, often giving the customer quantitative value in terms of number of figures crowded onto a bowl.

Perhaps the greatest contribution the Phoenicians made to civilization was their development of a syllabary from which the Greek alphabet was derived. It is known that they produced literature but it has not survived.[3]

The Phoenicians seem to have had friendly relations with the Israelites, who were consolidating and fighting the Philistines. Hiram the Great of Tyre (*c.* 970-936) was an ally of Israelite kings David and Solomon. Phoenicians provided skilled labor and timber to help Solomon build his temple in exchange for grain and oil. When the Israelite kingdom was divided between Israel and Judah in the late tenth century, the Phoenicians remained on friendly terms with both.

Assyria posed a recurrent threat. At the beginning of the 11th century Tiglath Pileser I reached the coast and possibly occuppied the part of Aradus that was situated on the mainland. He was content to receive the tribute of Aradus, Byblos, and Sidon. Later in the same century, under Assurnasirpal (1050-1032), the Assyrians threatened again, but once again settled for tribute from the Phoenician cities without invading them. Similar incidents of Phoenician tribute to Assyria occurred under Assurnasirpal II in 875, Shalmaneser III in 840 and 837, and Adadnirari III in 805. The records of Shalmaneser III describe battle with Syrian and Phoenician troops at Qarqar in 852 and the destruction of numerous cities in 840 when the Assyrians again received tribute from Tyre and Sidon, but there is no clear evidence that any fighting actually occurred in Phoenician territory.

There is little written about the Phoenician military except for their navy. As sailors they acquitted themselves well, though often in the service of other powers. When they needed soldiers they probably made use of small citizen armies or hired mercenaries.

The Phoenicians, then, emerge as a pragmatic, hard-headed people, uninterested in political expansion except where it may have been useful to trade, and tolerant in religion. Lacking a propensity toward the abstract, their greatest contribution, the syllabary, probably came from their desire to facilitate commerical communications. Unwilling to fight if it was cheaper to buy off an adversary, they showed fantastic tenacity when their personal property was threatened. They worked hard but also enjoyed their profits.

Termination

In the eighth century the Phoenician relationship with Assyria began to change. Under Tiglath Pileser III (754-727), the Assyrians had consolidated their holdings in Syria and come within striking distance of the coast, gradually incorporating Phoenician cities within their empire. Their method all along had been to establish tributaries first, then to convert them into provinces by replacing their kings with governors and ending home rule. So long as paying tribute left the Phoenicians free to carry on trade, they regarded it as a prudent business deal. But when the loss of their freedom to control commerce was threatened, they were willing to fight. King Luli of Tyre and Sidon, recently united under one monarch, now formed an alliance of Phoenician states and Cyprus. This in turn may have provoked an attack from Shalmaneser V (726-722). His siege of Tyre (722) was unsuccessful, but other cities were taken and, if the Assyrians were in form, the inhabitants who resisted were put to death, crops were ravaged and trees were cut down.

The peace was ended. Sennacherib (704-681) invaded in 701, taking all of the cities, including Tyre. In the following years, individual Phoenician cities revolted against Assyrian domination, but they were soon restored to submission. Major invasions from Assyria and Babylonia continued into the sixth century. After this peace was restored, but the history of Phoenicia became incorporated with that of the Chaldean and Persian empires.[4]

Possibly, if Tyre had not formed alliances, Shalmaneser might have withheld his attack. But Sennacherib was of a different stamp and the subtlety of diplomatic etiquette or the possible advantages of restraint would have eluded him.

Reflections

This is an unexpected and rather different type of peace from those of Egypt. It is unexpected because the history of Syria and Palestine has been the history of a battleground. We often perceive Phoenicia as the land of Baal, biblical symbol of religious idolatry. Dire things were continually prophesied for the wicked cities of Tyre and Sidon—indeed Tyre was the victim of several long, agonizing sieges.

The peace was different from the Egyptian in that it involved no empire and no highly organized political unification. The area in which peace was preserved was extremely small, hardly more than a thousand square miles, but there is no reason why the peace should have been less meaningful to the inhabitants than it was to those who lived in the larger Egyptian state.

The success of this string of cities in dealing with the outside world may be due in part to external circumstances. The two great powers in the region, Egypt and the Hittite Empire, were both on the decline. Assyria was for a long time erratic in her rises and relapses and, as it happened, only once expanded to the edge of Phoenician territory before the 11th century.

Even after the appearance of Assurnasirpal, the Phoenicians were able to buy a continued lease on independence and freedom for three reasons—their wealth, their diplomacy and their ability to defend themselves. Their wealth was of a kind that could not be retained through conquest, since it required a special kind of skill to keep it coming. A brutal conquest of Phoenicia would have been equivalent to killing a flock of golden egg-laying geese.

The Phoenicians made it easy for the Assyrians to settle for a tributary relationship, since they rarely participated in alliances with other cities. The Assyrians, who won all the battles, had no reason to pursue them as defeated adversaries. It was easier to accept tribute than to administer this diversified, inconsequential territory.

These rational considerations might not have impressed the Assyrian military leaders if the Phoenician city-states were less capable of defending themselves. The Assyrians had no navy and the successful invasion of cities receiving ship-borne supplies would have taken considerable time. Since these cities were also so far from the Assyrian power centers, they were not worth the trouble. There were always nearer and more pressing problems.

Given an appropriate set of circumstances, it appears that it is possible to buy peace by paying tribute and by acknowledging political suzerainty. It worked because both the greater power and the weaker powers preferred the advantages of nominal suzerainty to the difficulties that would have been involved for both in an attempt to achieve either complete conquest or complete freedom.

Besides maintaining peace with their powerful neighbors, the individual Phoenician cities had the problem of maintaining peace with one another. The primary factors contributing to the maintenance of peace among the cities themselves seem to be the superiority of defense over offense, mutual commerical ambitions and the prevalence of religious tolerance.

The superiority of defense is obvious. If great empires had such difficulty taking individual cities, what could an army of citizens do against another town? Even if they launched a naval attack, they would have to be able to use landing forces, a difficult operation even in modern warfare.

The influence of the merchant oligarchies of the towns must always have been toward peace. Why should one fight when the combination of peace and trade was accumulating immense wealth? And who would want to finance such a risky and uncertain undertaking as the siege of another city?

But such considerations might have been overridden if the Phoenicians had a religious temperament like that of their friends and neighbors in Israel. As world travelers, however, they had seen all sorts of religions and as businessmen they had to compete in a cosmopolitan world. Without accepting the concept of tolerance, they could not have been what they were.

6
The Athenian Peace
(683-513 B.C.)

The history of the Mediterranean lands can be traced back to the third millennium B.C. One of the earliest Bronze Age civilizations in this area arose on the island of Crete. There the Minoans achieved an advanced state of society, especially in the region of Knossos, from about 1800 to 1500. One might infer from their insularity, lack of fortifications, and unwarlike art that the Minoans had long periods of peace. However, at least until their Linear A script is deciphered, there is not enough evidence to put together a chronological history of the civilization and the idea of a Minoan period of peace, in the context of the present work, must remain speculation.

Some time around 1900 the Greek-speaking peoples apparently entered Greece from the north. They developed the Mycenaean civilization, which flourished from about 1600 to 1200. One might conclude from their extensive "cyclopean" walls, the predominance of war in their art, and the abundance of weapons buried in their tombs that the Mycenaeans were not likely to have experienced long periods of peace. The specific details of their history, however, remain hidden, even though their Linear B script has been deciphered. The Mediterranean area was the scene of extensive invasions at the end of the second millennium. Minoan and Mycenaean centers were destroyed, perhaps by the mysterious Sea Peoples who devastated the Phoenician coast around 1200. The last of the Greek peoples to enter the peninsula, the Dorians, filtered through most parts of Greece around 1100 and ushered in a dark age that virtually obliterated Greek culture for about three centuries.

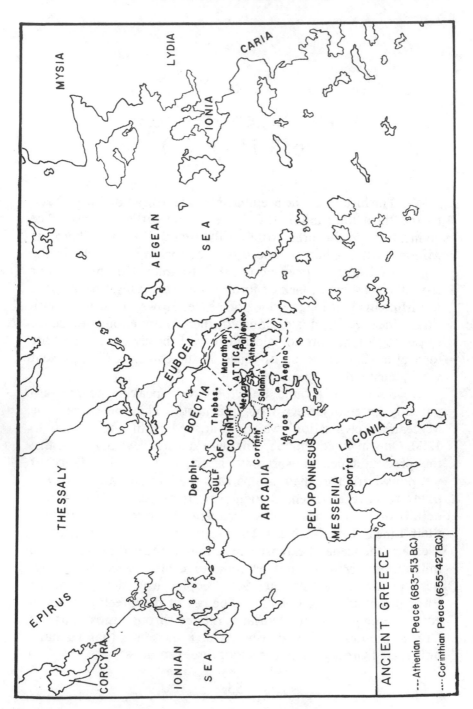

ANCIENT GREECE

---Athenian Peace (683-513 BC.)

·····Corinthian Peace (655-427 BC.)

As the misty curtain of the Dorians gradually lifted around 800, a distinctive Greek institution, the *polis,* or city-state, had already begun to emerge. Determined to some degree by the enforced isolation created by Greece's mountain barriers, the *polis* would serve as the chief vehicle for the development of Greek civilization. The city-state provided its citizens with a place of refuge, with economic opportunities, with social and religious identity, and with the chance for individual political participation. As the Greek *polis* emerged, most of the states underwent a change from government by monarchy to that of an artistocracy or oligarchy.

Usually a *polis* consisted of a city and surrounding territory. The extent of this territory varied from a few square miles to several hundred. Since the ideal for each city-state was to be small and independent, fighting among them must have been frequent. Usually it involved disputes about valuable farmland outside the cities, often between local farmers who brought their respective cities in to back their claims. Where a larger city did dominate smaller ones, it had to be constantly on guard against rebellion. The cities themselves were relatively safe from warfare, since other cities did not have the power or time to besiege them, though when the walls of a city were breached, furious fighting was likely to follow.

Origins

It is safe to say, taking Greek civilization as a whole, or even the Greek peninsula alone, that there was fighting going on much of the time, most of it at a local level. During this period mainland cities either remained separate and quarreled with their neighbors, or they were reduced to an uneasy, conditional and rebellious submission to the strongest regional power among them. Still there were undoubtedly some among them who were able to remain aloof from these disputes and develop peacefully. Two cities that appear to have experienced such periods of peace were among the most famous: Athens and Corinth. A third famous city, Sparta, may have had more than a century of internal peace between the second and third Messenian wars, but the documentation is insufficient. It is possible there were others, but little or no evidence has survived.[1]

The Athenians lived in Attica, one of the peninsulas in eastern Greece, punctuated with good harbors and somewhat cut off by mountains from other cities. They were blessed with the pleasant Mediterranean climate, which encouraged an open air society. The land contained marble, silver and fine clay. Its agricultural products included wheat, olives and grapes. Its area of about a thousand square miles was very large for Greece, comparable in extent to the entire area occupied by all the Phoenician cities.

Among the Greek mainland states, the Athenians were the most successful in uniting the surrounding country with what appears to be a minimum of duress and a maximum of trust and cooperation. All persons of Attica came to consider themselves Athenians, willing to fight border wars in any part of their state, and though some were inferior in class, they were not inferior because of the distance of their landholdings from Athens. The union of the various communites of Attica in one Athenian state, called *synoikismos* probably occurred gradually and was apparently completed around 700. Common adoption of local religious practices from the various districts of Attica served to unify the state. The state cults and religious festivals would continue to act as a unifying and stabilizing force throughout the period of the Athenian Peace. By the seventh century, when history becomes clearer, Greek separatist tendencies were so strong that political units that had not already been integrated were not likely to be united without resistance and rebellion. This particularism would result in numerous conflicts and would keep the Greek states relatively weak in relation to foreign military powers.[2]

Chronological history for Athens begins with the creation of the office of *archon* in 683. Peace may have existed before, perhaps for a long period before, but the historical records are not sufficiently clear to document it. Peace lasted through the development of an artistocracy and its overthrow by a tyrant. The artistocracy regained control of the government toward the end of the sixth century, but not without a three year conflict (513-510) that ended the peace.

Characterization

By the seventh century B.C., a cultural unity had come to exist among the Greeks. They shared a common tongue and literature, a common religion, and participation in festivals and competitions that were open to all who were recognized as Greeks. There was less fighting between states from different regions than there was among local cities supporting farmers struggling for land or resisting a stronger neighbor. Warfare in this period was carried on primarily between well-shielded, long-speared infantry units, the *hoplites*. Infantry formations provided a more effective method of fighting in a poor and mountainous country than cavalry, which was expensive and needed room for maneuver. Another factor was the spread of the use of iron, which reduced the cost of weapons and armor. This made massed infantry more feasible and by reducing the importance of the noble cavalry or of individual noble foot soliders, it democratized warfare. *Hoplite* battles resulted in fewer casualties since a defeated army could drop shields and run, easily out-distancing the formation of shield-bearing victors. In Mesopotamia or Persia they would be wiped out by pursuing cavalry, but not in Greece.[3]

The improved military position of the farmer apparently encouraged him to advance his political and economic position as well. Yet in 632, when an Athenian noble named Cylon tried to establish a tyranny by coup, he received no support from the farmers surrounding the city. On the contrary, they came to the aid of the aristocratic government. Cylon was able to seize the Acropolis with the aid of soliders sent by his father-in-law, Theagenes, the tyrant of Megara. This was a serious threat to the peace, but no actual fighting is described in the sources. The swarms of peasants rallying to the defense of the state were able to surround Cylon's troops and force them into submission. The subsequent execution of Cylon's followers when they were under the proteciton of the goddess Athena Polios, to whose temple they had fled, brought down the famous curse on the head of the *archon* Megacles and his entire Alcmaeonid family.

In the following decades, under the leadership of Draco and Solon, political and economic reforms were attempted that would improve the position of farmers, merchants and the poor without completely alienating the aristocrats. Draco and Solon provided changes in the system that enabled it to cope with the growing political power of the new farmers and merchants. Around 624 Draco codified Athenian law so that citizens would be free from arbitrary justice administered by the nobility. His homocide laws, although prescribing harsh penalties, made the important distinction between murder and manslaughter. Solon, as *archon* in 594, increased the power of the Assembly, which met more regularly, had an agenda prepared for it by the new Council of 400, and had the power to choose the *archons* from the nobles of the first class. He also created a new appeals court, the *Heliaea,* on which all members of the Assembly, including even the *thetes*, the lowest class of citizens, could serve. It received appeals from decisions of the magistrates and thus the average citizen could on occasion participate in overruling the nobility. The base of political power was extended from birth and wealth to wealth alone. As prosperity increased, more and more men became wealthy enough to qualify for office.

The problems that confronted Solon cannot be appreciated without considering the economic development of Athens. Seventh-century Greek trade consisted mostly of the exchange of primary products, though there was some manufacture on a small scale of luxury goods. Though the development of trade and industry reduced self-sufficiency, most states were still largely dependent on their own farming. Despite colonization and the acquisition of the nearby island of Salamis, agrarian problems were arising from subdivision of land plots in inheritance and the loss of this land through debt to larger estates.

Solon met this situation by canceling land debts, using public funds to bring debtors back to Athens, and forbidding the pledging of one's body as security. Then he barred the export of wheat, so that it had to be sold on the Athenian market, thus reducing the price for the poor and at least temporarily securing a local food supply needed for Athens's expanding population. Solon also stimulated trade, especially in olive oil, and is credited with introducing a coinage standard that would allow Athenian products to compete in a wider market. In addition, he at least partially accounted for the introduction of many of Corinth's best potters into Athens, a fact that could only hasten the approaching Athenian eclipse of Corinth in that trade. Solon probably also instituted a graduated income tax on the top three classes that might have shifted some of the burden of supporting government from the poor to the wealthy.

Solon's reforms were assailed by the poor as not going far enough and by the nobles as going too far, but this perhaps is a measure of his success in averting civil war and preserving the peace. He did not give in to the demands of the one for land redistribution, yet he succeeded in breaking the other's monopoly of wealth and political power without resort to violence. Although his reforms did not bring immediate calm to the Athenian state and factionalism continued, his basic moderation and justice did preserve the peace.

Civil strife between political factions resumed following Solon's reforms. It was characterized by three competing groups, somewhat organized along geographical, social and economic lines. The party of the Plain was centered on Athens and dominated by the noble familes, who generally desired a return to the pre-Solonian constitution. That of the Coast was located along the sea and included merchants, fishermen and city craftsmen who were pleased with Solon's reforms. The Hill party was based in the highlands of Attica and included small farmers, shepherds, the poor, and the discontented, and favored democratic reforms. The leader and probably founder of this faction was Peisistratus.

In his first attempt at establishing a tyranny at Athens, around 561, Peisistratus, claiming to have been wounded by his political enemies, convinced the Assembly to vote him an armed bodyguard, with which he seized control of the Acropolis. This lasted only a few years, during which the tyrant ruled well, before a combination of the two opposing factions ousted him. Peisistratus soon returned for a brief period around 556, with a tall young woman dressed as Athena riding in his chariot and sanctioning his resumption of power, before he was again forced out. His third attempt was more successful because he spent the interim period amassing wealth, making foreign alliances, and hiring mercenary soldiers, especially Scythian archers. Around

546 he landed his troops at Marathon and, in a battle at Pallene to the east of Athens, defeated his opponents and firmly established his tyranny. Pallene interrupted the peace in Attica, although peace within the city continued.[4]

To assure the continued ascendancy of his tyranny, Peisistratus maintained his mercenary forces, saw to the election of friends and relatives to office, and kept as hostages the children of many of his potential enemies. He also preserved peace, both at home and abroad. He allowed traditional governmental institutions to function, under his guidance, and in general he was very popular. He instituted traveling judges to settle minor disputes in the country, thus keeping discontented persons out of the city and strengthening both the system of justice and his central control. Peisistratus's religious policy emphasized the predominant position of Athena. He was probably responsible for placing her and her symbol, the owl, on Athenian coins and he rebuilt Athena's temples and increased the importance of the Panathenaic Festival. He also instituted the City Dionysia in honor of Dionysus, a festival which featured the "goat-song" (*tragoidia*) scholars generally cite as the forerunner of Greek tragedy.

Peisistratus favored the poor in his economic policies. Some land redistribution came out of confiscation of land from exiles or dangerous opponents. He also made loans at moderate rates for farm equipment, which resulted in an increased productivity and land tax revenues. He used some of the income to improve water conduits so that fresh water could be brought to the working class people living in the city. Both Solon and Peisistratus carried out commercial policies that encouraged production and the trade of luxury products for export and this led to an increase in wealth. Peisistratus used some of this increased wealth to launch a building program that provided jobs and beautified the city.

The transformation of class structure underlying these other changes has already been made evident. The old families whose wealth was based on land were being challenged by less wealthy farmers whose status was increased by the role they played as *hoplites* in the citizen army and by cash-crop farmers, manufacturers, and middlemen who were becoming well-to-do through trade. All these classes, however, had to deal with a poor class that was becoming poorer as others prospered. This class could have been competely subordinated or its rights and problems could have been dealt with. The Athenians chose the latter course and preserved their peace — whether because of or in spite of this decision is difficult to say with certainty.

The two leaders who stand out in this period, Solon and Peisistratus, were both nobles who had affinities with other classes. Solon achieved recognition because of his integrity and his intelligence; Peisistratus, because of his genial personality and his cleverness. They both had gained military fame; each in his own way was radical; each in his way, moderate.

The striking cultural and artistic achievements that have drawn attention to Athens came later. But they had their beginnings in the sixth century, in the splendid black-figure pottery and the archaically pure sculpture that arose when Peisistratus began to embellish his city. In putting an end to the strife of the artistocratic factions and weakening the power of the old nobility, while at the same time elevating the status of the Athenian middle and lower classes, Peisistratus's tyranny performed a necessary and positive role in preparing Athens for the democracy that would follow soon afterward.

Termination

When Peisistratus died in 527, he was succeeded by two of his sons, Hippias as political leader and Hipparchus as a junior partner. The two brothers generally continued their father's policies. They were particularly successful in attracting eminent literary figures to their court. However, foreign relations were changing rapidly with the threatening expansion of the Persians into northern Greece and the jealousy of both Sparta and Thebes regarding recent Athenian growth. The assassination of Hipparchus in 514 because of a personal matter turned Hippias into a cruel architect of repression. He instituted new taxes, reportedly even one on birth and death, in order to raise money to pay additional mercenary troops. He became more harsh, less approachable, sometimes almost paranoid. The position of the tyrant was sufficiently delicate that any sign of his weakening could encourage rebellion.

The Athenian nobility, led by the Alcmaeonid Cleisthenes, gained the support of the neighboring kingdom of Sparta through manipulation of the Delphic Oracle and began a rebellion against Hippias. The tyrant, in turn, was backed by another neighboring kingdom, Thessaly. The opposing forces were evenly matched and it took three battles, a siege of Athens and the withdrawal of Thessalian support, before Hippias was finally forced into exile in 510. The Athenian Peace had come to an end. Meanwhile, finding Cleisthenes too independent, King Cleomenes of Sparta switched his support first to a more conservative Athenian noble, Isagoras, and then to the exiled Hippias. On behalf of the dethroned tyrant, Attica was again invaded by the Spartans, this time supported by forces from Thebes and Chalcidice, before the struggle subsided with Cleisthenes still in control. The stage was now set for the establishment of Athenian democracy and for the advances in so many areas that would glorify the "Age of Pericles" in the fifth century.

Reflections

The peace survived as long as it did because of luck, dextrous handling of problems of Solon and Peisistratus, a pattern of settling disputes by nonviolent methods, and an external pattern of relationships that surrounded Athens with other small states engrossed by their own troubles, while larger states capable of destroying the city were too distant and the whole Greek peninsula was too obscure to attract much attention.

The history of Athens begins to be decipherable only after the conditions under which peace existed were already established. Therefore the founders and consolidators, if they existed, are not known to us. Solon and Peisistratus were reformers. Their problem was not the revitalizing and restoration of the old order, as it was for Haremhab, but the steering of a society through a political, economic and social transformation.

The problem was complicated by Athens' location in the midst of a multipower situation in some respects comparable to that which confronted the Phoenicians but involving many more states and these, smaller and more closely packed together. That they were not engulfed by a greater power is attributable to their remote location with relation to the centers of civilization in Asia, their poverty and their isolation by mountains and sea. That no Mentuhotpe II arose among them to attempt unification seems to be a matter of thought patterns, perhaps related to geography, that had become deeply rooted within the people, while economic necessity—if it is a cause of expansionist policies—was alleviated somewhat by colonization.

The behavior of the Thessalian barons and the Spartans in the crisis of 513-10 reveals something about the attitudes of the archaic Greeks, shows why wars of total conquest were rare, and possibly indicates that the pattern was in a process of change by the end of the sixth century. The Spartans intervened because they were repeatedly advised to do so by the religious Delphic oracle. If this story had come a couple of centuries earlier, we should have called it legend and attributed Spartan intervention to a desire for power or wealth. But the behavior of both Spartans and Thessalians is such that it is apparent that faith, honor, prestige and even sportsmanship played an important part in shaping their policy. The Thessalians beat the Spartans in one conflict, lost in a second, accepted the verdict and went home. While they defended their honor, it is almost as if they were good sports about it, perhaps feeling they could not win them all or that they had given the Athenian tyrant as much support as the issue warranted. To bring further troops in for a third conflict would have violated the tradition of moderation.

Yet it is also obvious that once he did become involved, Cleomenes hoped to gain political influence over the government of Athens. Certainly the oracle did not advise him to restore the man he had helped depose. It could be that this change of attitude reflects the end of the archaic phase of Greek history and the beginning of a more modern, power-oriented period.

7

The Corinthian Peace
(655-427 B.C.)

Corinth is located at the head of an isthmus that separates two gulfs linking the Ionian and Aegean seas. This position encouraged the Corinthians to build a navy and to concentrate on commerical enterprises throughout the Mediterranean Sea. Corinth became the major point of exchange for overseas commerce between the Aegean and Black Sea areas in the east and Ionian and western Mediterranean regions in the west. Their position astride the narrow connection between mainland Greece and the Peloponnesus likewise assured the Corinthians of an important role as a marketplace for trade over land. They exported large amounts of pottery and also bronzework. Rich and complacent, Corinth showed that peace could be established on a foundation of commercialism.

The aristocratic period of Corinthian history is more obscure than that of Athens. We know that it was dominated by the Bacchiads, an aristocratic clan, but we have no archonic dating to help us with chronology. Around 655, however, the Bacchiads were ousted by a noble named Cypselus, who established a tyranny.

As in Athens, the aristocracy eventually recovered power, but with much less conflict involved than in the corresponding overthrow of Hippias. Corinth, however, did not follow Athens in developing democracy. The aristocracy maintained peace until war involved most of the Greek states in the latter part of the fifth century. The Peloponnesian War brought the Corinthian Peace to an end in 427, when Athenians besieged the city.

Basically the change in structure of Corinth during the peace was much simpler than that of Athens. The territory involved was much smaller; Corinthian control extended little more than 100 square miles.

Characterization

Cypselus himself appears to have been a popular demagogue who was able to walk the streets without a bodyguard. His rule, in any event, was apparently more benevolent than that of the aristocracy he had overthrown. His son, Periander, was less popular, but not less effective. Both men sought religious sanction for their tyranny by constructing Corinthian monuments at Delphi and Olympia.

The Cypselids were not so subtle as the Peisistratids. If they aimed to keep the rich busy and subdued, it was not with an eye toward gaining the support of the poor. They simply aimed at holding power. To this end Periander limited the number of slaves a man could hold and discouraged excessive display of luxury so that no man would rise too far above others and attract a following. To this end also, like Peisistratus, he discouraged people from moving from the country to the city, where political activity was likely to take place.

When Periander died, around 586, he was replaced by his nephew, Psammetichus, who was killed after a brief reign. The tyranny was then replaced by a moderate oligarchy that continued to keep power concentrated. A council of 80 merchant aristocrats then ruled. The farmers and artisans had no part in the government.

Though the regime was occasionally oppressive, the city reached a high level of prosperity. A commercial empire was established extending into the Aegean and Mediterranean. One of the tyrants was likely responsible for the construction of the *diolkos*, a stone passageway across the Isthmus that allowed ships to be carried across land from one gulf to the other.

Although Corinth's two greatest colonies, Syracuse and Corcyra, were founded under the Bacchiads in the late eighth century, both Cypselus and Periander established important colonies, particularly along the northwest coast of Greece. These served as trading centers both along the routes to the west and for penetration into the less civilized interior. The two tyrants apparently built up Corinth's military and especially naval strength. Periander had close ties with the tyrant of Miletus and expanded trade with that part of Asia Minor and with Egypt.

Cypselus' apparent introduction of a sound coinage would also have increased Corinthian access to foreign ports. The benefits of her commercial wealth must have extended to a large percentage of Corinth's forty to fifty thousand inhabitants. Their lives were made more pleasant because the bulk of their unpleasant work was done by slaves. Thus Corinth had an aristocracy of landowners, but few problems with a class of rising farmers or urban poor.

Under the tyrant, Corinth, like Athens, engaged in great building activity and became a center for artists and poets. Periander brought to his court Arion of Lesbos, who is credited by Herodotus (I. 23-24) with developing the *dithyramb*, or choral song, used in the cult of Dionysus. He is also credited with introducing the Isthmian Games in honor of Poseidon. This soon became one of the great panhellenic festivals of Greece. Corinth also achieved recognition in temple architecture, particularly for the development of the pediment. Corinth dominated Greek pottery production and pioneered in using the colorful "orientalizing" style. Attic vase painting, however, gradually surpassed Corinthian in both quality and quantity during the late sixth century.

The Corinthians maintained friendly relations with their strongest neighbors, Athens and Sparta, into the fifth century and they fought with other Greeks to turn back a formidable Persian invasion before it reached the Isthmus of Corinth. There is no doubt, however, that Sparta and Corinth, by planning a defense at the Isthmus, were willing to leave Athens and other northern states to suffer invasion at the hands of the Persians. Corinth was concerned primarily with saving her own city and ports. This was a dangerous game, for without the support of the Athenian fleet Corinth might have been subject to invasion by sea, even though she still had her own formidable fleet available for defense.

Termination

As early as the last years of Periander's reign, the international importance of Corinth began to decline, both in trade and military affairs. By the middle of the fifth century, there was a deterioration in the relations between Corinth and Athens. Athenian encroachment in Corinth's immediate area was largely responsible for this reversal of what had been a friendly relationship. The Corinthians suffered greatly in commerical competition with the free and vital Athenians, who more than once increased antagonism by intervening in Corinthian colonial affairs and sending more and more of their vessels into the Gulf of Corinth. When Athens became an ally of Argos and then joined Megara, Corinth and Aegina decided that the Athenian presence in their region was too much of a threat to their commerce and their sovereignty and hostilities broke out in 459 or 458 in what is called the First Peloponnesian War. The battlegrounds in this war, however, were the Megarid and Boeotia and neither Corinth nor Athens was invaded. Although this struggle was officially ended with the Thirty Years' Peace of 445, the growing Athenian arrogance in relations with her Delian League, combined with the increasing Peloponnesian fear of Athenian strength, led to Athenian intervention in Corinth's colonial affairs, which sparked the outbreak of the great war between Athens and Sparta in 431.

The major Peloponnesian War went badly for the Corinthians in its early phases and after suffering a naval defeat they were invaded in 427 by the Athenians, who could not take the city but destroyed the surrounding countryside. Corinth survived the rest of this war, but shortly thereafter endured a domestic massacre and two invasions by Spartans and dissident Corinthians, which resulted in two breaches of their long wall to the sea, the capture of towns within the Corinthian sphere, and a bloody battle below the walls of Corinth itself.

The peace ended because the Corinthians felt they had to take a stand against their expanding neighbor. But they might have been able to protect their land from invasion if they had maintained their domination of the sea. That they could not was attributable not to their lack of power but to their inability to use it. They continued to use older tactics, based on the expectation of hand-to-hand battles between ships grappled together, while the Athenians developed ramming tactics, stressing speed and maneuverability and requiring seamanship rather than armed power. Just as the Athenians had shot ahead of the Corinthians in pottery making, they also outdistanced them in military tactics. In the end the Corinthian Peace seems to have been lost because of a decline in vitality and imagination and a corresponding failure to keep pace with a more vigorous neighbor.

Reflections

The Corinthians maintained their internal peace because their problem, compared with that of the Athenians, was simple. Those who were well off were satisfied with any government that would allow them to remain comfortable. Those who were poor or were slaves had no base of potential power with which to threaten their government. In addition, the state was so small that the government could easily maintain its control. A common religious and cultural tradition also contributed to the preservation of unity. Corinthian problems were primarily commercial and their leaders did not have to cope with complicated reconciliations of small farmers and landed nobility. Administrative difficulties were simplified by Corinth's mercantile orientation because most of the citizens were kept active and relatively satisfied. The Corinthians were also fortunate that Periander had been less popular than Cypselus. His successors, unlike those of Peisistratus, had little support when the aristocratic counter-rebellion took place and the peace was hardly rippled.

It is significant that the early years of the Corinthian Peace, as is also true of a large part of the Athenian Peace, took place under the rule of tyrants. In both cases, the tyrant's central control coupled with rule by and large for the good of the state was most likely an important factor. The tyrannies allowed both city-states to harness the power of their nobilities while bringing new groups of citizens into political, social, and economic participation.

The Corinthians remained free from alien attack for the

same reasons that served the Athenians: the local character of war during the period, their strong navy and the remoteness of the Greek peninsula from other centers of power. When the Persians finally reached Greece, the Corinthians benefited from the enterprising leadership of the Athenians and Spartans and from the geographical circumstances that placed their Isthmus beyond the region in which the battles of the Persian War were fought.

On the local level, Corinth was one of the major Greek city-states and was strong enough to resist any aggression on the part of her neighbors. In addition, the balance of power was such that, although Sparta was a dominant power in the Peloponnesus by the mid-sixth century, there was little danger that she would try to absorb her allies. Sparta had her hands full keeping Messenia subjected to her will. No state north of the Isthmus was powerful enough to threaten Corinth until the sudden spurt of Attic empire-building in the mid-fifth century altered the balance of power. Corinth's ties with Sparta within the Peloponnesian League also brought her the assistance of Greece's strongest land power. This naturally helped maintain stability and peace in the region, although the alliances would ultimately produce war with Athens on a greater scale.

There were probably other city-states in the eastern Mediterranean that managed to achieve a century or more of peace before the Persians invaded. This is likely because of their number and smallness. Though warfare was frequent, it was not ubiquitous. Any period of warfare, no matter how violent, will have its patches of peace. Where such cities were left alone by external opponents, they had a chance to maintain internal peace, again because of their smallness, since each government could be in touch with its population as no emperor could. Being in touch could mean very different solutions to problems, as the Corinthian solution was very different from the Athenian. One population might fare well under a generous distribution of power and another might thrive when political power was centralized. When one pattern of rule was losing its effectiveness, a transformation could be made to another when the desirability for such a transformation was accepted among elites.

8

The Achaemenid Peace
(520-331 B.C.)

The great clash between East and West, immortalized by Herodotus, pitted the largest empire yet to appear in western Asia, the Achaemenid Empire of Persia, against the independent city-states of Greece. For Western historians, the Persian Wars of 490-479 B.C. represented a crucial event, and threat to the whole future course of Western Civilization, for they were followed by the florescence of Greek culture and ultimately the Hellenistic expansion, the Roman Empire and the whole shaping of Western history. For the Persians, however, this was an unsuccessful peripheral adventure during a glorious period of history, the creation of a vast, intricately governed, stable and generally peaceful empire.

The geography of the Iranian Plateau region, relatively isolated and protected by surrounding mountains and deserts, appears to have helped prepare the Achaemenid Peace in much the same way that the physical features of Egypt contributed to her periods of peace. The records of the peoples of the Iranian Plateau are obscure except as they relate to Mesopotamia where the Elamites of the Zagros Mountains had fought or allied themselves with various small states for centuries. The Elamites were perhaps related to the Guti and Lullubi peoples of the Luristan Mountains who descended upon the Akkadian Empire around 2100 B.C. and together with the Kassites formed the ethnic background for the emergence of the state of Parsa under (the possibly legendary) Achaemenes in the seventh century. The Parsa (sometimes, *Parsua*) came originally from the Caucasus region

72

or from eastern Iran to Persis (Fars) where they settled. Further
north, between the Persian Gulf and the Caspian Sea, the Medes
became powerful. They conquered Parsa, and after some fluc-
tuations of fortune, united with Chaldean Babylonia to destroy
Assyria. They were then free to build an empire that extended
from the Halys in Asia Minor east to the Oxus in Bactria and
south to the Persian Gulf. The chief builder of this empire was
Cyaxares (625-585). His son, Astyages (584-550 B.C.), however,
proved incapable of holding his father's domain and his power
was destroyed after an alliance was formed between Nabonidus
of Babylonia and Cyrus II (559-530) of Parsa. Nabonidus swept
up the Euphrates Valley (555 B.C.) unopposed while Astyages
sent two armies against Cyrus. Both rebelled, and went over to
Cyrus, while Astyages was captured and his capital city, Ecbatana, was plundered (550).[1]

Origins

Cyrus and his son Cambyses II (530-552) pushed the new
empire even further than that established by the Medes, defeating
Croesus's Lydian kingdom and occupying all of Anatolia, extending their eastern boundary as far as the Jaxartes and Indus,
destroying the Chaldean Empire and sweeping on into Syria,
Egypt and Libya. But a succession dispute that brought Darius I
(522-486) to power resulted in an apparent breakup of the empire, with the Medes conquering Assyria and western Anatolia,
while Babylonia, Parsa and Elam rebelled under local leaders.
Significantly, Darius was able to defeat all his foes and reunite
the empire—which had taken Cyrus and Cambyses three decades to
assemble—in less than two years.[2]

The reconstituted empire was moderately successful in
preserving peace in its central areas—Mesopotamia and the
Iranian Plateau—from the victory of Darius in 521 until the invasion of these areas by Alexander of Macedonia between 331
and 328. In addition, peace was maintained in Syria and
Palestine, as well as in eastern Asia Minor, through the fifth century. Peace did not last very long in Egypt or western Asia Minor,
while the Indian portion of the empire broke away in the middle

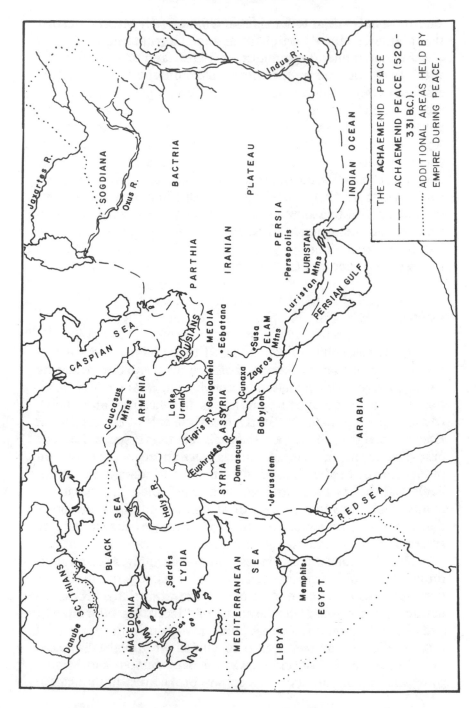

THE ACHAEMENID PEACE

— — — ACHAEMENID PEACE (520–331 B.C.).

· · · · · · · · ADDITIONAL AREAS HELD BY EMPIRE DURING PEACE.

of the fifth century. Even the center of the empire was occasionally affected by internal conflicts: rebellions of Bactria,
Cadusia, Elam and Babylon itself as well as a major battle in 401
fought at Cunaxa, 60 miles north of Babylon, was the culmination
of a succession struggle. (This battle was followed by the famous
march of the 10,000 Greek mercenary soliders back to Greece
under Xenophon.)

While these were significant interruptions to the imperial
peace it must be borne in mind that they occurred over a period
of two centuries within an area of more than a million square
miles. The achievement of the Persians in creating such a large
area of peace for so long is still most impressive.

Characterization

The Persian kings struggled to hold together an extremely
diverse region, and to do so they employed a quiverful of
methods. On one hand they were capable of conciliation and
tolerance. They were willing to employ local kings as dependent
rulers (*satraps*), where they felt these would be accepted, even
though this policy could result in rebellion, as it sometimes did.
Relatively monotheistic themselves, they were tolerant of
regional polytheism, so that Cyrus was able to present himself as
a defender of local Babylonian cults in contrast to the centralizing Nabonidus, who liked to have all his divinities at hand.
Men of talent—Sogdianan, Lydian or Egyptian—were offered
opportunities to rise in government and military service. The
Persians treated surrendered populations humanely and
established a reputation for keeping their promises. Inhabitants
that had been deported by previous dynasties, such as the
Hebrews in Babylon, were given permission to return to their
homelands.

But running through this pattern of tolerance and
humanity was another contradictory pattern of vengefulness and
brutality. Rebels, traitors and even mildly corrupt officials were
subject to brutally imaginative tortures and executions. Locally
appointed *satraps* who allowed or encouraged rebellion were
replaced by centrally appointed men who were instructed to

govern harshly. Rebellious populations were transported to distant parts of the empire. Garrisons, consisting of permanently settled soldiers, with their families, were established to control areas that had a reputation for rebellion. Thus a policy of tolerance and humanity was also one of expedience and it could be quickly reversed if it failed to produce satisfactory results. The policy of tolerance must have been the dominant one, however, for no previous empire attempted to bring together under one rule so many different nationalities.[3]

The bureaucracy that managed this system of *satraps* does not appear to have been exceptional. Men made their way to the top by merit, to some extent, but part of this merit must have been an ability to keep out of trouble. It was less important to take the initiative than to obey rules. Thus, according to Ctesias, a *satrap* named Megabyzus almost lost his life for shooting a lion that was about to dine on his king. The king, Artaxerxes (465-424), ordered him beheaded for violating a rule that stated that no one should kill an animal in a hunt before the monarch had killed one himself. Megabyzus was saved only by intercession of certain ladies of the court and was merely exiled for his crime. There was a good deal of nepotism within the court and Persians and Medes held a disproportionate share of offices. Some of these offices appear to have been hereditary.[4]

In order to maintain some monitoring of the activities of his *satraps*, Darius developed a system of special inspectors, "The King's Eyes," to report on the conditions in the provinces and the loyalty of his officials. It must be supposed that as time went on, the Persians would have had to face the problem that developed in New Kingdom Egypt: collusion between central and provincial officials.[5]

Like preceding governments of Babylonia and Assyria, the Persian government maintained irrigation and roads. The latter were not as good as those of the Assyrians in terms of paving or milestones, but they were well-traveled, well-policed and equipped with adequate inns. A highly efficient postal service was maintained with mail carried from station to station on horseback.[6]

Darius updated the legal code of Hammurabi, which had served Babylonia, Assyria and Persia. The laws continued to be very specific and to prescribe punishments that were often severe. Great emphasis was placed, at least in Darius's time, on the honesty of the judges, who were given lifetime appointments and high honor, but severely punished for taking bribes.

Darius also standardized weights and measures, the values of metals and coinage for the empire. Although the coinage reforms may not have affected the Persian peasants to a great degree, the general policy of standardization was important not only for merchants involved in trade, but also for the empire as a whole in that it provided a more uniform tax structure. Collection of taxes, under the direction of each individual *satrap*, was fairly equitable and provided the monarch with a regular source of precious metals and agricultural products. He used both in supporting the administration of his empire and was still able to accumulate a large stockpile of the former in his treasury. Overtaxation would eventually sap the strength and loyalty of the satrapies. Government involvement in business and trade increased dramatically under Darius, raising prices to high levels and generating economic dislocation for the future.[7]

Although the Persian homeland was characterized by seminomadic bands of herders, the empire had swallowed the highly urbanized and economically advanced areas of Mesopotamia and Egypt. Here business and trade flourished and social gradations, including a large slave population, were highly developed. The Persian monarch took particular care to maintain control in these regions and expected increased taxation proportionate to an area's wealth. Darius's standardization of coinage and weights, however, and his construction of a canal between the Nile River and the Red Sea, combined with the maintenance of an effective road system and the general peace created by Persian control, apparently benefited economic life in these regions.

The absence of long periods of peace in the Near East may be attributable in part to the introduction of iron in the 12th century. This made it possible to arm many more men, so that battles could no longer be decided by a small cavalry of nobles. For some time this may have worked to the advantage of the outlanders, who armed as many men as they could, while the nobles hesitated to arm their peasants for fear of losing control of them.

By the time of the Medes and Persians, however, the creation of large armies began to work to the advantage of centrally organized empires. The Persians were able to create a much larger standing army than had been known before, greatly superior in organization and fire power to any force a group of nobles could hope to muster. The standing army was organized around the 10,000 Immortals, so called because their force was never allowed to drop below that number. This was an elite of Persians, Medes and Elamites. The Immortals were supported by contingents from other parts of the empire. Though the army as a whole was organized into regiments and companies of thousands and hundreds it was never integrated into a national force. So long as battles were fought in open terrain, this army seemed invincible. It relied on the use of arrow volleys, and its firepower was so great that the ranks of enemy cavalrymen and infantry were decimated before they were able to close in for battle. The power of this army may have helped maintain peace among *satraps* who otherwise might have considered rebellion.

The great weakness of the army was that it was terribly difficult to supply. The emperors Darius I and Artaxerxes II (404-359) found themselves foiled respectively by the Scythians of the Black Sea area and the Cadusians of the Caspian, because these foes would neither fight nor surrender. And the one thing such a great army could not do was to remain idle: it was too difficult to feed. For the same reason, Xerxes (486-465) had to retreat when the Greeks cut off his naval supplies by winning the battle of Salamis. But this weakness merely set a limit on Persian expansion, it did not affect control of areas nearer the center.

Once the administrative system was established, it seemed to carry along on its own momentum. After Darius there were no outstanding monarchs, although no one who was outstandingly incompetent lasted very long either. The succession system, though clear enough in theory, worked badly in practice. Only in the cases of Cambyses and Xerxes did the designated successor take the throne without great difficulty. The successors of Xerxes — Artaxerxes I, Darius II (423-404) and Artaxerxes II — all had to battle or conspire for the throne. Several monarchs and contenders for the throne were either assassinated or executed. Palace intrigue was a constant threat to Achaemenid stability. The influence of dominant women in the royal family over the

Great King on several occasions deprived the monarch of capable generals and *satraps,* who were executed to satisfy the jealous desires of queen mother, queens, or princesses.

We have already observed, in discussing Persian tolerance, that the monarchs were nominal monotheists. Possibly their Zoroastrian belief in Ahura Mazda as the supreme god might have strengthened the image of the appropriateness of an absolute monarch. But certainly the emperors never let their religious convictions get in the way of their policies and as time went on, Ahura Mazda became, as Olmstead puts it, a remote monarch with a harem full of mother goddesses. This may have been bad for the purity of Zoroastrianism but possibly it contributed to the tranquility of the empire.[8]

Persia's rapid expansion from a small primitive state to a vast empire encompassing areas with long established cultural patterns naturally restricted and channeled her own development. However, the Achaemenid artists adapted Babylonian or Assyrian models to their own purposes, especially to create the image of imperial grandeur, strength, and unity. They displayed great artistic skill in the construction of magnificent palaces and state buildings, in high quality relief work, and in the minor arts, particularly in cylinder seal engraving, in jewelry, and in various metal utensils. Art and architecture both served as vehicles for proclaiming the power, the order, and the unity brought to the empire by its King of Kings.

Termination

The peace came to an end with Alexander's invasion of Mesopotamia in 331 and his victory at Gaugamela in Assyria, followed by his destruction of Persepolis and his crushing of resistance in Bactria and Sogdiana. Alexander confiscated an enormous treasure as he marched through Babylon, Susa, and Persepolis and he soon became the Great King himself.

The Persians were defeated, certainly, because of a deterioration in the quality of leadership. Darius III (336-330) was consistently ineffective and out-generaled, lacking both in ability and courage. And certainly he was in power as the result of harem intrigue, the chosen candidate of Bagoas the Eunuch, who had murdered the more capable Ochus (359-338). Probably the Persians should not have engaged the Macedonians in Asia Minor at all, at least not on such a large scale, since the cities in the area were disloyal to Persia. A continuing guerrilla campaign might have worn out the invaders, draining their supplies and weakening their forces until attrition became a Persian ally. But if Darius had let Alexander take Asia Minor without opposition, he almost certianly would have had trouble keeping his throne in Persepolis. In addition, Alexander had the advantages of a new and superior technique. The Macedonians were accustomed to work with the Thracian cavalry and the Greek phalanx. Alexander's father, Philip, had combined the two: charging with massed, shielded cavalry, backed up by the power of the phalanx. They could run down the Persians with a massed attack before the enemy arrows could take effect. In short, the Persians were attacked by a formidable opponent using novel techniques at a time when their leadership was weak and their bureaucracy was in need of revision.

The Persians were world travelers who were concerned with military techniques and had ample opportunity to try them out. That they did not experiment extensively with military tactics might be attributable to the tendencies of bureaucracies, military as well as civil, to establish vested interests in existing techniques. Just as 20th-century armies persisted in employing cavalry and teaching bayonet skills long after they became irrelevant, so the commanders who had been schooled in arrow volley warfare must have been strongly reluctant to abandon them for the combined phalanx and cavalry attack.

Reflections

In the establishment of the empire there emerges once again the foundation-consolidation pattern. Cyrus was certainly more than a great conqueror; his instincts always worked toward conciliation and consolidation. Nevertheless, the main organizational job fell to Darius. He established the bureaucracy, instituted a revised law code, stabilized the economy, organized the army on a basis of hierarchy as the Assyrians had done, and initiated the system of special inspectors. With Xerxes we already have the magnificent monarch, an Amenhotpe III reaping the rewards of his predecessors' work. His successors we might call mediocre. They manage so long as nothing exceptional is required of them. But when it is, like Darius III they go down ignominiously. No Haremhab appears to reform the bureaucracy, but considering the size of the empire, it would have taken countless Haremhabs to go to each province making effective, personal inspections. The nearest to a reformer to come to the throne was Ochus, more of a Senwosret III, forceful and aggressive, able to dam the tide, but not to divert it.

It would appear that a clear succession system is not necessary for peace. Possibly such a system would have brought a series of very weak monarchs. Possibly having to fight for power insured the survival of the fittest, as in the case of Darius I and Ochus. Of course it could also be that a lack of vigor on the part of some monarchs helped preserve the peace where effective collection of taxes would have brought rebellion.

Against internal weaknesses the early kings were able to build an image of just and tolerant leadership combined with the threat of an army of overwhelming power and rapid mobility. They got the obedience because their rule was not unbearable and because they offered some advantages to the obedient, while promising severe punishment to the disobedient. The image of justice, however, was by no means a product of cynical politics. On Achaemenid documents there runs a conception of ethics that is not to be found among the rulers or scribes of Babylon or Assyria.

The problem of regional control was greater for the Persians than it had been for any of their predecessors. They tried all sorts of devices: a well-maintained system of communications, the transportation of rebellious populations, the settling of garrrisons in remote parts of the empire, governing with regional authorities to instill regional support, governing with central authorities to prevent regional rebellion. Yet they were clearly overextended. They could consistently maintain peace only in regions nearer their center of power.

The fact that Darius revised a system of law does not tell us much about the relation between law and peace. Hammurabi's legal code does not appear to have preserved peace for his empire. Probably the system of law that exists must be appropriate for the times. Since a transition from time of conflict to time of peace means a general alteration in the kinds of problems arising, a need for change in law may be felt.

The legal reforms of Darius seem consistent also with the desire of early Persian monarchs to build up an image of temperance, integrity, and justice in the central government. The expectation that justice could be obtained might increase the support it received. The same is true of tolerance. Newly-conquered peoples could be assured that if they offered no resistance and paid their taxes, their way of life would not be interfered with.

The virtues of the empire must have outweighed its defects. By the time Darius came to power, the possibility of a widespread empire had been established by the preceding conquests of Cyaxares and Cyrus. Once established, the benefits coming from the empire to aspirants to military, governmental and priestly positions, as well as to the merchants of Syria, Phoenicia and Mesopotamia, must have created a powerful and influential desire to perpetuate it regardless of deficiencies to be found at Persepolis. In addition, a conscious policy of religious and cultural unity and an excellent communications system, along with an efficient administration and omnipresent army, helped to preserve the Achaemenid Peace.

9

The Ptolemaic Peace
(332-216 B.C.)

Origins

Alexander of Macedon died less than a decade after his conquest of the Persian Empire had opened Egypt and Southwest Asia to Hellenic culture. The lands he conquered were divided, not without extensive conflict, among his generals. If two of the ultimate victors, Antigonus and Seleucus, were unable to establish poltical entities capable of maintaining peace in Greece or the lands east of the Mediterranean, it was otherwise with their colleague, Ptolemy Soter, first *satrap* and later (305) king of Egypt. Although Ptolemy was involved with the others in a series of wars to acquire footholds or extend holdings, he focused his attention on consolidating his control of Egypt and strengthening his fleet to win the Mediterranean territories necessary to protect the Nile Delta. By the time of his abdication in 285 he had achieved these objectives.

The peace period began before Soter arrived. It can be traced back through Alexander, who entered the country in 332 as liberator and was not resisted after his victorious siege of Gaza on his way to Egypt, to the Persian reconquest of Memphis from the Greek mercenaries under Amyntas several months earlier. This general, who had deserted both Alexander and Darius, invaded Egypt later in 333 or early 332 and gained control of both Pelusium and Memphis. The Persians under Mazaces, however, counterattacked following their defeat in a battle near Memphis and succeeded in regaining control of the city after killing Amyntas and many of his followers. The peace

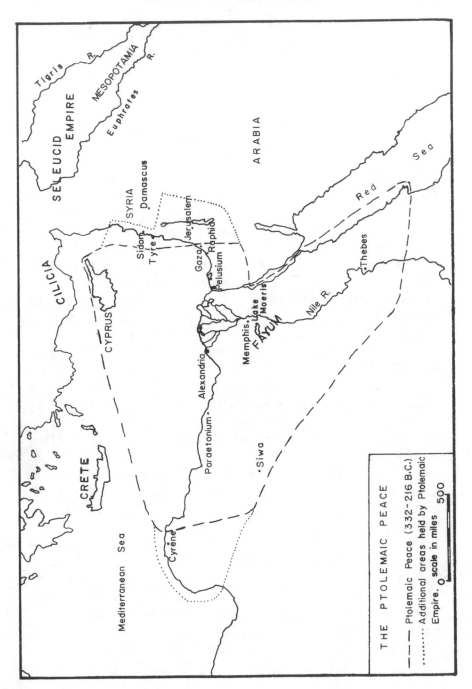

THE PTOLEMAIC PEACE

— — — Ptolemaic Peace (332–216 B.C.)
·········· Additional areas held by Ptolemaic
Empire.

scale in miles
0   500

lasted, then, from 332 until the first of many Egyptian rebellions against Macedonian rule in 216.

Characterization

A policy of frequent but limited engagements was followed by the Ptolemies. Egypt could be invaded either by land from Syria or by sea on the Delta. Ptolemy I therefore sought to build a strong navy and to control the coasts of the Mediterranean on both sides of the Delta as well as Cyprus. Control of the Mediterranean meant also that he would have access to Greek and Macedonian mercenaries, and these he attracted by his liberality. The Egyptian empire was compact, for generally the Ptolemies did not seriously try to hold territory that was not essential to their defense or to the carrying on of trade. Ptolemy III Euergetes (246-221) did attempt an expedition into the heart of the Seleucid Empire, but this was an uncharacteristic involvement in a succession struggle rather than an effort to extend territory. In execution it resembled a grand tour by a popular and friendly foreign sovereign. The Ptolemies were continually involved in secondary skirmishes and maneuvers in the Eastern Mediterranean area.[1]

Within their land, the first two Ptolemies, Soter and Philadelphus (285-246), established a far-reaching system of state ownership designed to exploit the wealth of the country for the benefit of the Macedonian rulers. The king, like the pharaohs before him, owned the entire Nile Valley. Supervision of its production was carried out in remarkable detail under what W.W. Tarn calls a "thoroughgoing system of state nationalism."[2] Its operation required a tremendous number of officials, Greek at the upper levels, Egyptian at the lower. They maintained minute supervision of post offices, roads, canals, dams and taxes. The Ptolemies kept the old Egyptian system of *nomes*, but these were further subdivided on the village level. To keep accounts, a remarkable collection of statistics was gathered in each village, forwarded to the *nomes*, and finally redigested in Alexandria. A separate finance minister presided over another set of officials who employed these statistics for the collection of taxes. There were so many positions to fill at the lower levels that officers had to be conscripted.

The Ptolemaic dynasty was regarded as the richest in the world. Its wealth came from lands, taxes, monopolies and trade. The land owned by the king was supervised by his retainers and occupied by *fellahin*, Egyptian serfs. Other land the king leased to temple priests, retainers or mercenaries, who paid him rent for its use. This land was also minutely supervised. One could not cut a tree without the king's permission and all pasturage had to be rented from the king. The mercenaries were given land as an incentive for entering the service of the Ptolemies and to keep them occupied during peacetime. Their rent was not so high since military service was part of their obligation. Every parcel of land was registered, so that a yearly count of houses, population and livestock was maintained. Even fish were counted. Instead of selling fishing licenses, the government sent an agent along to take a percentage of the angler's catch.[3]

Along with a heavy tax on farm produce (often the government would tell farmers what to plant), there were poll taxes, sales taxes, house rent taxes, inheritance taxes, slave taxes. All trades and industries paid license fees.

Besides being the greatest wheat merchant in the world, the king had a monopoly on oil, mining, salt and papyrus. He fixed the quantity of each item that would be produced and paid a set price for it, selling at the inflated price what the deliberately reduced supply would bring. Thus the king either owned all the land and all business or he received a part of every transaction.

Trade flourished in the Hellenistic world and Egypt could trade surplus grain, flax and papyrus for exotic meats, fish, oil, honey, wine, fruits and timber. Copper came from Cyprus and, with the clearing of the old canal from the Nile to the Red Sea, gold and spices from Arabia and ivory, pearls and cotton from Africa and India. Alexandria was the busiest industrial and trade center in the whole world.

A money economy continued to develop during this period. Two main currencies were used throughout the Hellenistic world and regular banks were established in the commercial cities. In the provinces money remained scarce and brought very high interest rates.

Public works carried out by the government were designed to improve trade or to increase the amount of productive land. Lake Moeris was drained to recover the fertile Fayyûm land, the canal between the Red Sea and the Nile was restored, caravan routes were equipped with wells and block houses, and official postal service, modeled on the Persian, was established with the innovation of a parcel post. All of this was carried out under the first two Ptolemies.

The Ptolemies tried to support their position through religion, philosophy and setting. They followed the policies of preceding pharaohs by making themselves and their ancestors gods. They built temples and paid homage to Egyptian deities, even while they strove to reduce the power of the priesthood. They supported their position through the advocacy of Hellenistic political theory, which glorified the idea that one man, the best, should be leader of his people, their protector, paymaster and benefactor, while at the same time conducting himself as a gentleman and supporter of the arts and sciences.

Ptolemy I had intercepted Alexander's body on its return trip to Macedonia and interred it temporarily in Memphis pending the construction of a magnificent tomb in Alexandria. Ptolemy II later moved the remains to their final resting place, thus adding to the luster of the capital and increasing the legitimacy of Ptolemaic rule.

The Ptolemies made Alexandria a cultural as well as political and economic center of the Hellenistic world. They attracted poets, philosophers, scientists, and mathematicians from various areas to their capital and constructed the Museum and the Library to provide the proper materials and environment for their work. Three of the greatest figures in Hellenistic literature, Callimachus, Apollonius Rhodius, and Theocritus, were associated with the Ptolemaic court, the first two having directed the Library. And yet, their poetry is not specifically Alexandrian, but characteristic of the age as a whole. An Alexandrian style does develop, focusing on detail and relating stories within stories, but this has no direct connection to Egypt. Several of the Ptolemaic scholars also contributed to textual criticism and commentary on great works from the past.

The Ptolemies also established Alexandria as a center of

Hellenistic science, attracting leading figures to work at their court in such fields as medicine, geography, astronomy, botany, zoology, physics and mathematics. The achievements of Euclid and Apollonius of Perga in geometry, the work of Hipparchus in trigonometry, Eratosthenes's close estimate of the earth's circumference, the discoveries of Archimedes in mechanics and mathematics, and Aristarchus of Samos's heliocentric theory of the universe all reflect some glory on the Ptolemaic court. In short, despite the fact that cultural and scientific developments in their capital are more reflective of a Hellenistic than a specifically Egyptian spirit, the early Ptolemies succeeded in establishing Alexandria as the world center for arts and sciences, yielding preeminence only in the field of philosophy and only to Athens.

The structure of the Ptolemaic kingdom was one in which Greeks numbering in the thousands ruled Egyptians numbering perhaps seven to nine million. The Greeks who were brought in as civil servants and mercenaries were at first determined to maintain their own way of life and, during the reigns of the first few Ptolemies, refused to learn the language of the Egyptians or to fraternize with them. But toward the end of the third century, Greek provincials began to marry Egyptians and adopt their religion and customs. Even the kings accepted the Eighteenth Dynasty custom of brother-sister marriage. The Ptolemies were viewed as a new line of pharaohs. They supported Egyptian religious cults, especially that of Serapis, and were depicted in temple art dressed in ritual garb. After 217, however, when the Egyptian rebellions began, the Greeks again drew together to defend their privileges against Egyptian encroachment.

Despite some dispute at times over which son would succeed to the throne, the Ptolemaic father-to-son succession system functioned very well during the peace period. In the second and first centuries B.C., however, the system would break down and become a source of intermittent discord.

The lives of the Egyptian workmen and *fellahin* must have been difficult. Taxes were so high that the peasant was left with no seed and the king controlled its supply. Wages were so low that there was very little incentive to use slaves. Workers often went on strike, taking refuge in temples.

The existence of the two segregated classes required two

systems of justice, one for natives and one for Greeks. A further judicial subdivision was created between the Greeks in the cities and those in the country and a separate system developed also for Jews. The amount of litigation was apparently so heavy that the ubiquitous administrators more and more encroached on the territory of the courts, acting as arbitrators to speed decisions.

There were three external threats to the Ptolemaic Peace, not counting Alexander's welcomed invasion. These were led by Perdiccas in 321, by Antigonus I and Demetrius in 306, and by Magas in 274. All three invasions were ended prematurely by a combination of Egyptian geography and the Ptolemies' defensive forces before a battle could take place. The weakening effect of a long trek across the Sinai, the difficulty of crossing the Nile, and the lack of harbors along the coast which could provide shelter from Mediterranean storms for an invading fleet all contributed to the security of Ptolemy's kingdom.

Termination

In 217 B.C. the fourth monarch, Ptolemy Philopator (221-204), had to defend against an attack by an energetic Seleucid, Antiochus III. This was the king who would later provide an external threat to the Roman Republican Peace. The Ptolemies, in order to enlarge their army, supplemented their Greek mercenaries with 20,000 hurriedly-trained native Egyptians.

Apparently the Ptolemies could not find enough mercenaries. This might have been a consequence of a naval defeat inflicted by Antigonus Gonatas of Macedonia in 245. After that Egypt no longer dominated the sea and recruitment may have been more difficult. It may be also that they were running out of land to offer the mercenaries as an inducement for settling in Egypt. They probably could not displace the *fellahin*, who were already living at subsistence level, without creating a dangerous landless peasantry.

When they met the Seleucid army at Raphia, the Ptolemies were apparently outnumbered by about 68,000 to 55,000 men—and 102 Indian elephants to 73 African elephants.

Although the Indian elephants chased their African counterparts back upon Philopator's troops, a late rally by the Ptolemaic center and right wings saved the day.

But not the peace. For Raphia proved to be the catalyst that was to bring about a new phase of conflict between Greeks and Egyptians. Having played a role in defending Ptolemaic holdings, the Egyptians demanded greater rights and better conditions within the empire. The problem was compounded because mercenaries are accustomed to receiving rewards for victory, but in a successful defense there is neither land nor booty to award. In any event, rebellions occurred all along the Nile, starting in 216, and continued interspersed with major succession struggles throughout the second century and into the first. The rebellion caused great disruption to the African trade even as the Second Punic War interfered with trade to the west. From this time on there was also a decrease in the average amount of land under production. Internal unity was not to be restored again until Egypt came under Augustus' control and received the benefits of the Pax Romana.

Certainly, considering the discrepancy between the Egyptian peasants and Greek landowners and merchants, there was plenty of cause for rebellion. It may have been, as Rostovtzeff suggests, that as the Greeks and Egyptians intermingled, the Greeks no longer seemed to be conquerors but intruders who had grabbed the best land. The fact that the Greeks did not feel able to defend themselves without Egyptian help may have torn away the last vestige of Greek pretense to superiority.[4]

Reflections

The Ptolemaic bureaucracy seems to have administered in great detail, even as its Egyptian predecessors had done. So long as leadership remained strong, it was possible to keep the relatively small and compact territory of Egypt suppressed by total administrative supervision and the presence of a powerful military force.

Geography also again contributed to an Egyptian peace period. The obstacles presented to a potential foreign invader by the Nile, by extensive desert border areas, and by an almost harborless coastline are difficult to surmount. Combined with this natural defense system were the activities of the Ptolemies' fleet, which dominated the Mediterranean until 245, and the active presence of their large army.

The early Ptolemies appear to have been good rulers in comparison with the Persians who preceded them. They at least secured the peace of the country, which is more than the Persians could manage. But as a memory of the Persians faded, comparisons were made instead between the condition of the Egyptians and that of the ruling Greeks.

The Macedonians and Greeks were also aided by the recurrent pattern of peace in Egypt. By adopting the customs and remoteness of the pharaohs, the Macedonians succeeded for a time in establishing themselves as traditional rulers. The pattern of obedience and cooperation, born of living on the Nile, came naturally to the Egyptians, and more physical hardships apparently did not ordinarily disturb their optimistic dispositions. This is somewhat more striking when seen from the Greek side, since no other Hellenic area of comparable size seems to have been able to achieve a century of peace until the Romans united them all. That Egypt should be the only Hellenistic area of peace would indicate that more than coincidence was involved.

While the Ptolemaic empire was very rich, property was shared only at the upper level. The peasants lived in exceptional poverty. This social situation did not lead to conflict so long as classes remained separate and comparisons were not invited. The fact that peasants could go on strike and find sanctuary in the temples may have acted as a safety valve for their discontent. They had an alternative to physical violence that sometimes produced at least some limited results.

Though the peace began under the Persians, the founder of the Ptolemaic peace would appear to have been Alexander III of Macedonia. This is somewhat surprising since he is generally remembered either as a conqueror or as the creator of an idea of world peace that never existed. Were he to conceive of himself as the founder of a century of peace for a parochial region, he would doubtless regard that as a poor consolation prize. But if the founder-consolidator pattern is typically a charismatic leader followed by a meticulous organizer, Alexander the Great and Ptolemy Soter certainly fit that pattern.

Soter must rank high among consolidators. He was persistent enough to gain the necessary military objectives to maintain the organization of his state without being drawn too far into endless Asian conflicts. He lived long enough to complete his objectives, and to establish himself as a patron of letters, the builder of Alexandria's great library, and a competent historian whose relatively objective account of Alexander's campaigns was a major source for Arrian. Finally, at the age of 82, he abdicated in favor of one of his younger sons, Philadelphus, and lived long enough to assure a quiet succession.

Philadelphus played the role of magnificent monarch, presiding over a splendid cosmopolitan court that was somewhat dissolute, but hospitable to artists, writers, scholars, and scientists. He did find time, however, to continue his father's policies, consolidating control of the kingdom and expanding land reclamation and irrigation programs.

One figure who does not appear—we might have looked for him at the death of Alexander—was a native leader, a Kamose arising from Thebes to throw the invaders out. That spirit seemed dead, although it arose somewhat feebly in the second and first century rebellions, when Thebes was partially destroyed.

In foreign affairs we once again have an example of discriminating foreign policy. The Ptolemies acquired the territory and kind of power needed for defense and then avoided extended involvements in more distant territories when it became apparent that the resources they would have to commit would not be worth the results they could hope to obtain.

The Phoenicians did not attack their neighbors. The Middle Kingdom did not get into foreign military involvements and Akhenaten apparently withdrew military support from Syria and Palestine when difficulties appeared at home. It would appear that in the foreign policies of all of these states there was an element of caution, an avoidance of alliances, military entanglements, a wariness of overreaching. This caution, in these cases at least, seems to have aided in the preservation of peace.

10

The Roman Republican Peace
(203-90 B.C.)

Origins

The Second Punic War (218-201 B.C.) was a life-or-death struggle for both Rome and Carthage. To the victor would go virtual predominance in the Mediterranean and to the loser, subjection and eventual oblivion. In the early years of the war, one defeat after the other brought the Romans to the brink of disaster and made it appear that Hannibal would soon even capture Rome itself. However, despite heavy losses and the scars of battle left on the Italian countryside by fifteen years of ravage by the Carthaginians, the Roman people refused to yield. Their strong resolve slowly turned the tide in both Spain and Italy and finally forced the recall of Hannibal's troops to defend the Carthaginian homeland, where the Roman forces shortly afterwards won the decisive battle at Zama.

The victory over Carthage had forced the Romans to accept an international role as the Mediterranean's policeman, especially in relation to the constantly-bickering states of Hellenistic Greece and the Near East. During most of the second century B.C. Rome was involved in various foreign struggles, including three Macedonian wars and single campaigns against the Seleucid kingdom of Antiochus III, against the states of the Achaean League, and against Carthage. Despite repeated attempts to secure Greek independence, the Romans finally came to realize that the Greeks were incapable of self-rule and they annexed the troublesome Macedonian kingdom to provide closer supervision over affairs in Greece. The intentions of the Romans

93

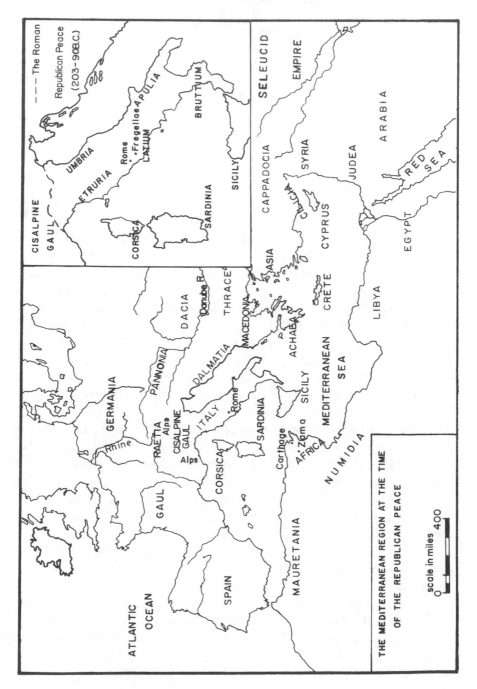

--- The Roman
Republican Peace
(203-90B.C.)

CISALPINE
GAUL

UMBRIA

ETRURIA

Rome
·Fregellae APULIA
LATIUM

BRUTTIUM

SICILY

SARDINIA

CORSICA

SELEUCID

EMPIRE

CAPPADOCIA

SYRIA

CILICIA

CYPRUS

JUDEA

ARABIA

RED
SEA

EGYPT

LIBYA

CRETE

MEDITERRANEAN

SEA

ASIA

THRACE

MACEDONIA

ACHAEA

DACIA

Danube R.

DALMATIA

PANNONIA

GERMANIA

RAETIA
Alps

CISALPINE
GAUL
Alps

ITALY

Rome

SARDINIA

SICILY

Carthage

·Zama

AFRICA

NUMIDIA

Rhine

GAUL

CORSICA

MAURETANIA

SPAIN

ATLANTIC

OCEAN

THE MEDITERRANEAN REGION AT THE TIME
OF THE REPUBLICAN PEACE

scale in miles

0   400

were chiefly defensive and not aggressively imperialistic. They were mainly interested in providing peace and security and on several occasions carefully avoided annexing territory after military victories. Rome also spent most of the century fighting to subdue the rebellious native tribes of Spain, thus consolidating her control of her two provinces in that region.

In spite of Roman military involvements abroad, peninsular Italy entered a period of peace and security after the departure of Hannibal's troops in 203. The area certainly needed a rest to recover from the destruction of the war. Italy in the past, however, had not known long periods of peace. It was thus particularly significant that the Romans succeeded in establishing a lengthy peace there.

Perhaps the most important factor in creating peace in Republican Italy was the system Rome had used to unite the diverse parts of Italy around her. From the early fifth century B.C. the Romans had thrown off Etruscan domination and formed a Latin League with other towns in Latium. Although the league had begun as an association of equal powers, Rome soon emerged as the dominant force, in 338 forming a new Latin Confederation, which recognized her superior status. The Romans set up a system for gradually bestowing Roman rights and privileges on her allies. Generally those towns or areas closest to Rome and of Latin stock were favored over more distant, non-Latin regions. Even the Italic allies with the fewest Roman rights, however, benefited from the arrangement. The Latin Confederation was not a subject empire paying tribute for the sole profit of its conqueror. It was a group of reciprocal alliances between Rome and numerous Italian cities and regions that served all concerned. The Roman allies gave up a measure of their independence and provided military service in support of Rome. In return they received trading rights, a share in the spoils of war, the protection of the strongest state in Italy, and general peace and security. The best measure of the success of Rome's system for uniting the Italian peninsula under her direction is the fact that even in the darkest days of the Second Punic War, when Hannibal presented them with the opportunity for freedom if they would rebel, most of the allied states loyally stayed by her side.

The graduated system of admitting the allies to Roman rights by stages prevented them from arriving at a feeling of unity among themselves as subjects and rebelling against their common master, at least for the time being. The seeds of the destruction of the Roman Republican Peace, however, were already present before its inauguration. When the Italian allies would tire of waiting patiently for full rights and despite numerous attempts at making their sincere grievances heard in Rome would have their hopes for fair treatment dashed by senatorial intransigence, then they would find a common bond and strike out violently against their oppressor to secure what they believed was due to them. In 203, however, when Hannibal left Italy to defend Carthage against Scipio Africanus, these seeds were ungerminated. They were to grow during the century of peace that was to follow.

Characterization

Peace was successfully achieved in peninsular Italy during the second century B.C. for a variety of reasons. The decisive victory in the Second Punic War established Rome's predominance in the Mediterranean. With the threat of Carthage removed, there were no other powers strong enough to contest Rome's position and threaten her homeland with external attack. The Romans made sure that this situation remained by forcefully maintaining stability, and relative peace, in Greece and the Near East. Before any imperialistic ventures could gain enough momentum to endanger Italy, they were firmly resisted by Rome and her allies, as in the cases of Philip V of Macedon and the Seleucid King Antiochus III. The Roman military forces had emerged from the Second Punic War with expertise and greater flexibility, under the skilled leadership of Scipio Africanus. Although the Romans still did not establish a standing army, the numerous campaigns against rebellious tribes in Cisalpine Gaul and in Spain and the frequent wars in the Greek world kept a large number of citizen-soldiers active enough to qualify them as professionals. The strength of the legions, whether in accompanying a *consul* or *praetor* to a particular trouble spot in a given year or in carrying out longer campaigns abroad, was a major factor in maintaining the peace in Italy.

Once the various parts of peninsular Italy had been united in the Latin Confederation, geography also contributed to preserving the peace. The mountainous terrain of central Italy had been a major obstacle to Romanization as late as the early third century and the mountain tribes of Cisalpine Gaul continued their resistance throughout much of the second century B.C. However, the peninsular nature of Italy left only the region in the north open to land invasion and with Cisalpine Gaul soon to be tied to Italy, the Alps would prove to be a strong northern boundary. The extensive Italian coastline may appear at first glance to have invited attack by sea, but there were few good harbors and the rivers were scarcely navigable. An invader would also have to land enough troops to engage the Roman legions in their own territory, where supplies of men, weapons and food would come readily to their assistance. Although geography had not significantly contributed to the establishment of the Republican Peace, and in many ways had earlier hindered Roman control in Italy, it did further the preservation of peace.

According to Polybius (*VI*, 11, 18), one of the sources of Rome's strength was what he viewed as its "mixed constitution," a fine blending of the elements of monarchy (*consuls*), aristocracy (Senate), and democracy (assemblies). The government did divide power between these three elements but, in reality, for most of its history the Roman Republic was governed by an oligarchy with the Senate usually in full control. The executive power in the state was held by two consuls elected annually. The consulship was the chief goal of the Roman noble's political career and the intense competition for the position generally precluded the election of anyone without the pedigree of a distinguished *gens* (family). Most of the consulships were held by as few as ten or fifteen extended families. With the magistrates changing every year and the assemblies of the people too unwieldy for sustained, effective action, power devolved upon the Senate, whose members were usually experienced former magistrates serving for life. The Senate deserved much of the credit for holding the state together during the crisis years of the Second Punic War and was largely responsible for the successful outcome of the struggle. In the postwar period the Senate emerged with even greater prestige and a dominant role in the administration of the Republic. The Senate usually decided which "provinces" needed the presence of a *consul* or *praetor* and his legions in a particular year. The system of sending off armies to deal with various trouble spots, whether in Italy or abroad, was an important factor in maintaining Rome's defenses and preserving peace and stability.

An important by-product of Roman involvement in the first two wars with Carthage was increased exposure to and interest in Greek culture, particularly in the field of drama. The extensive military service of Romans in the Greek towns of Sicily and southern Italy during the First Punic War was especially important. From the late third century on, Romans began to adapt Greek literary models in comedy, tragedy, poetry, history and oratory to the Latin language and tradition. Livius Andronicus, Naevius, Ennius, Plautus, Terence, Fabius Pictor, Cato the Elder, Polybius, and others, although most of them were Greeks or Italians who had moved to Rome, rather than natives, had all made significant contributions to Roman literary development. In satire and legal commentaries, Roman authors achieved greater originality in fields that were distinctly Latin, rather than Greek. Art, painting and sculpture were already in an advanced stage by the second century and reflected some Etruscan influence. The portrait-masks of a noble's famous ancestors emphasized realism and portraiture became one of the greatest achievements of Roman artists. In the field of architecture, the Romans built fine temples and public buildings and, with the use of their engineering skills and the arch, constructed excellent bridges and aqueducts. Roman culture would not reach its highest point of achievement in many areas until the Age of Augustus, but it was already very productive by the beginning of the second century B.C.

Though Greek culture was dominant, the Latin language became increasingly widespread. As Roman control of Italy grew, Latin gradually ousted the numerous Italian tongues, although some would persist, at least in rural areas, into the Empire period. Roman magistrates compelled petitioners to make their representations in Latin and it became increasingly the language of commerce, just as Roman coinage replaced the Italian issues.

Polybius (VI, 56, 6-15) cited Roman religious practice as the most important element in holding the state together. Although the state rites, handled by the pontiffs and augurs, offered little or no satisfaction through the participation of individual citizens, religion continued to play an important role on the family level, especially in the rural areas. The crises of the early years of the Second Punic War caused panic and spread superstition. Frequent consultation of the Sibylline Books introduced into Rome foreign rituals and even the Phrygian goddess, the Great Mother. The fact that most religious offices were held by political figures created the opportunity for religion to become a tool of politics, but this abuse was not really common until the first century B.C. Shared worship had been one of the major purposes for the original Latin League and Rome's willingness to accept into her pantheon the deities worshipped by her allies or subjects made religious bonds an important source of cohesion among peoples of diverse backgrounds.

The Hellenistic philosophies of Epicureanism and Stoicism were attractive to some Romans of the second century, although abstract philosophy and science were not fields of great interest for the practical Romans. Epicureanism, in superficial interpretations, may have reinforced selfishness and lack of social concern. Stoicism, on the other hand, was developed and modified by Panaetius, and may have supported the older Roman tendencies toward duty and responsibility.

It could be said that in the second century there was a general decline in social responsiblity or an increase in individualism or selfishness. There was a tolerance of many ways of life but with this, a growing indifference to others, not only to their beliefs and practices but to their miseries. The influence of the Roman family began to decline and divorce became more common. Bribery and corruption became part of the social fabric as the traditional Roman values weakened.[1]

The struggle between the patrician and plebeian orders had been extinguished by a series of legislative concessions ending with the Hortensian Law of 287. Other social distinctions remained, however. Assignment of each citizen to one of 35 tribes, generally in relation to the district where he owned land, proved to be a source of social conflict, particularly when large groups of people were enfranchised and added to the citizen rolls. The heads of the smaller rural tribes, attempting to preserve their personal control and political power in the popular assemblies, usually fought to have new citizens enrolled in the four huge urban tribes, where they could least affect the *status quo*. The new citizens normally desired some political voice to express their views and needs and so naturally requested enrollment in the 31 rural tribes. With the *centuriate* assembly, where the *consuls* and *praetors* were elected each year, the citizen population was divided into five basic classes, according to wealth. The 18 *centuries* of knights, or equites, whose members were very wealthy and served as cavalry troops in the army, in combination with the votes of the two wealthiest classes, would often create a majority in an election or on a given legislative proposal and so prevent the other classes from even voting. Social conflict was also caused by the growing number of slaves introduced into the Roman world as a result of foreign conquests. The facility of earning manumission to the status of freedman injected a large number of people of eastern origin into the citizen population, thus increasing the diversity of the ethnic and cultural mix.

A major economic change in the second century involved the gradual disappearance of the smaller farmers, the men who in previous centuries had provided the people of the Italian peninsula with food and who in war time had formed the backbone of the legions. Many had been killed in the Punic Wars and many others had been away from their farms for several years and found it difficult to bring their small plots into production once again. The devastation of their lands by Hannibal's troops, continually recurring absences from their farms because of conscription for military campaigns in the east, and competition from cheap grain produced in Sicily all combined with the use of slave labor on a large scale to squeeze the small farmers off the land. The large estates swallowed up many of the small farms and, using slaves, could afford to enter the more lucrative areas of olive and grape cultivation or sheep and cattle raising. These economic changes made a few large landowners very wealthy, depleted the ranks of those subject to military service, cut down on local grain production, and swelled the masses of unemployed in the cities. Rome's foreign conquests had caused economic, political, and social problems that threatened her internal stability.

Roman commerce and industry were not highly developed. It was considered beneath the standards of the senatorial class to engage in profit-making occupations. The equestrian class became commercially-oriented towards the end of the second century B.C. The Greeks of south Italy carried on some overseas trade, but the Roman economy in general was very localized. Most industry and crafts were handled by the lower classes, producing and marketing their wares in small shops. Roman coinage had replaced most Italian issues by the second century, but trade over long distances was still infrequent. Free laborers in various trades were also often displaced by slaves, who were frequently very skilled. As the slave population had increased greatly from overseas conquests, the yeoman population was disappearing and in Rome there was a growing population of displaced and often unemployed former yeomen, soldiers and freedmen.

If distribution of wealth was skewed, the quantity increased during the second century. After 167 so much was brought in from the provinces in taxes and loot that the war tax on property was discontinued within Italy.

The increased concentration of wealth had consequences for life style, particularly in Rome. Ostentatious living replaced the austere customs of the yeomen. Slaves themselves were wealth, taking on all menial duties and pampering a new generation of plutocrats.

By contrast, the lot of the urban poor grew steadily worse. As more and more ex-farmers swarmed to the city, where they generally could not find work because of competition from cheap, skilled slave labor, housing became overcrowded, thus increasing the destructiveness of Rome's frequent fires. The growing numbers of urban poor gained increased importance in the popular assembly and they became a political force to be reckoned with.

The ruling oligarchy attempted to calm the growing and often unemployed city populace by selling cheap grain or by sponsoring festivals and lavish spectacles, such as triumphant entries of victorious generals. It is not certain that this "bread and circuses" policy contributed to the uneasy peace of the capital, but it was later to play a part in the collapse of that peace.

The unification and Romanization of the Italian peninsula, which had been instrumental in the establishment of the Roman Republican Peace, continued to develop during the second century B.C. and reinforced the stability of the period. The planting of colonies, both citizen and Latin, was important in establishing greater military control, in bringing additional land under cultivation, and in strengthening Rome's ties to a more unified Italy. The construction of roads, bridges, and aqueducts, in which the Romans excelled, further bound diverse parts of Italy to Rome, provided a communications network that encouraged internal travel and commerce, and facilitated the spread of the Latin language and of Roman law, institutions, and culture. Internal unity, in combination with a strong military defense, allowed peace to flourish on the Italian peninsula.

Termination

Many of the problems resulting from Rome's foreign conquests combined to create a social, political, and economic crisis that would bring the peace, and ultimately the Republican system itself, to a violent end. There were a few instances during the second century that foreshadowed the chaos of the following century. One threat to the peace came from the discontent of slaves with their mistreatment. There were minor servile uprisings in Etruria in 196 and in Apulia in 185, both of which were crushed by *praetors*. A major rebellion of slaves took place outside Italy in the province of Sicily in 134-132 and again in 103-101 and the revolt of Spartacus would plague the Romans the following century.

Another threat to the peace came from the increasing use of violence in politics. The cause of the growing ranks of urban poor was taken up by the idealistic *tribune* Tiberius Gracchus in 133. Gracchus saw the growth of huge estates, farmed by slaves, and the related disappearance of the small landowner as the chief evils facing Rome. He proposed a legislative solution that would enforce old restrictions on the amount of public land that could be held and redistribute the excess to the urban poor — restoring them to farms to increase agricultural production and also bolstering the dwindling number of landowners subject to military service. In his haste to pass the agrarian law, however, he disregarded several Roman traditions. He ignored the Senate, which was bound to oppose him, and took his bill straight to the people's assembly, where it passed. When another tribune, Marcus Octavius, vetoed his law, Gracchus unconstitutionally deposed him by another vote of the people. Gracchus saw the need to continue in office to carry out his program, but reelection without a sufficient interval between terms also violated Roman tradition. Leaders of the Senate murdered the *Tribune* and many of his followers to end what they viewed as a threat to the state. The intransigence of both sides, a total disregard for legality and tradition, and the violent reaction of the Senate benefited no one and set the stage for the political and military disruption of the following century.

The growing dissatisfaction of the Latin and Italian allies was ultimately to destroy the Republican Peace. Although the war with Hannibal had proven the success of Rome's system of organizing the peninsula through the allegiance shown by most of her allies to Rome even in her weakest moment, the second century revealed the slow dissolution of what had been a mutually beneficial relationship. There were several cases of abuse by Roman leaders treating allies as subjects instead of friends. The allied share in the spoils of war was often reduced to a minor portion. The Romans began to resist further grants of citizenship and Latin rights. Many Italians and Latins found it easier to migrate to Rome and gain citizenship illegally rather than to wait for a hope that seemed to grow increasingly distant. Many allied areas lost considerable numbers of their population and yet the Roman demand for their troops remained stable or even increased. The agrarian legislation of Tiberius Gracchus threatened many allied landowners with the loss of public land. The benefits of a close relationship with Rome were quickly disappearing and there was little hope that the situation would improve. The allies began to find unity in their discontent.

Scipio Aemilianus defended the allies against the encroachment of the Gracchan land commission. In 126, however, a bill to expel aliens from Rome caused further disaffection. Fulvius Flaccus as consul in 125 raised the hopes of the allies by introducing legislation to give them the coveted Roman citizenship, but this measure made no headway. A revolt on the part of Fregellae for independence from Rome was quickly put down by a *praetor's* forces in 125. Flaccus as *tribune* in 122 joined his colleague Gaius Gracchus in support of a bill to enfranchise the allies. This was only part of a broad program of reforms that was introduced by the younger Gracchus and included the sale of grain in Rome at about one-half of the prevailing market price. Gaius Gracchus met the same intransigence his brother had faced and the Senate skillfully undercut his power base and caused his defeat in an attempt at a third consecutive term as *tribune*. Gracchus committed suicide in the midst of a violent clash between his partisans and those of the Senate.

The expectations of the allies were raised and dashed one final time during the tribunate of M. Livius Drusus in 91. Included in Drusus's reform package was a bill to enfranchise them. When the legislation was blocked and Drusus was killed, the patience of the allies broke and an independent confederation of Italian states was established. The war which followed, called variously the Italian, Marsic, or Social War, lasted from 90 to 88 B.C. and was only ended after a series of laws offered the Roman franchise to the Latin and Italian allies. However, the bitter fighting had shattered the period of Roman Republican peace and stability was not to be restored for long periods again until the bloody civil wars ended in one man rule in 31 B.C. The problems of the allies may have been temporarily solved, but the use of violence in poltical disputes, continuing economic problems, and the new volunteer army system introduced by Marius, whereby soldiers developed allegiance to powerful generals instead of to the state, would all combine to send Rome through the chaos and destruction of a series of civil wars. The Senate had been discredited, the people were only too willing to sell their political power to any leader who would promise them a larger grain allotment or other prizes, and a republican government established for a city-state proved itself no longer capable of administering an empire.

The only external threat to Italy during the peace period

came from a major force of Cimbri and Teutones, Germanic tribes originally from the Baltic coast, who invaded Gaul and defeated a major Roman force in Provence in 105. They threatened an invasion of Italy, but quick action by Marius eliminated them in separate battles in 102 and 101, thus postponing barbarian invasions of Italy for several centuries. The unprecedented series of consulships and the volunteer army that had contributed to Marius's victory, however, were soon to contribute to the internal dissolution of the Republic.

It is somewhat ironic that Rome's relationship with her allies in Italy was partly responsible both for the establishment and the destruction of the Roman Republican Peace. However, the reversal of her attitude in this regard, from one of amicable supervisor to that of domineering master, parallels other changes going on about the same time in Roman values and interests. As Rome expanded to become a dominant international power, she opened herself to the influence of social, religious, cultural, and moral values alien to the spirit that had achieved her success. Although victorious and almost invincible on the surface, Rome unintentionally subverted her traditions, religion and moral fiber. Her traditional values of harmony, personal sacrifice, duty, devotion to state and adherence to the customs of the ancestors gradually gave way to internal strife and pursuit of self-interest. Just as the agricultural functions of the small farmer were taken over by large-scale operations using slave labor, his role as the backbone of the army was assumed by the volunteer soldier fighting not for the preservation of his system but for personal gain.

Reflections

Of all of the various factors given as responsible for the Roman Republican Peace, probably the most important were political and military. A stable republican government, with most power exercised by an aristocratic Senate and with annually-elected magistrates able to command armies and deal with areas of potential trouble, ably maintained the peace as long as internal harmony was preserved. The government was responsible for fostering the political, economic, social, and cultural unity of Italy, which established and protected the peace. The Roman armies, based on service by landowners with loyalty to and a vested interest in the survival of the state, were successful in winning peace and stability abroad before any foreign aggressor could threaten the Italian homeland. The maintenance of a strong defense and the use of a powerful offense when necessary proved to be effective in the organization and continuation of the peace period.

As in the cases of the Phoenicians, Athenians and Corinthians, the members of the Latin Confederation had to cope with a double set of relationships: those within a group of small neighbors and those with the outer world. But in the other cases, the relationships were among equals, whereas in the Latin Confederation, Rome was the dominant power. The dominance became increasingly pronounced in the second century. The Romans treated their nominal allies as subjects and for several decades the allies accepted a situation in which they had little more than nominal autonomy.

The seeds of destruction for the Roman Republican Peace were already present at its inauguration. It took a long time for them to bear fruit, in the expanded use of slave labor, the disappearance of the small farmers, the introduction of landless volunteer soldiers, the increased use of violence in politics, the growth of an urban mob, the abuse of a close relationship with the allies, and the disregard for tradition and morality. However, once internal discord grew, it proved that the Republican government without the loyalty of its citizens was incapable of coping with the problems of an empire. The only solution appeared to be recourse to the sword. It would be more than fifty years before Italy would finally emerge from the exhaustion of civil war and once again enjoy, under a very different political system, the benefits of peace.

11

The Pax Romana
(31 B.C.-A.D. 161)

The *Pax Romana* ("Roman Peace" in Latin) is perhaps the original peace period in the sense of a society's being consciously aware of living in an epoch enjoying the benefits of peace. The Romans had a visible symbol of peace and war in the doors of the temple of Janus. These were left open if Rome was involved in armed conflict and ceremoniously closed to signify to the people that Romans were everywhere at peace. The Pax Romana is by far the best known of all peace periods, both ancient and modern. It has stood for centuries as a model of administrative efficiency because such a vast area of diverse nations was united in relative harmony under a government directed from one city and by one man. It has been particularly meaningful to western civilization because it brought together in harmony geographical areas that had previously known incessant warfare and that have been both fragmented and plagued by war regularly since Roman times.

Origins

The man responsible for creating the Pax Romana is the first Roman emperor, Augustus (27 B.C.-A.D. 14). He was able to emerge as the sole leader from the long years of civil war, which had put an end to the Roman Republican Peace and which had finally destroyed the Republic as well. Augustus was particularly successful in reestablishing stability in Rome because he

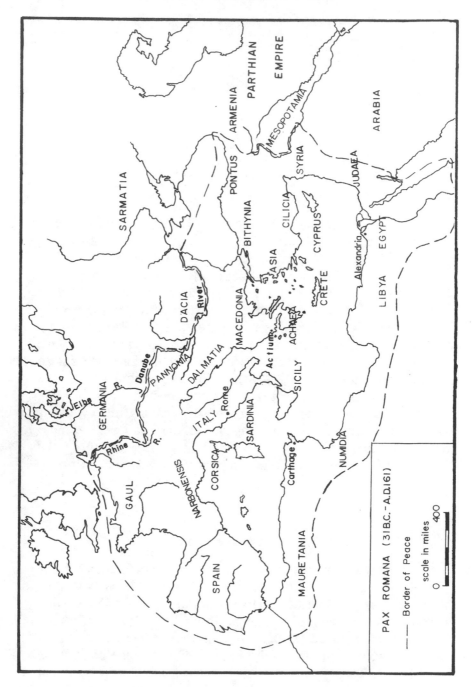

PAX ROMANA (31 B.C. – A.D.161)

——— Border of Peace

scale in miles

0   400

was able to learn from the mistakes made by his great-uncle, Julius Caesar. The Roman world lay in ruins before him and he had the ability to reconstruct it by carefully using his leadership and control in various areas. His new constitutional system, generally called the *principate*, on paper appeared to function as a partnership between the emperor and the Senate. In reality, however, real power rested in the hands of the former. Under Augustus, the Roman world gradually recovered from the long years of civil war. The size of the military was greatly reduced, soliders were settled in colonies around the empire, disruptions in the outlying provinces were suppressed, a large-scale public works program gave jobs to the unemployed, the financial system was reorganized, commerce increased, and peace settled upon the land. The peace begins, then, with the victory of Augustus over the forces of Mark Antony and Cleopatra in the battle of Actium in 31 B.C.

The immediate successors of Augustus extended Roman rule into Britain, established a frontier along the Rhine and Danube rivers in central Europe, and generally consolidated control of the provinces. After about a century of peace, the stability of the empire was shattered by the disruptions of A.D. 68-70. Various frontier armies marched against one another, each trying to make its general the new emperor. Virtual anarchy was ended, and peace and stability restored, by the swift actions of one of these generals, Vespasian. Peace and prosperity again embraced the empire under the rule of the Flavian and Antonine emperors until external pressures along several borders brought the Pax Romana to an end.

Peace was preserved, then, except for the interruptions of a major civil war from A.D. 68 to 70 and a few isolated disturbances along the borders, from the victory over Mark Antony in 31 B.C. until a Parthian invasion of Armenia and Syria in A.D. 161 marked the beginning of a long series of invasions and rebellions that would disrupt the stability of the empire.

Peace was provided for an estimated 100 million persons living in a wide band of territory surrounding the Mediterranean. Excluding Dacia and Mesopotamia, where Roman authority was not undisputed for long, and Britain and Judaea, where there were intermittent disruptions, the imperial peace covered an area of nearly three million square miles, of which about one million was the sea itself. Included were Spain, Gaul to the Rhine, Italy, eastern Europe to the Danube, Greece, Asia Minor, Syria, Egypt, and the north African littoral.

Characterization

Augustus had to solve the problem of transforming a republican structure designed to govern a city and dominated by a landed nobility into a form appropriate for administering an empire. This he managed by retaining the republican forms of government while at the same time exercising most political and military power by himself. Under Augustus the Senate and even the Assembly continued to meet and elect magistrates and other officials. In reality, however, the Assembly soon withered away and the Senate, although it may have claimed the respect of being the emperor's equal partner, usually only ratified Augustus' legislative wishes and exercised elective choice only from among lists of candidates commended by him. The emperor was careful to cultivate the support of the senatorial class by seeing that its members had access to the traditional republican offices so necessary for the prestige of the old noble families. He wisely avoided excessive display of his power and projected the image of a Senate continuing to play a vital role in the state. The equestrian middle class, or knights, Augustus assisted by establishing opportunities for lucrative careers in the growing imperial bureaucracy. Many freedmen likewise discovered the benefits of loyal service to the emperor.

The governmental structure that Augustus established was retained by his successors, though the balance between emperor and Senate tipped even more noticeably in favor of the former, since he had the support of the army and his sources of revenue from the imperial provinces were far greater than those available to the Senate. Thus the emperor's power was not greatly inferior to that of the Achaemenid kings, but the machinery that surrounded his position was more complex and at the same time relatively subtle. The wonder of the Roman imperial system is that despite the weakness or blatant misrule of a particular emperor in Rome, the government of a vast empire would generally continue to function well.

Both Rome and the provinces were usually governed more ably by the imperial civil service than they had been by the agents of the Senate. The imperial provinces were administered by governors appointed by the emperor and responsible to him. The Senate continued to control some of the less critical provinces through governors selected by lot from lists of eligible former magistrates. In the imperial provinces, financial matters were generally handled by *procurators* of equestrian rank. Governors and procurators served as checks upon each other and the increased accountability to the emperor raised the efficiency and quality of provincial administration. Provincial taxes were based on a census of the empire and usually collected by a permanent civil service, not by the tax-gouging farming system.

Throughout the entire history of the Roman Empire, one of the major weaknesses in the governmental system was the lack of a successful policy of succession. Augustus had originally intended a hereditary *principate* and had shared some powers with a series of designated successors. At the same time, however, a tradition had developed where the Senate and Roman people were responsible for the bestowal of the emperor's powers. Although until the civil war of A.D. 68-70 the emperors were all members of the Julio-Claudian "family," as early as 41, with the Praetorian Guard's choice of Claudius, the powerful role of the military in an emperor's selection was revealed. The second century Antonine emperors carefully established close "family" ties with their designated successors and associated them in the imperial rule so as to preclude military initiatives in the selection process. The succession problem was never really solved and it contributed greatly to the anarchy of the third century.

The delicate relationship the emperor had to maintain with the Senate of Rome on one hand, and with the imperial forces on the other, became evident in A.D. 68 when a provincial governor in Spain was moved by events in Rome under the emperor Nero to march on the capital city. This produced a reaction in the armies on the Rhine and Danube and a civil war among them before the candidate of the Danubian army, Vespasian, was finally placed on the throne as the fourth emperor of the year 69.

He suppressed revolts in Gaul and Germany, ordered the rebelling city of Jerusalem razed, and restored peace. By controlling the office of *censor*, which was concerned with the Senate roll, he managed to create a Senate favorable to him while maintaining control of the army. The reorganization of imperial finances was a major factor in his restoration of stability to the empire. The Pax Romana was interrupted by the disruptions of 68 and 69, but the peace had already lasted almost exactly a century and was destined to last more than 90 additional years. Vespasian appropriately built a temple to Peace in honor of its restoration.

The military policies of most emperors, Trajan (98-117) excepted, were predominantly defensive. Augustus aimed at getting defensible frontiers. Failing to achieve the Elbe, he accepted the Rhine. In the east he came to terms with the Persians of Parthia, both empires agreeing on the establishment of buffer states between them. Domitian (81-96) built a line of forts along the Rhine-Danube Frontier and Hadrian (117-138) strengthened them. Where the adventurous Trajan had expanded into Dacia, Armenia, Arabia and Mesopotamia, Hadrian withdrew to the line of Octavian. After Antoninus Pius (138-161), when the peace had been broken, the emperors spent much of their time and financial resources trying to maintain the established borders. Many of them would purchase the services of or otherwise negotiate for protection by Germanic tribes, which would serve as federated troops and defend the empire against other tribes.

The military structure of the empire consisted of standing armies in the east and along the northern river frontiers, with smaller garrisons occupying other frontier provinces. The emperor also had his own Praetorian Guard, recruited entirely from the Italian peninsula to defend Italy. The standing army, recruited voluntarily as far as possible, consisted of about 150,000 legionaries and a like number of auxiliaries. The auxiliary soldiers, on completion of service, were granted Roman citizenship for themselves and their families.

After the conflicts of 68-70, Vespasian restored army discipline and loyalty and brought the soldiers back under control. He practically closed the legions to Italians, since he could draw a better class of soldier from the provinces, where the middle class was still attracted to the reward of Roman citizenship.

He also broke up groups of auxiliary troops from one local area to prevent further threats of nationalistic rebellion. His army proved to be more efficient and cohesive than that recruited during the Julio-Claudian period.

The years through about A.D. 100 saw increased prosperity throughout the empire. Large-scale farms predominated in Italy, then spread to Gaul and Spain. The peace and political unity and stability of the empire encouraged commerce. Grain, manufactured articles and raw materials made up the bulk of the trade. Italy prospered from the export of wine and oil. During this period the state intervened very little in economic development.

In the second century, large-scale farming continued to expand, with the result that most small farmers moved to the cities or became tenants, and commerce, even the wine and oil trade, had already shifted away from Italy to the flourishing provinces. The campaigns of Trajan were economically damaging, resulting in depopulation, requisitions by military commanders from the surrounding populace, and general discouragement. But Hadrian apparently repaired the damage by encouraging agriculture in the provinces and granting permanent tenure to the settlers on certain lands of his imperial estates. Peace and prosperity continued through the reign of Antoninus Pius.

The first century saw a decline of the old families that had dominated politics under the Republic. Many had died out in the civil wars or through failure to produce or adopt male heirs. Loyalty to the emperor became more important than noble birth as a criterion for government service. At the same time the need for many administrators strengthened the equestrian class, which was reorganized by Augustus and given greater opportunities. Prosperity led to the increase of a middle class living from the proceeds of industry, commerce, or land investment and of wealthy freedmen, who served imperial interests while also controlling much of the industry in the provinces. Social mobility increased greatly in the first century and, under Claudius, freedmen assumed a major role in government. But the slowing of industrial growth was occurring as more and more small farmers were selling out and moving to the cities. The result was an increase in unemployment and a consequent growth in the pauperized mobs who were fed and entertained by the emperors.

Though economic problems were obvious, for a long time the general prosperity spread even to the tenants and paupers. There was, moreover, a strong social spirit operating among members of the middle class who were generous in making local endowments for public baths, libraries and the care of needy children. There was a relatively high level of concern for humanity in this period.

The state religion continued to be strong during the Pax Romana and emperor worship served as a unifying factor to tie the more remote and backward parts of the empire to Rome. The more exotic "mystery cults" from the East gained many adherents, who generally sought a personal involvement and hope of salvation not offered by the state cults. Except for some conflicts with Jews and Christians, Rome's toleration of religious diversity proved successful in furthering peace and unity in the empire.

A flexible system of Roman law was already developed before the establishment of the empire. Its flexibility was attributable to yearly edicts of the *praetors* who, at times with the advice of a council of learned men, would modify and reinterpret laws enunciated in previous edicts. Under the empire the *praetors'* edicts tended to become less interpretive, but they were replaced by imperial edicts and rulings, also given with the advice of a learned council. The edicts of the *praetors* were codified by Salvius Julianus at the direction of Hadrian.

The Romans tended to be more pragmatic than theoretical. The philosophy of stoicism, insisting on man's duty to others and state, may have fit in with the somewhat austere and philanthropic qualities of the nobler Romans of the period. A cult of emperor worship may have provided some unity through the establishment of closer ties between the provinces, particularly those in the Greek east, and Rome. The emperors of the peaceful period seem to have been tolerant of exotic religious cults of the East, providing they did not interfere with administration.

The Roman interest in the practical was reflected in remarkable achievements in engineering: wide stone roads, many of which are still in use today, splendid stone bridges, tunnels projected from two sides and meeting in the middle, and aqueducts that brought more than a million gallons of water an hour to Rome. The Romans were interested in drainage, public health and public hospitals. They enjoyed specific information, such as is reflected in the motley collection of scientific knowledge and myth in Pliny the Elder's *Natural History*. Taking philosophy, religion, and science together, a materialistic, practical atmosphere seems to have prevailed.

The culture of this period was impressive. Much was achieved in the literary genres of poetry, essays, drama, satire and epigrams by such great writers as Vergil, Horace, Ovid, Martial and Pliny the Younger. There was also the sweeping history of Livy, and the vivid, almost contemporary, history of Tacitus. The greatest period of literature (Vergil, Horace, Ovid, Livy) came during the Augustan Age, under the emperor's patronage, but this golden age did not survive Augustus. The sometimes-called Silver Age included such figures as Martial, Juvenal, Persius, the two Plinys, Quintilian, Tacitus, Lucan, the two Senecas, and Petronius. It was a productive period in several literary areas, but generally of a quality inferior to that of the Augustan Age.

Imperial architecture tended to be massive, elaborate and secular. The reign of Augustus was one of extensive building activity, which supposedly converted Rome from a city of brick to one of marble. Many temples were restored or rebuilt at the emperor's personal expense. The Altar of Peace (*Ara Pacis*) and Forum of Augustus stand out as landmarks of the period. The Flavians erected the magnificent Colosseum and Trajan added baths and a large forum, among other things. Throughout the empire Romans displayed their architectural and engineering talents in the construction of bridges, roads, aqueducts, commemorative arches, temples, baths, theaters, and amphitheaters.

Sculpture was often realistic and unflattering, as in the Republican period, though the imperial style also shows traces of Hellenic idealization. There is a bust of Vespasian that wonderfully combines the real and the ideal, the vulgar, the majestic, humor and beauty. The Romans showed great skill in their development of sculptured portraits and in the techniques of relief work. Their painting was lively and colorful and very much a part of house interior decoration, as can be seen from numerous examples in Pompeii and other towns preserved by the eruption of Vesuvius in A.D. 79. Roman art and architecture ably reflect the extent, the prosperity, and the general glories of the Pax Romana.

Termination

The reign of Marcus Aurelius (161-180) was disturbed by invasions of territories included in the peace. At the outset of his reign, in 161, the Parthians broke into Armenia and ravaged Syria. It was two years before Roman generals were able to drive them out. A few years later barbarian tribes from eastern Europe crossed the Danube, overran the provinces of Pannonia and Noricum, and captured Aquileia at the head of the Adriatic. Marcus Aurelius was hard pressed to raise troops to drive them out and it was five years before he reached the Danube. He was to spend most of his reign in campaigns against various Germanic tribes along the borders.

During the reign of Commodus (180-192), there were serious outbreaks of tenant gangs that roamed throughout Italy and even captured some cities and waged open war against government forces in Gaul. Commodus, far from attempting to deal with these problems, confined his attentions to the pleasures and vices of Rome, until he was strangled on New Year's Eve of 193 by a companion who had the backing of the Praetorian Guard.

In the succession struggle that followed the frontier armies became involved once more. After a civil war much more far reaching than that of the first century, Septimius Severus (193-211) marched on Rome, packed the Praetorian Guard with his own men, and turned back to defeat his rivals in campaigns involving Gaul and Asia Minor. These conflicts were followed by major wars with Parthia, large-scale executions (a reported 20,000) carried out by the emperor Caracalla (211-217), and 50 years of anarchy following the death of Alexander Severus (222-235).

The end of the peace came as a result of difficulties with

the army, which could no longer maintain a strong defense against increasing external attacks. A break in the succession caused rival legions once again to struggle with each other in a civil war. Still, the failure of Septimius Severus to reestablish a lasting order, as Vespasian had a century before, suggests that this time the root of troubles was deeper and more far reaching.

One of the basic problems was that the emperors depended for financial support upon the Romanized or Hellenized urban population, and to broaden this support they encouraged the establishment of cities. But these city dwellers had to be supported by agriculture, and the process of urbanization without proportionate improvement in farm effectiveness resulted in an increased strain on the farms, particularly on the tenants, freedmen and slaves, whose land was owned by men living in cities.

By the time of Marcus Aurelius many of these displaced men were drawn into army service. By the time of Severus these soldiers, drafted from the rural provinces and living for years on the barbarian frontiers, had become more like the barbarian they were supposed to fight than the people of the cities they were supposed to defend. The result was a long period of strife in which conflicts among regionalized armies for power alternated with military raids by the rural soldiers on the wealthy cities.

The desperate Severus, trying to recreate an army to deal with the situation, requisitioned property in lieu of taxes, thereby destroying capital, while production fell as trade came to a standstill, and currency depreciated as the quantity of goods available fell and the government issued more to pay the debts of army and bureaucracy. The middle class was wiped out, and men resorted to subsistence farming and municipal militias where they could. Fifty years of anarchy was the understandable result.

The Roman era of peace was based on the organization of a large number of Hellenized, cosmopolitan cities that were more like Rome itself than the provinces around them. The cities spread and reinforced the ideal of peace and civility. Yet as they grew, they made greater demands on the resources of the provinces, and increased the social gap between the city middle class and the farmers and militia who supported and protected them. The weakness was endemic in the system, but without the system there would not have been a Pax Romana at all.

Reflections

The Roman empire resembles the Achaemenid in that it covered a very large area and came into existence after a period of severe conflict, when regional leaders were willing to sacrifice power to the man who could bring survival. It differs from the Achaemenid in its geography, in that its center was linked by sea as well as by land routes. Since sea routes were superior to land routes for moving troops or articles of commerce, this made possible the encompassing of an even larger geographical area that the Perisans could manage.

Like the Persians, the Romans had put together a peaceful empire administered in an orderly way by a professional civil service, with provincial officials given a great deal of local autonomy. The empire was linked by fast, safe communications, peaceful trade, a universal currency, and the widespread adoption of the Latin language in the west and the Greek in the east.

Through much of their history, the Romans depended on a multiplicity of leaders rather than the domination of one man. Outstanding men like Augustus and Hadrian did arise, but the peace continued under some incompetent emperors and began to break up despite the valiant efforts of a leader such as Marcus Aurelius. There were many who contributed to the foundation of the empire. Augustus was undoubtedly outstanding as a consolidator, since the mechanism that he had to work with was extremely subtle and the land that was to be united was diverse and exceptionally prone to political division. The Emperor Nero (54-68) resembled the "Magnificent Monarch," Xerxes, using the wealth accumulated by his predecessors to build monuments to himself rather than increasing imperial capital. His excesses, however, led to the great succession conflict that was finally stemmed by Vespasian.

Vespasian and Hadrian are the principal reformers. Vespasian had to reorganize tax collection, reestablish relations with the Senate, and reconstitute the Guard so it would be less of a menace. Hadrian had to consolidate defenses, personally review the organization of the provinces, and reconstitute the provincial economy. Septimius Severus, of course, resembles Vespasian to some degree, but the cards were stacked against him.

Antoninus Pius might have been the "magnificent monarch" of the Antonine period, but he did not have the temperament. He governed from Rome not because he loved to preside over pomp and luxury but because he felt imperial visits were too expensive for the provinces. An unusually incompetent monarch, Commodus, appeared at a crucial time. He didn't even attempt to cope with mounting internal problems, but instead engaged in debauchery, which could have been forgiven, and descended into the gladiator's ring and made a fool of himself, which could not be forgiven. Not that Commodus was the only incompetent monarch. Many of the Roman emperors seem to have been well below mediocre but others appeared during periods when the empire was either sufficiently strong to carry them or already on the rocks.

Peace seemed to have held up regardless of the exigencies of succession in the first century. The problems of removing and then replacing Nero created the disruptions of A.D. 68-69 that shattered the peace, but otherwise succession worked fairly well during the century. The effectiveness of the succession system in the second century was remarkable since it operated with a dearth of monarchs' sons, usually considered essential to peaceful succession in Egypt and Persia. However, the nonexistence of sons proved to be a great blessing, since there could be no desperate succession struggles of the type that gave so much trouble to the Achaemenids. An emperor was also given time to select a successor whom he could trust. When normal succession was restored, when a natural son succeeded his father, the result was Commodus.

Each central administration must come to terms with its elite. Amenemhet I found it necessary to sacrifice much of his regional authority. The Ptolemies had to satisfy their mercenaries. Solon had to reapportion power to accommodate the newly rising hoplite class. Augustus had to control his legions on one hand and appease the civilian city elite on the other. The appointment of emperors who appeared to represent both elites simplified the problem in the second century.

The political power that the army was capable of commanding always remained a threat to the stability of the empire and the peace. The Guard and the legions could make or break emperors and this knowledge led to repeated imperial donatives to gain the approval of the troops. Severus' deathbed advice to his two sons was to coddle the soldiers and forget everyone else. The army would continue even in the fourth century as both a tremendous financial burden and a constant threat to peace and stability.

The Antonine system of the *alimenta* ("nourishment"), which granted loans to farmers at low interest and used the interest to care for the poor children throughout Italy, was one of several welfare acts which, although well-intentioned, contributed to the growth in the cities of mobs of idle men who, as in the second century B.C. in Republican Rome, were ready to follow any dynamic, generous, unprincipled leader.

The Romans, unlike the Achaemenids, felt no need for complete law codification during their peace period. But the device of praetorial and imperial edicts was admirably constructed to allow the law sufficient flexibility to meet new situations, yet to remain constant enough to supply the security of a frame of reference.

Vespasian's policy in employing provincial soldiers throws some light on some of the side functions of the army that may have been operative in the Achaemenid Empire as well. Employing many men from the provinces, and moving them to all parts of the empire, must have increased the exchange of ideas within the empire and contributed to its homogeneous, cosmopolitan character. When troops are left too long in the garrisons, however, they lose their cosmopolitanism and acquire tastes and sympathies more like those of the lands beyond the border.

Among empires, periods of peace seem generally to have been congenial to cultural development. The Roman Peace seems to coincide at its beginning with the greatest period of Roman literature and architecture and both seem to be fading long before the peace comes to an end. This parallels somewhat the experience of the New Kingdom and the Achaemenid Empire. The quality of cultural pursuits remained relatively high throughout the entire period, however.

Despite the end of the Pax Romana in 161, the Romans had over three more centuries left to their empire. They would rebound to temporary stability under emperors such as Severus

Diocletian, Constantine, and Theodosius I. They even made significant further contributions in areas of art, architecture, literature, religion, law and political administration. They would never again achieve, however, any kind of lasting peace for their empire.

This Peace stretches our criteria a bit. The period before the disruptions of A.D. 68-69 lasted 98 years and the period after, 92 years. We could say those disruptions were not sufficient to end the peace but they seem to have been violent and extensive. Perhaps it is best to admit that by including the Pax Romana we are granting a variance from the criteria established for other periods of peace because it comes so close to meeting the requirements, because it was really a splendid as well as famous case, and because, had it not existed, it might never have occurred to us to look for any others.

12

The Hispanic-Roman Peace
(19 B.C.-A.D. 409)

Origins

The Pax Romana was broken in the late second century, but parts of the empire staggered on for more than another millennium through administrative division, transfer of power center, succession struggles, religious persecutions, civil wars, and invasions by Asians and Europeans, Persians and Moslems.

Each of the territories of the empire had its own special problems, but by the third century almost all of them had succumbed to one kind of conflict or another. The one exception was the Iberian peninsula, at the western extremity of the empire, which remained at peace until the fifth century, when it suffered successive invasions of Suevi, Alans, Vandals and Visigoths.

Spain had been so difficult to subdue that it would seem more likely to be the first area to rebel than the last to lose the peace. Army after army had been sunk into it in the last two centuries B.C. and it had been regarded as the graveyard of military and political reputations. Central and western Spain were refuges for rebels along with native Iberians, Galicians and Cantabrians. Roman armies often marched among them but as soon as they were gone the natives rearmed and resumed raids against pacified areas. Spain frequently was a battleground during the Roman civil wars of the first century B.C. In the 13 years between the death of Julius Caesar and Actium, six Roman governors had announced "decisive" victories and still little progress was made.

Spain was not pacified until well after Actium, not until

Augustus had made a long visit to organize the province and until his greatest general, Agrippa, had quelled the last of a long series of major rebellions. This last pacification was completed by 19 B.C. The peace was then maintained, with occasional but not devastating interruptions, until A.D. 409, when the first wave of Vandals crossed the Pyrenees.

Characterization

The Iberians were difficult opponents for the Roman legions because of their character and style. They valued personal daring and hardihood, regarded warfare as part of life and did not care how long it lasted. Thus they fought a continuous series of hit-and-run little wars (*guerrilla* was the Spanish word) of the same kind that the Achaemenids found impossible to deal with in their unsuccessful campaigns against the Scythians and Cadusians.

Augustus met the problem by modifying methods developed by his great-uncle Julius Caesar in pacifying Gaul. Like Julius, Augustus combined ruthless severity against rebellion with broad generosity for submission. Caesar had already established in both Gaul and Spain cities called *municipia*, which, by presenting the comfortable Roman way of life, were designed to attract the Spaniards to more settled ways. But where Caesar had emphasized municipal self-sufficiency, Augustus stressed conformity to imperial decree in exchange for economic prosperity and security.

Augustus and Agrippa built roads between chief cities, and established garrisons or colonies at key points. As brigandage was reduced and as prosperity increased because of general need in the empire for the products of Spanish agriculture, more Spaniards settled into farming and soon came to prefer their new security and prosperity to the older, more hazardous ways of gaining a living.

Spain had two distinct geographical advantages that favored peace once it had been established. First of all, her isolation at the western tip of the known world often separated her from any involvement in the contests of the central

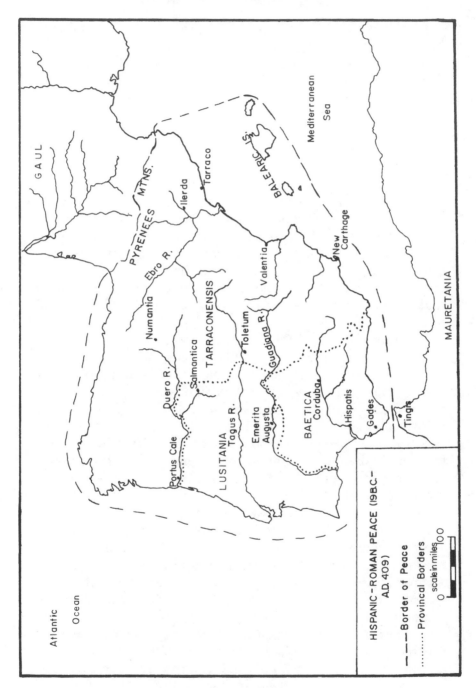

HISPANIC - ROMAN PEACE (19 B.C.-
                       A.D. 409)

--- Border of Peace

.... Provincal Borders

scale in miles
0   100

Mediterranean area. Second, the borders of the Iberian peninsula consisted on three sides of water and on the fourth side of the steep Pyrenees Mountains. The mountainous terrain along the coastline also protected Spain against a sea invasion. This situation, similar to that of the Roman Republican Peace, helped preserve stability once internal control had been established.

Following the Roman acquisition of Spain at the end of the Second Punic War, the peninsula had been divided into two provinces: Hither and Farther Spain. Augustus reorganized the area into three provinces: Baetica, Tarraconensis and Lusitania. Roman customs and the Latin language became the speech of garrison and colony, then of all administration, then of education, and finally of all the peninsula.

Baetica was so peaceful and settled that Augustus felt it needed no Roman military presence. He therefore allowed the Senate to administer Baetica as a senatorial province. Augustus maintained Lusitania in the west and Tarraconensis in the northeast as imperial provinces, stationing a total of three legions in Spain to patrol these two areas. The emperor wisely recruited these troops mostly from the two provinces themselves, thus furthering both local acceptance and romanization.[1]

The cities of the northeast coast became extremely wealthy if not so elegant as those of Baetica in the south. The uplands of Lusitania and Tarraconensis, retaining national and tribal aspects, did not attract Roman settlers but raids on the cities were replaced by economic exchange.

Although the Spanish garrison had revolted and put forth Galba, the governor of Tarraconesis, as its candidate for emperor, Spain was little affected by the disruptions that broke the peace in other parts of the empire in A.D. 68 to 70. Vespasian reestablished Roman control and made major contributions to both the romanization and peace of Spain. His grant of Latin rights to the entire free population of the peninsula brought the Hispanic Romans close to full citizenship, led to the creation of many new towns and the reorganization of older ones along Roman lines under municipal charters, and in general spread the influence both of the Latin language and of Roman customs. Vespasian's building activities and the privileged position among the provinces that Spain now occupied encouraged further economic prosperity.[2]

As the first century progressed, wealthy Roman families began to appear in the Hispanic cities, and by the second century these families were playing an active part in Roman political life: the emperors Trajan and Hadrian both came from Spain. One's key to advancement and success was to become a Roman, taking advantages of the opportunities for political, economic or military advancement offered by the empire. To maintain local customs became boorish, provincial.

Yet local peculiarities were retained. Under Roman administration the city was the basis of administration, and this fit the pattern of Iberian development. The village had been and still is the natural political unit. While Romans brought some general law, they did not interfere with the structure of the basic system. They really did not want to create united provinces that might be able to organize formidable opposition against the empire.

The combination of Roman style and municipal structure created a considerable municipal spirit among the elites. They were given privileges and honors in return for which they took on such tasks as improving the water supply or organizing grain distribution in times of high prices.

Agriculture, trade and industry flourished. Prosperity was based on the cultivation of grain, on high quality yet cheap olives, and on flax and mining. Wine was also produced for domestic consumption, though Domitian tried to reduce Spanish production in order to protect the Italian wines as a cash-crop product and to increase grain production. Though this may have reduced second century prosperity somewhat, it may also have insured Spain an adequate supply of grain when the imperial market collapsed in the third century.

The river system in the Iberian Peninsula facilitated the movement of goods from the interior to the coast for export. The building activities of Roman emperors, especially in the construction of roads, bridges and aqueducts, also increased commercial development in Spain, while at the same time advancing Roman political and military control and the general unity of the area.

Many but by no means all of the Spanish farms were owned by Romans. Labor for their estates and the mines was probably supplied by Spanish natives. But many Spanish natives owned property, becoming romanized as they grew rich.

Spain was favored with mineral wealth. Her supply of metals, particularly gold and silver, had attracted Phoenicians, Greeks, and Carthaginians before the Romans gained control of the region. Mining was a major source of revenue in Spain and most of the profits went directly to the imperial *fiscus*. Spain supplied the rest of the empire with metals and emperors carefully controlled the production of her mines. Besides gold and silver, the Spanish mined lead, copper, tin, iron, mercury, and cinnabar.[3]

As with the rest of the empire, creativity reached its peak during the first century and declined with each succeeding century. Spain produced fine mosaics, sculpture, wall-paintings, ceramics, earthenware and metalwork. Architecture and the plastic arts were simply variations of Roman style but in literature there seems to have been a marriage of Spanish and Roman style. This turned out to be the first of several periods of development in Spanish literature in which the original impulse came from abroad. Many of the contributors to the Roman "Silver Age," including the two Senecas, Quintilian, Pomponius Mela, Martial, Lucan and Columella, made their way to the capital from Spain.[4]

In the area of religion, Roman gods rapidly replaced native ones in the most romanized parts of the peninsula. In the more remote areas, the names of native gods persisted, often in combination with those of Roman deities. When Christianity began to spread through the empire, it developed in Spain much as it did in other areas, first in the cities and towns. Spain also had its share of martyrs, particularly those persecuted under Diocletian as the fourth century began. The extreme asceticism advocated by Priscillian and his followers caused a rift in the Spanish Church in the 380's which led to the suppression of the Priscillianists by the emperor Magnus Maximus. In addition, despite the fourth century Christian takeover of the empire, native rites and customs were to remain alive in Spain and in other areas for several centuries.

The second century, which brought an end of peace to the empire as a whole, brought many changes to Spain. New economic and political problems arose, worsening through the third and fourth centuries. Levies of troops and taxation increased, while trade and population declined. By the third century, municipal life had clearly lost its vitality. Residence in towns was made compulsory in order to end tax evasion and, as in other parts of the empire, men were compelled to stay in craft guilds in order to maintain the tax base. Municipal offices, once an honor, became a hereditary responsibility.

The second century was less peaceful than the first. Raids by African Moors along the coasts of Baetica began around 170, causing that normally peaceful region temporarily to become an imperial province. During the chaos of the reign of Commodus, an army of freebooters led by Maternus moved from Gaul to Spain, around 187, plundering and burning as they went. But the worst period for Spain occurred during a period of general anarchy in the 250's and 260's. Suevi and Franks invaded Tarraconensis for a period of nearly 12 years, causing extensive damage in the major city of Tarraco. This looked like the end of the Spanish peace, but a recovery followed. Though economically and politically Spain did not recover its vitality, it was spared further major invasions for more than another century.

A brief incursion by Franks around 310 provided a pretext for Constantine to occupy the area. In the early fifth century the Spanish historian Orosius could still believe that Augustus had brought eternal peace to the Iberian peninsula.[5]

Termination

The end of the Hispanic Peace bears some resemblance to the end of the Phoenician Peace in that both were products of transformations in external conditions. Spain had been protected from enemies to the north by the power of Rome in Gaul. Even when the northerners did break through, there was plenty of Roman wealth in Gaul to satisfy their avarice.

At the beginning of the fifth century, however, Gaul was stripped of its soldiers by the Roman (Vandal) general Stilicho, who was defending Italy against the Visigoths. Meanwhile a pretender named Constantine invaded Gaul from Britain and advanced into Spain. His armies were victorious over Hispanic Romans in Lusitania, but the governor left in charge launched a rebellion of his own and invited the support of German tribes from Gaul. By the time imperial armies could be brought to the rescue, armies of the Vandals, Alans and Suevi were in control of much of the peninsula.

"Rescue" is perhaps a loaded term. By the fifth century the decadence of Italy had led to the appointment of incapable or self-seeking governors in Spain; these were unable to stem the deterioration of the municipal system and their rule was such that many of the Spanish provincials welcomed the Vandals and others as deliverers.

The invasions from the north marked the end of peace in the Iberian peninsula and the end of the Ancient World in the West. Ancient traditions were continued for some centuries longer in the Byzantine Empire but its history seems more closely related to that of the Medieval West, and in any event does not seem to include long periods of peace.

Reflections

Spain had been protected from invasion by its remoteness. Britain experienced a shorter period of peace in the third century for the same reason but the islands were soon subjected to Saxon sea raids. Spain, however, was too long a sail down the Atlantic coast. This remoteness may also have kept Spain out of the fourth-century power conflicts, as it did Britain.

It would seem that in time of stability, peripheral locations may be unfortunate, because stable powers tend to use these regions for a battleground. Syria and Mesopotamia have often been in this position. But Spain was not involved in this kind of conflict because it was not between powers; it was located at the end of the world.

In time of internal conflict peripheral locations may be more favorable, since warfare at the center will decide control of the provinces anyway, providing there are no strong regional ideologies involved. In this case the romanized Spanish elite wanted most a strongly centralized, peaceful trading empire.

Perhaps the key to the longevity of the Hispanic Peace was the intricate political and social relationship that had been established between the imperial center and the province. On one hand there was opportunity for Spanish Romans to become members of the Roman equestrian and senatorial classes and to exercise their rights in Rome as Romans and not Spaniards. On the other hand there was a strong municipal spirit, reflected for example in spontaneous gifts to towns by affluent citizens. Thus a balance of loyalty to the central government and concern for the municipality was for a long period maintained.

Spain avoided most of the internal political disturbances during the third and fourth centuries because her city elite had no strong economic or political reasons for rebellion. The Hispanic Romans were producers of grain and as such, less subject to famine or economic breakdown than Italy or Greece. They had the political organization and military power to defend themselves against raids from agrarian and pastoral peoples and sufficient wealth to make trade more attractive than unsuccessful war.

It is interesting that the decline of population, in the third and fourth centuries, attributable in part to pestilence, did not break the peace. Widespread disease and demographic losses were characteristic of the empire as a whole in this period. A decline in population, whether the result of disease, famine or warfare, must often accompany the waning of effective authority. But the Spanish example suggests that a rapid decline of population need not be, in itself, a cause of internal conflict.

The Hispanic Romans did have political problems. They protested imperial military requisitions but the advantages provided by the empire were apparently greater than the inconvenience of the levies. Tribal and sectional differences may have caused some internal troubles, but perhaps the cities, by wealth, political organization and military power, were better able to defend themselves and to offer more attractive economic alternatives to rebellion. Roman political and cultural influences also created unity among the diverse parts of the Iberian Peninsula.

13

Settings

The cases of peace in the Ancient World presented here should indicate that peace is not an altruisic idea whose time has not yet come. Peace is very old.

In the horticultural and agrarian societies studied here, peace appears to have been normal, war an exceptional activity. The Ancient World was normally at peace. Most of the time, even if war was occurring in some society, it was not in most other societies. Peasants farmed much more than they fought. Kings fought occasional campaigns, but they spent much more of their time eating, sleeping, making love, collecting taxes and reviewing petitions. At any particular time, if somewhere a boundary was being violated, tens or hundreds of others were being respected.

It is true that periods of peace, as they are defined in this study, were rare. They were exceptional historical achievements and it is for that reason that they have been singled out for special attention here. But hundred-years wars, defined in terms of spatial and temporal unity, might be even more difficult to find.

It is not easy to discern any particular pattern in the location of these ancient societies with relation to others. Only two, the Roman and Achaemenid Empires, could be said to be of such size and power that they were virtually unchallenged by any other external political entity. Their situation was such that most problems of peace and stability were internal. External problems were remote and unimportant.

There were others, however, less concerned with external problems because of geographical remoteness. This could be said of the Middle Kingdom, the Phoenician and the Hispanic-Roman societies. The Phoenicians, it is true, had the powerful Assyrians to contend with, but part of their success was attributable to their own remote location with reference to the center of Assyrian problems. The Middle Kingdom had on its borders decidedly weaker powers and Spain was at the edge of the Roman world, with only less civilized peoples to the north to fear. All three of these societies were at the edge of a configuration of power but fortunately not caught between two such configurations.

There were, however, an equal number of societies that were generally involved with other powers, and for whom foreign affairs must have been a continual problem: the New Kingdom, Athens, Corinth, the Ptolemaic Empire and the Roman Republic. Each of these societies was in a situation in which external attack was possible though except for the Ptolemaic Empire and Ramessid Egypt none was hard pressed.

Another way of looking at relations with other states is to consider the extent of influence the society had regarding configurations of power around it. Of the ten, only the Hispanic society lacked autonomy. All the others, whether powerful or not, were clearly self-governing. And all of these, except the Phoenician, had the political power to influence or change the system or systems that adjoined them. Two states, the Middle Kingdom and the Roman Republic, were dominant powers in their areas. The New Kingdom, the Ptolemaic Empire and the two Greek city-states were involved with several competing powers in their respective systems.

In what kind of environments did these societies exist? Of course they had to exist in environments in which there would be some conflict or else the environments would have been part of the peace. The Hispanic Peace was protected during its earlier phase by a general atmosphere of peace in the Roman Empire. And the Phoenicians, at the other extreme, lived at the edge of a highly conflict-oriented society. But the others existed in environments of which warfare was a reality but not an overwhelming aspect of political relations. There was fighting going on but it was accompanied by trade, touring and other normal and peaceful activities. The environments were generally not conflict environments.

The settings, then, varied considerably. Some of the societies were protected by isolation, some were not. Control of great areas, overwhelming power, or isolation may have helped in some instances, but in others, none of these conditions was present. Peace did not require any recurrent combination of circumstances. Men were able to forge long periods of peace under a number of different conditions.

If we turn to physical boundaries, however, most of the societies seem to have been in a favored position. The Phoenician cities were surrounded by water, Spain and Italy were peninsulas, Corinth was on an isthmus. Athens and the Egyptian states had water boundaries. What was not protected by water in Spain and Italy was cut off by mountains, while Egypt was protected by desert and marsh. Only the two great empires transcended the advantages of geographical protection.

We have to be cautious about claiming a great principle of peace, however, because the Ancient World surrounded the Mediterranean Sea. Water was as important as land as a supporter of life in the Ancient World. In addition, the territory around the Mediterranean happens to be rich in both mountains and deserts, yet the inhabitants of such territories do not seem to have enjoyed any special inclination toward peace. Still, though geography may not have created peace, it may have been very important in providing opportunities.

Climate was perhaps a factor in the success of the development of civilizations in the Mediterranean area, but once civilization had been established, the climate was not greatly different for any peaceful society. There were floods on the Nile and dry spells in Egypt and Spain and there were storms at sea but for the most part the climate was favorable and supportive. There was no great challenge that people had to resolve, once the management of the Nile had been mastered by the Egyptians.

The physical setting, then, was generally supportive to a thriving society. To some extent the geography helped defend the integrity of the individual societies, but on the other hand, the weather did little to discourage military campaigns during most of the year.

It appears that ancient peaceful societies did have some advantages in geographical situation. Their political situations varied greatly, however, while climate was neutral. It would appear that in the settings, there were no prerequisites for peace.

14

Leaders

It is possible that in writing history we have had a tendency to focus excessively on individuals. Just as people in the past have attempted to provide answers to mysteries by creating gods and heroes, so many historians have euhemerized historical figures, attributing to them mythical powers to achieve all the glories and evils of epochs.

If we are aware of this today, in an era in which the writing of social history is forcing a reconsideration of political history, still we are dependent on many earlier historians who have written in a different epoch. Periodic reevaluation and reinterpretation of all periods of history is both healthy and necessary. It is also probable that in ancient history, where inference often must be used more frequently than in analyses of the more recent past, euhemerization may have been particularly tempting.

So it is not surprising, perhaps, that individual leaders should be so evident in these histories, or that certain roles seem to have been recurrently played. Possibly it is least surprising to discover that several of the peaceful societies trace their origins back to warriors. Every peace period, after all, must begin with a resolved conflict.

Sometimes the leader who is later perceived to have contributed most to the establishment of the peace, the founder if you will, enters the historical scene as leader of one of two factions that have already been victorious in a previous set of conflicts. He then leads in victory over the other faction and follows with some mopping-up operations that may be extensive.

In the case of Cyrus of Persia, the mopping-up occupied

134

his whole career, once his chief adversary, Astyages, leader of the Medes, had been conquered. He was not the kind of person a modern peace group would invite in as a speaker. Though his sphere was less extensive, Mentuhotpe II seems to have been engaged in a similar campaign in behalf of the Theban faction against the faction at Heracleopolis, in the founding of the Middle Kingdom, and his role was repeated 500 years later by another Theban general, Ahmose, who drove out the last of the Hyksos. The conflict of factions and a decisive victory are also repeated in Augustus' defeat of Antony at Actium. But in that case the victory was final as well as decisive, few mopping-up operations were required, and Augustus does not have the conqueror image of the Persian and Egyptian leaders. The victory of Cypselus over the Bacchiads in Corinth could have been the same kind of triumph in miniature. Scipio, hailed as the savior of Rome, was also the founder of the Roman peace, which actually began two years before his final victory at Zama.

In two cases, however, the winners of the final victories were never perceived as founders of anything by anyone. Mazaces of Persia and Agrippa of Rome put down the last of a series of revolts in what were to become Ptolemaic Egypt and Roman Spain.

There have been leaders in the ancient world such as Cyrus and Mentuhotpe II who conquered in great swathes around them. Assyrian history is rich in such leaders. The memories of these founders would not be associated with peace except for what happened after them.

Of Augustus, of course, there is much more to be said than that he was a conqueror. That role was almost incidental. He was an extraordinary organizer, a man who could establish structures to be managed by other people. We remember him not because he was a victor but because he was able to consolidate what had been won. If we are to have heroes in peaceful societies, it is to those who were able to consolidate their polities that we should look. Such consolidators, you might say, created the founders in retrospect.

While Augustus was supreme in organizational capacity, in designing political structures that were relevant to situations, and in choosing managers of those structures, other peaceful societies seem to have been blessed with leaders of similar capacities. Darius appears to have played such a part in the Persian Empire and Ptolemy Soter is a clear example of the type in the kingdom that was appropriately to bear his name. Other founders, like Augustus, could prove themselves as consolidators, for such seems to have been the case with both Ahmose and Cypselus, who were blessed with energetic and capable successors Amenhotpe I and Periander. Amenemhet I and Senwosret I fulfilled this role in the Middle Kingdom, though, as with Darius, not before there was a threat of resurgent anarchy that had to be quelled with yet more fighting.

In other cases no particular consolidator appears. In Spain, of course, Augustus performed the same role he performed in the Pax Romana. In Phoenicia and Athens we do not know whether there was any one person responsible for the two very different kinds of politics that emerged. In the Roman Republican Peace, the formula had been developed considerably before the peace and remained only to be carried out after the departure of Hannibal. The Senate probably deserves most of the credit for consolidation in this case.

What the consolidators actually did varies with the situation. We shall attempt to generalize about their handling of poltical centralization, policies for stabilization, systems of justice, economic policies and so on. But what matters is that these leaders had a realistic sense of the situation they were attempting to manage.

They were similar in type. Taking Augustus, Ptolemy Soter and Darius as the leaders we know most about, they seem to be sober, industrious, prudent, far-sighted. They were not charismatic types, though Augustus and Cypselus, at least, seem to have been highly respected and had something of a common touch: Augustus refused to accept exalted titles, Cypselus walked the streets safely alone. The consolidators may have had temptations to enjoy the luxuries that go with power, but they seem to have preferred problems of work to the joys of leisure. They must have been good judges of character and willing and able to delegate power (though Soter showed some reluctance here, setting a pattern that was to limit the length of the peace he created).

There is a resemblance in character type, perhaps, between the consolidators and at least two figures who appeared late in the peace periods, the reformers Haremhab in the New Kingdom and Vespasian in the Roman Empire. They too seem to have been practical, prudent and perhaps a little dry. The reason for the resemblance, possibly, is that they faced similar organizational problems. The reason that there are more successful consolidators in this book than reformers is that we began by studying successful peace periods, so that we have ten cases out of possibly hundreds of attempts in which a successful consolidation was managed. If the odds are against consolidation they are also against reform. The failure of capable monarchs like Akhenaten may serve as a reminder that no reform is wrought without considerable opposition and often such opposition includes violence and civil strife.[1]

Successful reconsolidations did take place in the New Kingdom and the Roman Empire, perhaps in the Middle Kingdom and in Roman Spain. It may well have happened during the long period of the Phoenician Peace, but that was decentralized and we lack information about leadership. As for Roman Spain, the problem is that some of the responsibilities for administration lay outside the territory. For instance it could be argued that Diocletian was an administrative reformer for Roman Spain, in that his reorganization of the empire made possible or at least supported the retention of peace in Spain for another century. If so, Diocletian seems to fit the personality type of the reformer-consolidator.

But what of the situation itself? What do the founders and consolidators of peace have to cope with? The situations that existed in the Ancient World might be classified in three ways: the conquest of new land by an external invader, the defeat of an invader or conquerer, or the resolution of a succession struggle among domestic contenders. There are 13 cases that might be considered: the origins of the ten periods and the restorations of peace in the New Kingdom, Pax Romana, and Roman Spain, which we may call the Ramessid and Flavian-Antonine Restorations, and the Hispanic Revival. These may be classified as shown in the adjoining table.

Conquest of New Land	Conqueror Defeated	Succession Struggle	Unknown
Achaemenid	Phoenician	Middle Kingdom	Athenian
Ptolemaic	Roman Repub-	New Kingdom	
Hispanic-Roman	lican	Ramessid	
	New Kingdom	Corinthian	
	(Thutmosid)	Achaemenid	
	Hispanic Revival	Pax Romana	
		Flavian-Antonine	

Though succession struggles occurred more often than not, there was no clear cut pattern of conflict preceding the establishment of a peace period.

Once peace was established, in our case areas, the quality of leadership generally declined somewhat. At least the nominal leader was likely to be less important to the maintenance of the peace period. He may have flowed with the situation, enjoying his perquisites and allowing the mechanisms established by his predecessors to run as they would. Xerxes historically provides the model for the magnificent monarch; Amenhotpe III in the New Kingdom and the Roman Emperor Nero seem to have been such monarchs as perhaps, on thin evidence, was Hiram the Great of Tyre.

These magnificent monarchs have drawn more attention than a larger series of mediocre leaders who appear at less affluent stages and who were ordinary men inheriting a position they could not have earned. They were not powerful enough to assert themselves but the system was strong enough to support them. If, as happened often in Persia, they were assassinated, the system was affected little more than if the chairman of the board resigns or retires from a modern corporation.

This is not to say that every nominal leader was mediocre after the early part of a peace period. Quite a number were obviously competent, but they tended to administer the system they inherited rather than to modify it. There are three choices open to a leader who inherits a stable system with a capital surplus. He can bank the surplus, holding his reserves for future times of troubles; he can invest it, building capital, constructing roads and aqueducts, protecting shipping, and supporting agriculture by draining marshes or subsidizing irrigation; or he can spend it by building glorious edifices, or endorsing military adventures into distant lands. A fourth choice would be to reduce taxes, leaving merchants, craftsmen and peasants to decide whether they will spend, invest or save. The magnificent monarchs spent, as did monarchs like the Thutmosids, Ramesses II or Trajan, while monarchs like Amenemhet III in the Middle Kingdom, or the Antonine Emperors after Trajan, were savers or capital builders. Lowering taxes does not seem to have been an option chosen.

For the most part, failure to maintain peace in times of crisis cannot be attributed to inferior leadership. Darius III of Persia seems to have been mediocre but for the most part these times of crisis seemed to bring out the best in leaders and the roster of the unsuccessful certainly is impressive in quality. There were creative leaders like Akhenaten in the New Kingdom, the Gracchi in the Roman Republic and the Roman emperor Marcus Aurelius. They were unable to transmit their visions to their countrymen. There were more pragmatic, steely, tough leaders who were both capable and courageous: such as Merenptah and Ramesses III were not able to stem the New Kingdom collapse, while Ochus was deprived of the chance by assassination, and Ptolemy IV Philopator was successful in battle but not in peacemaking. We may well wonder if Philopator in particular contributed to mounting problems by his rigidity, but the others seem to have done their best with a situation that was slipping away.

What did the leaders, particularly the successful consolidators and reformers, actually do about ordering the polity? In answering this question, we are not likely to discover any formulas for peace. We are not going to be able to say that a government that decentralizes, codifies its law system and provides a certain kind of succession system has, let us say, a certain percentage chance of producing a century of peace.

Rather, by reviewing the variety of situations we can suggest a range of effective responses. Moreover, in focusing on the Ancient World we can perhaps suggest the problems that are timeless, just as reading Plato helps us sort out universal problems from the problems peculiar to industrial societies.

This generalization can be made: As far as we are able to penetrate the mists of ancient history, allowing for the gaps in information and the inevitable blurring of facts and introduction of speculations by the most careful of historians, it would seem that the successful peacemakers had a reordering of polity as a priority. This means that they were operating consciously to make political changes. They were not accepting the conditions of the past as given. In almost every case, their knowledge of history would be knowledge of conflict and chaos.

The one exception to this generalization might be Roman Republican Italy, where it could be said that the mechanism for peace had been created before the chaos and the history of the peace is the gradual institutionalization and disintegration of that mechanism.

Sometimes, as in the case of Phoenicia and the New Kingdom, and very likely Athens and Corinth as well, the chaos had been produced by external forces that now had waned, providing an opportunity that had not been made by the peacemakers. At other times, as in the Roman Empire and Republic, the Middle Kingdom, Ptolemaic Empire and Persia, the inheritors of the new situation were very much the creators — if not they themselves, then their immediate predecessors.

What the consolidators and successful reformers did have in common was an effective understanding of the situation in which they found themselves. This may seem both banal and tautological. Who does not succeed without understanding his situation? And how do we judge effective undestanding except by success?

Akhenaten may have understood that his situation called for substantial change, but he did not have an *effective* understanding. He seems to have combined political and religious reforms, succeeding in neither. Cyrus, by contrast, succeeded without profound understanding. He understood military tactics and organization, he understood that men would follow his leadership, he could establish a basic political organization and he must have understood that there was no other military organization in range that could challenge him. But that kind of understanding is less subtle compared to that which was required of Darius, who had to understand a thousand nuances, to know whom to trust, when to withdraw, when to temporize. Comparing the two is like comparing a successful hunter who has to know how to kill as many deer as he can and a successful ecologist who has to figure out how many deer an area can afford to lose and then arrange so that the successful hunters take no more and no less.

We have referred and we shall refer again to this sense of the situation. It is probably the most important theme in this analysis. The men who individually or collectively made peace were realists who understood the limits and possibilities of their power. They were not historians, but they did have some sense of history, enough to tell them that the past provided some clues to understanding but no guidelines to policy.

They were men who had some sense of the future too. They did not set out to establish a century of peace, but they set out to build a political structure well, so that it could cope with foreseeable problems and, with the exception of the Ptolemies, they allowed enough flexibility for future modification.

What they did, they intended to do. Their aim was to organize and structure a particular entity. Peace was very much part of their planning. Their perception of order included peace. Augustus and Amenemhet I did not seek to expand the glory of the political system they dominated. We call them consolidators, because consolidation rather than expansion was a central feature of their policies. They were leaders who did not allow prestige and glory to blind them to the need for less spectacular but more lasting achievements.

15
Polities

We have indicated that the sense of situation was more important than the creation of a particular structure. That said, it would follow that there would be a diversity of political structures. And so there seem to have been.

In horticultural and agrarian times, given history in general, one generally expects to find monarchy as the normal form of government. Among the peaceful societies there were a number of monarchies to be sure, but there were other forms as well. The Egyptian and Ptolemaic kingdoms had monarchs. The Phoenician states had kings but no Phoenician king ruled over all; they were really a federation of king-led entities. The Roman Republic was a federation too, though its propensity to federate decline rapidly. It was also a republic, as was Athens for part of the time. Athens and Corinth were also ruled by tyrants, for a period, and Corinth had an overblown oligarchy besides. The Roman and Achaemenid periods of peace were the creations of empire, though the Achaemenid rulers may have called themselves kings. And Spain was administered by provincial governors. It would be very difficult to say, then, that any particular form of government is essential to peace.

We have already implied in Chapter 13 that the size of a political entity does not seem to have been a crucial factor. The Roman and Achaemenid empires were very large, the Athenian and Corinthian systems were very small and the other entities were comparable in size to medium-sized modern states.

You might expect that the regimes of peaceful societies would be exceptionally stable. We have no control group operating in this study, so we cannot comment on how excep-

142

tional the stability was, but it doesn't appear to have been extraordinary. The Roman Empire itself was rocked by an explosive series of coups and counter coups right in the middle of peace, and the most serious of these was generated from the government of Spain, another of our peaceful societies. The Persians were plagued by battles among claimants to the throne and by assassinations once the claimants came to power. Assassinations were also common in the Roman Empire and Phoenicia. The New Kingdom suffered a major internal struggle during the height of its power, with a resulting change in dynasty. Power in Athens was usurped by a despot while Corinthian despots were upset by a cumbersome oligarchy. The Roman Republic rumbled with power struggles long before the storm really broke.

One might expect peaceful societies to have developed effective succession systems. But if the governments were not especially stable, neither were their succession systems. The succession system that seems to be most familiar in history is the one we have learned about from the English and French monarchies, where the oldest son or sometimes daughter of a king or queen is normally the successor. But this policy does not seem to have been followed very often in ancient times. The Egyptians did except when there was no male heir or when the heir was too young. Egyptian kings often shared their thrones for a time with their successors, insuring a smooth transfer of power and giving the future ruler experience. Some Roman emperors were victims of intrigue in the first century, but the system became more stable in the second when a series of emperors adopted successors not related by blood. The Persian succession often went to the most effective organizer and warrior among the sons of a monarch. Corinthian and Athenian tyrants were unsuccessful at passing on their power beyond a generation. In Athens and the Roman Republic, though the Areopagus and Senate provided some stability, leadership succession was annual and by election—about the most unstable system that could be conceived, unless it were the imperial system in Roman Spain of allowing governors to recoup the expense of gaining office from the wealth of their temporary subjects.

One problem that would seem to affect all peaceful societies was the degree to which power was to be delegated in each. Some kind of decision had to be made about the extent to which each society would be centralized or decentralized. The answer in the case of the ancient states seems to be strongly on the side of decentralization. With the exception of the Ptolemaic state, which had strong centralizing tendencies, the ten societies studied herein tended to be considerably decentralized throughout their period of peace, or to lose their status of peace after becoming more centralized.

The Phoenician state was the most decentralized of all, each city retaining its own sovereignty. The Middle Kingdom, with its *nomarchs,* was strikingly decentralized when compared to the Egypt of the Pyramids. The Roman and Achaemenid empires delegated immense power to their imperial administrators.

The impression that decentralization is important to long periods of peace is strengthened by the cases that began with peaceful disintegration and terminated after power consolidation had been effected. The Roman Republican Peace began with a confederation, but Roman consolidation gradually extended until toward the end of the peace period the federation had ceased to exist. The Athenian state emerged as a peaceful oligarchy, but eventually tyrants usurped power and ultimately lost the peace. The New Kingdom began with considerable delegation of power to viziers. As time went on, more power came to be concentrated in the hands of the Theban priesthood of Amun until a virtual theocracy eventually undercut the monarchy. In the early days of Roman Spain, local peculiarities were retained and nurtured. But by the third century, municipal life had lost its vitality and rule was maintained by compulsory centralization. Corinth is the exception to this pattern, beginning as a centralized tyranny and later giving way to oligarchy.

The attempts by central powers to increase authority were generally followed by threats and disruptions to peace. It may be, however, that decentralization was natural in stable situations and that centralization was a response to, rather than a cause of, crisis.

Closely related to the problem of degree of centralization was that of the place of elites. To what extent were elites brought in with new leaders; to what extent were they left undisturbed? To what extent did they share power or were they given only the appearance of power?

Augustus managed to transform a republic into an empire while continuing to share the appearance of power. The Senate, in particular, continued to function as it had under the Republic, to meet and make decisions, but the range of those decisions was narrowed and controlled by the *princeps*. Augustus, like Ammenemhet I in the Middle Kingdom, inherited a position with considerable tradition behind it. But Amenemhet shared power as well as prestige, because the *nomarchs* of the Middle Kingdom retained a large measure of domestic sovereignty.

The other empire, the Persian, inherited no such central institution as the Roman Senate. But the Achaemenids had to preside over diverse regions, including kingdoms that had long traditions of their own. Here they were willing to accept the leadership of local elites, bringing in outside *satraps* only after the local rulers had proved incapable. The Roman system, by contrast, was more centrally administered, more professional. There was less emphasis on maintaining regional identity. A local leader would have more chance of maintaining family power and prestige by enrolling his sons in the imperial service. This was also true under the Ptolemies, where association with the Greek rulers was the only route to prestige and power, and in the New Kingdom, where the old dynasty had been alien and the new dynasty brought with it a new elite.

In Corinth and the Roman Republic, the trappings of power were shared by existing elites but social mobility was restricted. The Athenians too shared power among a relatively small and homogenous elite.

In the Ancient World, there is little approaching popular democracy. The Greek tyrants and the Roman Gracchi courted popular support, challenging the elite, and making themselves heroes of popular movements of the future. The Gracchi were significantly unsuccessful. Their approaches were inappropriate for the situations they faced. The Greek tyrants soon created an elite of their own.

Generally, where an elite group was already established, new rulers left to it prestige and even some local power where it would have been awkward to challenge. New leaders, on the other hand, generally brought in their own elite. Where there were extensive territories to rule and it was necessary to subdivide power over areas, a variety of approaches were tried. Sending out governors from central areas worked for the Romans and Ptolemies, though the latter experienced recurrent and growing rebellion shortly after the first century of peace. Decentralization worked in the Middle Kingdom and Persia, though the Persians frequently switched to centrally appointed governors.

The questions of centralization and elites are almost inextricable, and in the Ancient World it is difficult to generalize about them. We know that in what seem to be similar situations, leaders took different approaches, all of which led to the continued maintenance of peace. We can see, in the case of Egypt, that leaders tried different approaches in the same land, but always the situation was different: once there was a native dynasty seeking native support; once a native conqueror of an alien dynasty; once an alien conqueror of an alien dynasty. It would seem that greater knowledge would not have helped the peacemakers of the Ancient World. No matter what information they had about successful approaches in other situations, successful leaders still needed a sense of their own situation.

Five of the peace periods of the Ancient World are associated with law. The Persian, all three Roman, and the Athenian peaces all reflected significant developments in the law. Roman codification, along with the laws of Draco and Solon of Athens, have also have a direct bearing on the later development of law in the western world. What is the relationship, then, between law and peace? Did the codification of laws cement the peace periods or did the peace periods provide the opportunity for the codification of the laws?

Both positions probably contain some truth. The Roman codification did not take place until well into the second century, in the second phase of the Pax Romana. However, law had been a basic, cohesive force in Roman life, at least from the time of the 12 tables in the mid-fifth century B.C. The guardianship of the laws probably prevented some disputes from breaking out into violent disturbances and thus helped to preserve peace. The Persian codification took place early in the time of Darius. The Persian laws, however, were harsh and uniform. The Roman laws were liberal and flexible, subject to praetorian and imperial reinterpretation. This contrast is combined in Athens, where Draconian severity was followed by the Solonian reforms, which gave greater flexibility.

This suggests that the function of law is to provide some kind of standard of justice. The laws of Draco and Darius released people from arbitrary decisions of regional nobility. If law could be tempered with flexibility, perhaps with a system of appeals, so much the better. A government that had established authority was expected to provide justice. Providing justice affirmed and supported the authority.

Law figured heavily in the Ptolemaic Kingdom, where there were separate law systems for Greeks, Egyptians and Jews, which suggest that legal systems have an organic origin and it is better to cultivate and modify them rather than to replace them with novel or alien systems. The Ptolemies did not think it necessary to divide political power or even prestige. They were the most meddlesome, intrusive and neurotic of all rulers, but they did not choose to unify or transform existing systems of law.

If the authority of a government had been established, if arrangements had been made with regard to distribution of power, it was not necessary that the government be popular. But many governments were popular: Cypselus in Corinth, Peisistratus in Athens and a number of kings, archons and consuls as well. In the case of the Gracchi, however, such popularity was perceived as a danger to the state and threatened peace rather than reinforced it.

If many governments were popular, many were also oppressive. The Ptolemaic government was relentlessly intrusive; Persian justice could be harsh. Egyptian governments kept a close reign on the productive functions of farmers and laborers. The Greek, Roman and Phoenician governments, however, were milder in administration of laws and general controls.

The wisdom of the ages yields no easy answers. It is difficult to generalize about forms, stability, succession, centralization, elites, law, popularity or oppression. One combination of approaches worked in one society, another in another.

16

Economies

The basic question, probably, is how peace affected economics in each of the periods. It would seem as though peace should encourage prosperity. Once peace came to be accepted as a normal condition, people could make long-term economic plans, expecting to reap what they planted, to sell what they had made, to receive the benefits of long-term captialization and to be at their business posts when their ships came in.

And, in the Ancient World, this common sense hypothesis seems to be verified. Each of the societies experienced a period of prosperity that became evident some decades after the establishment of peace. The Egyptian societies were all productive and wealthy, especially the Ptolemaic, though in that case wealth may have been a function of inadequate distribution as well as of a world in which opportunities, communications and interactions between states were unusually favorable. Travelers through the great empires remarked on their prosperity; the Phoenicians were especially known for economic skills; and the Greek states, Roman Republic and imperial Spain all experienced periods of economic recovery and development.

But if prosperity becomes possible because there has been a period of peace, it would follow that it should continue as long as peace itself continues. The record in the Ancient World, however, indicates otherwise. In every case except Persia there were signs of economic decline before the termination of peace.

Sometimes the government was sharply increasing tax collection (New Kingdom, Athens, all the Roman polities), but this usually was the result of some other economic problem. There were problems of land distribution in the Ptolemaic and

148

Roman empires as well as in the Roman Republic. These led to landless tenants inundating the cities in great numbers in the Roman states. Agricultural productivity was down in the Republic and later in the Empire and this led to a decline in trade. Trade disruption was also a problem in the Middle Kingdom, Phoenicia and Corinth, though the causes were different. In some instances (Ptolemaic Egypt and the Roman cases), economics deeply affected all classes, while in others (the Middle and Thutmosid New kingdoms, the small Mediterranean states) it is not clear that economic problems were more than nagging: elites may have felt that times were not as good as they had been. In the Persian case, though Persia always looked unstable and vulnerable, there does not seem to be any marked decline in productivity or trade, nor any sharp change in distribution. It may be that if one is invaded by Alexander the Great, one is in for a bad time no matter what the condition of the economy.

In dealing with the relationship between economic health and the termination of peace, we have implicitly suggested provisional answers to several other aspects of the economy. The later increase in government taxation implies moderate policies toward economic enterprise. Certainly the Phoenicians seemed to be free of government interference. The Roman emperors' policies, in Spain as elsewhere, generally were supportive without being intrusive. They constructed roads, bridges, aqueducts; improved inland waterways, and most important, provided protection. In Persia the situation seems to have been similar. If governors and *satraps* enriched themselves, they left plenty for local elites. The government of the Roman Republic possibly did not interfere enough, allowing increasing inequity without doing much about it. This, of course, generally benefited the senatorial oligarchy in power.

The governments of Athens and Corinth, on the other hand, intervened to insure a wider distribution of wealth. In the case of Solon, we view this as far-sighted policy; in the cases of Cypselus, Periander and Peisistratus it seems to have been politically motivated but the result may have been to encourage varied kinds of investment since display of affluence was dangerous. The Egyptian governments, of course, had supervisory functions in the nature of their special economy but, in the

Middle Kingdom especially, economic control of farms and trade ventures was left to nomarchs.

Government intervention, then, seems to have had positive effects where it encouraged economic distribution but negative effects where increased taxes led to narrowed distribution and increased impoverishment or unemployment. In all cases except the Ptolemaic and Roman Republican, a relatively wide distribution of wealth was characteristic. And these two peace periods, as it happens, were among the shortest of the periods studied. To say that there was relatively wide distribution does not imply equality. But the classes that could be influential had some economic opportunity and those that did not at least had subsistence employment.

The early Egyptian societies were horticultural, the Phoenician, Corinthian and Athenian societies were maritime, the others were agrarian. All but the maritime societies would have had more than 90 percent of their populations involved in farming. The farmers who worked in the fields were generally peasants, though they have been serfs as well, or slaves—it did not seem to matter, so long as there was land enough to support such a population. Generally, when there was not enough land, there was social conflict. We do not have much information about population but where there was a shortage of land, it usually appears that policies of land distribution were a major factor, though there may also have been increasing population as well, as a result of the long periods of peace. We do know that there was a combination of ineffective government economic policy and falling population in Spain during the long later period of the Hispanic Peace, which makes one wonder if rising population could have been a factor in other cases.

As for the maritime societies, there have been relatively few in world history. The absence of land distribution problems may have been a factor in these peace periods. So, perhaps, may have been the fact that maritime people can move elsewhere more easily than inhabitants of horticultural or agrarian states.

In discussing the decline of economies, we noted that several were having problems with trade. The implied converse would seem to be that peaceful societies were often trading societies and this appears to be the case. But, once again, we need to remember that the Ancient World was located around a great sea, and the sea was a principle means of communication. The Mediterranean world, therefore, was one in which trade was normal. Since peace was also normal, peaceful societies normally would be trading societies. For the small Mediterranean states, particularly in Greece, trade was essential. The Phoenicians could not have survived, and the Athenians and Corinthians would have been much impoverished if they were prevented from trading.

The empires, particularly the Roman, provided attractive areas that drew traders and the wealth of the Ptolemaic and New Kingdom were greatly enhanced by trade. The Roman Republic, however, does not seem to have been much involved in commerce despite its power and favorable location nor, comparatively, was the Middle Kingdom. Though geographical isolation may have been a factor in establishing the peace of some of the ancient societies, they were not generally isolated in their economic relations.

Trade requires efficient systems of transportation and these were plentiful in the Mediterranean world. The Mediterranean Sea, the Nile and the road systems of the great empires supported transportation, as did the probability of a peaceful trip. Still, traveling across a system as large as the Roman Empire was not comparable to a modern business trip. Braudel writing about the Mediterranean in the 16th century, estimates that traveling from Spain to the Levant might have taken two to three months.[1] Moreover, storms and currents made even shorter journeys highly unpredictable as to time and very dangerous as well.

Trade requires specialization. Either there must be resources not available elsewhere or there must be specialized production. There was a good deal of both among the peaceful societies. The Phoenicians and Athenians, for instance, developed special techniques, taking advantage of local resources. These activities were intensified by trade, which made such activities profitable. The Egyptians produced grain surpluses because of the Nile and the empires had access to wide range of resources.

But there were the normal activities of men of the time. Traders were encouraged by peace, and their schemes were more frequently successful. Areas with no special advantages in terrain or location, like Spain, became prosperous because people could devote their time to problems of agriculture and commerce.

Such activities could be carried on in time of war as well, so long as the warfare was intermittent. The Hellenistic world and the world of New Kingdom Egypt were worlds of frequent conflict, not to mention piracy, but the states involved had plenty of time and manpower to continue to grow and produce and a sufficient expectation that most of their ships would get through.

It was the case with economy, as it was with polity, that no special kind was essential for peace. Most were involved in agriculture, manufacturing and commerce, though some might specialize more in one area than another. It seems clear that given peace and expectation of peace, economies tended to function for themselves. If governments intervened, they could do so most effectively by favoring wider distribution. Economic prosperity, then, was to a great extent a function of peace.

Declining prosperity, on the other hand, was likely to be an indication of other kinds of problems in the political and social system. Though economic decline frequently preceded the termination of peace, it was not likely to be the sole precipitating factor in that termination.

17

Societies

Can each of the ten cases of peace be described as a peaceful society? Is there a Roman Imperial society, a Hispanic Roman society, a Corinthian society? Or are these simply areas definable on a map but lacking social coherence?

If a society is a social system in which there are extensive, internal human relationships, in which there is distinct autonomy, and in which the combination of autonomy and relationships is widely perceived within and without, then the cases presented here were societies. If the criteria had been to find areas without conflict, that might not have been so, but the criteria also included the idea of finding distinctive, coherent units. There may have been areas of the Chaldean or Parthian or Sassanian empires or among other Greek city-states that had more than a century of peace, but we could not isolate them or locate sufficient documentation.

Eight of the ten cases were themselves political units. The exceptions were Phoenicia and Spain, the one including a number of political units, the other being a region of a larger unit. But the Phoenicians recognized the cultural relationship among themselves and it was generally recognized by contemporaries and has been by historians. Though Spain was romanized and divided into provinces, it too was always perceived as having social unity, though it lacked political autonomy.

Probably the most important question to ask about the societies is what were they like to live in? What kind of life did they provide? The answer to this question is disappointing. We cannot always be sure. Much of the chronological history of the Ancient World is political and economic. When we get to social

153

history, it is likely to be for broad periods and it is not easy to sort out what applies to the peaceful periods and what to the societies in general. Moreover, social history is likely to be more conjectural than political history, it is likely to be more complete on urban classes and elites than on rural classes, peasants and artisans. The life of peasants everywhere could not have been easy but it is difficult to translate what that life would have been like.

Probably the first several decades of peace were the best. Older people could remember times of strife and appreciate the change. Possibly they could transmit their memories to the next generation. Then, as economic prosperity increased and there was some distribution, at least there would have been less hunger.

Changes in art and artifacts in Egypt indicate that the Middle Kingdom artists were reasonably cheerful and outgoing, though New Kingdom artifacts indicated a great preoccupation with the hereafter. Which preoccupation brings greater rewards is not clear, nor is it certain that artists accurately reflect the spirit of a society.

We do know that the Athenian elite participated in the government of the society and this appears to have been a healthy, social and status-supporting activity. Free men living anywhere in the Roman Empire could receive citizenship and travelers from the outside perceived the society in a positive light. The concept of *ma'at*, at least in the Middle Kingdom, promised an equality of rights for even humble people and the rulers seemed to be strongly influenced by humanitarian principles. The Phoenicians, being a maritime society, were not oppressed by a landed nobility and obviously there must have been many opportunities for men with imagination. Also their religious toleration suggests a mild society. Tolerance was also characteristic of the Persians, despite the harshness of their justice, and the Bible indicates that life was much better for minority peoples ruled by the Persians than it had been under the Babylonians. Corinth, though arid in some respects, may have been a pleasant place to live in, even if the pleasantness was based on the work of slaves. The latter, of course, were ubiquitous in the Ancient World.

If you had a chance to live for a year in one of the peaceful societies, you would probably not choose to chance the New Kingdom or the Ptolemaic Empire. The change in atmosphere of the New Kingdom may have pervaded the society. There may have been a loss of confidence, a fading of optimism, that went to the roots of the society. The meddlesomeness and intrusiveness of Ptolemaic government looks totalitarian and this must have been made worse by the fact that the Ptolemies were an alien dynasty who favored alien Greeks over native Egyptians.

Life, in peaceful societies, does not appear to have been exceptional. In some it was pleasant, in some, unpleasant. Peace provided opportunities but the results are less clear than they were for the economies. The outcomes seem widely different and the measuring devices seem less precise.

The social structure of the Ancient World was fairly rigid. Those who were born into the elite generally remained so, those not, did not. The elites generally came from government officials, landed gentry, the military and the priests, what Carroll Quigley has called "the quartet." Merchants often became wealthy, and in maritime provinces could enter the elite; there was a small percentage of artisans who constituted a distinct in-between class along with stewards, perhaps. The majority of people were peasants and there was a larger number of slaves.[1]

Most of the peaceful societies operated within this master pattern but there were considerable variations. Though we know little about the Phoenicians, it seems likely merchants must have fared better there, or perhaps merchants were also landowners. Several of the societies made much of citizenship and in Athenian and Roman societies this extended to those of little property or wealth. Slaves were common in all of the societies, although they may have been more numerous in those areas which had the opportunity to acquire large numbers of foreign slaves through military conquest.

It is difficult to delineate the social structure without touching on the social environment. The peaceful societies, again with the possible exception of the Middle Kingdom, existed in a cosmopolitan world. There was a great mixing of ethnic backgrounds, races and even civilizations. If there were a social barrier beyond class, it was likely to be between cosmopolitan and provincial, between the person who had been to Heliopolis, Susa, Alexandria or Rome and the provincial landowner who knew only seasons, seed, grain or grapes. This cosmopolitanism was as common in the politically divided Hellenic world as it was in the empires. The major exception, perhaps, was the failure in the Ptolemaic Empire of Greek and Egyptian to merge, and this failure certainly contributed to the dissolution of peace after Raphia.

The peaceful societies were, on the whole, hospitable to social mobility. At the elite end of the scale, they provided many roads to power and wealth. The robes of Roman imperial office could be achieved by any man with power, ambition, loyalty, luck and certain kinds of charm. The empires had countless governorships and satrapies to fill. In Athens and the Roman Republic, the top position rotated so rapidly that many ambitious politicians had a chance to fill them. When Corinth had a ruling council of 80 members, the opportunity for citizens to get to the top must have been much greater than it would be for citizens of most modern countries to achieve membership in even the national legislature. Among the Phoenicians, wealth may have been valued more than power and there were considerable opportunities to achieve it that would not have been enhanced by seizure of political power. In the Middle Kingdom the provincial leaders retained an unusual amount of power and in the Thutmosid New Kingdom there were at least three major changes in monarch-elite relationships (Hatshepsut, Akhenaten and Haremhab), and each change would have allowed the fortunate and astute a chance for advancement.

There were also opportunities at lower levels. Slaves could become freedmen in most of the ancient societies. In the New Kingdom, the life of the average free peasant laborer was little different from that of the slave laborer, but the possibility for individual elevation did exist. In the trade-oriented societies, there were always possibilities of making (and losing) fortunes rapidly. Land reform programs under Solon and Peisistratus made more land available to poor farmers, as it must always have been available in the empires to the farmers who were willing to become pioneers and move to new frontiers. Problems that arose in the Roman Republic and Ptolemaic Egypt because of a reduction in available land indicates that the opportunity to develop land was an important route to social as well as economic well-being.

The mention of trade already suggests that there was a considerable degree of horizontal mobility in the Ancient World. One could travel to trade, or one could travel for a new footing, leaving dissatisfactions behind, taking hope along. There were other places to go and means to get there. Even for punishment the city states used banishment, forcing dissidents to travel for the good of themselves and the state, and at the same time often leaving land and property to be distributed to others.

In the sense that the same classes prevailed in most societies, and most people in any class remained what their parents had been, the social structure of the peaceful societies of the Ancient World was relatively rigid. In the sense that there was always scope for the most restless or ambitious to move horizontally or vertically, the social structure of these societies was quite flexible.

18

Religion and Civilization

Culture is difficult to deal with: It has to do with shared ways of seeing life that give a people a collective character and make them unique and they contain subcultures having characteristics that make them different from the culture and similarities that identify them with the culture.

The largest cultural delineation that is generally made is that of a civilization. In Toynbee's conception, a civilization is the largest area you need to study in order to comprehend a particular history. In order to understand the Romans, you need to understand the Greeks, but it is much less important to understand the Egyptians. From this frame of reference, there are three civilizations involved among the ten cases: the Classical, the Egyptian and the Mesopotamian. The Phoenician and Persian societies were Mesopotamian, the Egyptian societies were periods of Egyptian civilization and the Greek and Roman societies were Classical. The Ptolemaic case is one in which a Classical dynasty rules an Egyptian society.[1]

The interaction of civilizations generally does not seem to prevent peace. In the case of the Ptolemaic society, it is true, Egyptian and Greek did not mix, and that caused problems shortly after the first century of peace was completed. The New Kingdom interacted with other civilizations, sometimes peacefully, sometimes in battle, but the level of conflict does not seem greater than that experienced by its Ptolemaic successor in a predominantly Classical world. The Phoenicians traded peacefully with other civilizations and had most to fear from the Assyrians, a major power in their own civilization. The Greek

158

and Roman peaceful societies, on the other hand, were embedded in their own civilizations, despite contacts with others, and the Roman and Persian Empires provided unified wholes for single civilizations, however tolerant and cosmopolitan they may have been.

Toynbee has contended that civilizations go through periods of particularly vigorous conflict that he calls "times of troubles." These usually last some centuries. They are preceded by periods of growth and followed by peaceful empires, which ultimately disintegrate in a period of conflict, revolution and invasion.[2]

Using Toynbee's classifications, eight of the ten societies achieved peace during periods of general civilizational peace. The Athenian and Corinthian societies achieved their peaceful periods during growth periods of Hellenic civilization and the Phoenician during the growth period of the Syriac (roughly, a Mesopotamian offshoot). The Middle and New kingdoms formed the universal states (*i.e.,* empires) for the Egyptiac civilization; the Achaemenid for the Syriac; and the Roman, including Hispanic Rome, for the Hellenic.

Only the Ptolemaic and the Roman Republican, the two shortest and perhaps most troubled of the ten periods of peace, existed during a time of troubles — in this case for the Hellenic civilization. The termination of two other periods of peace that had begun in times of growth — the Phoenician and the Corinthian — came during subsequent times of troubles. And the long Hispanic period came to an end about three decades after the Roman universal state had entered its final dissolution.

It certainly would seem as though there is a strong relationship between civilizational phase and peace. Long periods of peace were easier to achieve and likely to be maintained longer during peaceful phases of civilizational development. Peaceful periods were likely to be shorter and more difficult to maintain during conflict stages.

Most civilizationists agree that higher religion plays an important part in the formation of a civilization, and that the civilization is likely to carry the imprint of that religion thereafter.[3]

Mesopotamian civilization linked the Phoenician and the

Achaemenid societies. One was small and one was large, one was mercantile and one was agrarian-imperial. But both were polytheistic, pragmatic and tolerant, more inclined to incorporate new religious ideas and deities than to reject, ban or attack them. This is one reason for believing that Iranians and Phoenicians shared a Mesopotamian outlook.[4]

Classical civilization was also tolerant. But where Mesopotamians were inclined to incorporate the alien, the Greeks and Romans were likely to be indifferent. Their souls were not strongly stirred by religious differences, so they were not threatened if others, entering their cosmopolitan world, happened to be serious about individual religious pursuits.

Religion was a unifying factor in a Greek world of independent, competitive city-states. When a mother city established a colony, religious ties between the two were carefully maintained, while political bonds were not. Cautious people ascertained the will of the gods before plunging ahead into the dangerous unknown. And yet, religion could be turned to serve political or personal purposes. The story of Athena sanctioning Peisistratus seems more like a homey politician providing floats and entertainment than a serious use of religious sanction for government. The extreme anthropomorphism and ribald mythological tales might make one question the religious devotion of the Greeks. However, the time and expense spent in building lovely temples for putting on festivals and in carrying on the day-to-day ritual between gods and men shows religion to have been more than just incidental to Greek development.

Religion also proved to be a source of unity for the Roman Republic. The Romans gradually accepted anthropomorphism and Greek ideas, but they continued to be concerned with scrupulously maintaining the proper relationship with their gods. The Ptolemies, being alien rulers, had a special problem. Their solution was what you would expect of Greeks: when in Egypt, do as the Egyptians do. The state gods do not seem to have been taken seriously by the urban imperial Romans and emperor worship does not seem distinct from the widespread homage given most monarchs. However, cults offering individual participation and immortality attracted many followers and the local and family gods maintained their strength long into the

Christian period. In Hispanic Rome the peace continued into the Christian era and here, as elsewhere in the empire, the new Near Eastern faith provided a threat to peace.

The polytheistic Mesopotamian societies, Phoenicia and Achaemenid Persia, seem to have been more serious about religion than the Greeks and Romans. The Phoenicians, being traders and businessmen, maintained a cosmopolitan tolerance. The Persians, though nominally Zoroastrians, were also pragmatic, and permitted all sorts of religious practices, so long as they did not interfere with domestic rule. They were infuenced, perhaps, both by Mesopotamian tolerance of polytheism and by their imperial system, which like that of the Roman emperors was essentially pragmatic. Centuries later, their Sassanid successors were more ardent Zoroastrians but were less successful at maintaining internal peace.

Religion seems to have been more important to the Egyptians than it was to either the Greco-Romans or the Mesopotamians. The stress on the divine nature of the pharaohs was stronger and more ubiquitous. This had the advantage of providing support from the priestly elite but the disadvantage in the New Kingdom of allowing that elite to threaten the dominance of the government. The intricate process of mummification, at first reserved for the royal family but eventually extended to all wealthy enough to pay for it, bears witness to the strong Egyptian concern for the afterlife.

On the other hand, the pharaohs were willing to compromise. The Twelfth Dynasty was able to combine Amun and Re to widen its basis of support. When the intellectual Akhenaten attempted to revolutionize the state religion, relying primarily on the power of ideas, conflict inevitably arose. It required the pragmatic Haremhab to restore peace.

It would appear, then, that religion is strongly interwoven with the pattern of civilization. Generally governments had to consider these religious patterns and to work within them.

Where the religious patterns were weak, they could be ignored, unless the area to be controlled was large and heterogeneous. In that case government would be tolerant if there were diversity, or would acquire the trappings of religion where the general impulse was weak.

Where the religious patterns were strong, government would adopt them, advocate them: where they were weak and varied, government would tolerate diversity or reconcile the major differences through mergers.

Where religious patterns were strong and varied, it was difficult to preserve peace. Tolerance of divergent views would lead to conflict; merger was impossible; adoption of one view by government would lead to conflict between government and the proponents of minority views. Hence Akhenaten's solution was unworkable—and the intrusion of Christianity into Classical civilization was not resolvable without conflict.

19

Creativity and Outlook

How creative were the ancient peaceful societies? Does peace challenge the imagination, or does it dull the creative urge by failing to provide any challenge? Can we gauge from their art and literature what kind of societies they were? Do art and literature reflect the atmosphere of the societies? Do they tell us about the outlook of the societies, their world views, their values?

These questions are more difficult to answer than political or economic questions, more difficult even than social questions. We have to deal with fragmented art, we have to look at it with Western eyes, and often we cannot look at it directly. We have to make do with pictures, or descriptions or summaries.

When we have none of these problems, when we can see art directly in our own society, we still have difficulty interpreting. Is the United Nations Secretariat Building a triumph of beauty and simplicity, a prime object around which a whole art develops, or is it an ecological disaster reflecting Western man's alienation from his own society? If we are not certain about that, what can we make of pictures of weathered ancient ruins?

Let us see what we can do. To begin with, there does seem to have been a quantity of art produced. If these peaceful societies were not the most creative centers in the Ancient World, neither were they dreary backwaters.

Several of the peace periods coincide with periods of active and lively production. Both Egyptian periods created a quantity of interesting art. The Middle Kingdom art was naturalistic, delicate and vital, more in scale than the massive, stylized art and architecture of the Old Kingdom. In the New

Kingdom, it is true, an almost manneristic revolution in art was accompanied by social conflict, but there followed a period of fresh creativity in the early Ramessid period. The Achaemenids did not produce a spectacular period of original art, considering the size of the empire, but they did build a number of striking buildings and decorated them with impressive reliefs. The Pax Romana corresponded closely with the greatest period of imperial aesthetic development. Though the Romans were more likely to express themselves in literature: epics, history, poetry, drama, satire, their architecture, sculpture and painting are impressive. Among the more successful Roman artifacts were likely to be the rugged and realistic busts of statesmen, but even more impressive were some of the products of Roman engineering, a form of unconscious art. Spain participated actively in the Roman Silver Age of literature and produced fine mosaics as well.

Some of the other societies were not known for their aesthetic achievements and yet they were productive during their peaceful periods. The Phoenicians and Corinthians are often protrayed as Philistines, markedly inferior to the Athenians in their arts and crafts. Yet the Phoenicians did produce some fine craft work, even if much of their work was inclined to be mass produced and overdecorated. Development of the syllabary that led to the Greek alphabet was, of course, a significant achievement. The Corinthians in peace produced outstanding pottery, even if they were later outstripped by the Athenians.

As for the Athenians themselves, they seem to be the one society in which art and drama were developing toward the end of the peace period, and later, during periods of conflict, reached higher levels.

Several of the peaceful societies seem to have been centers of art. They attracted artists, writers and philosophers from other parts of the Ancient World. This was the case of Corinth under Periander, who was attempting to build a cultural center of Athens under Solon and Peisistratus, of the Roman Republic and especially of the Ptolemaic capital at Alexandria, which became the cultural capital of the Hellenistic world. These areas were not only peaceful and prosperous but attracted artists because of the opportunities offered in building and supporting arts and, in the case of Alexandria, science.

It is difficult to classify the kinds of creative activity that took place. Most polities, in early phases, engage in a considerable amount of building. The building in turn provides opportunities for architects, sculptors and probably painters. This was the case with most of the large and medium-sized polities. In the small ones there does not seem to be as much evidence of building activity except in Corinth, where the activity came later and was the result of the tastes and policies of a particular leader.

Where trade occurs, crafts are encouraged. The Ancient World was a trading world, so most of the societies encouraged craftsmen. The Ancient World abounds in relics of fine imagination and workmanship. The peaceful societies certainly produced their share.

Literature and philosophy are not found everywhere. They seem to be particularly the style of the Greek, Hellenistic and Roman worlds. The writing of the earlier societies seems to be pragmatic, although there is great literature from the Egyptian periods. Then there are special achievements that seem to be the mark of a particular society, such as the Phoenician syllabary and the scientific discoveries of the polynational scientists who convened at Alexandria.

This portrayal of creativity in the Ancient World would not be in balance if we were to ignore the considerable quantity of dull, boorish architecture and sculpture and the impressive quantity of potboiler crafts that were also produced. The Ramessid New Kingdom and Achaemenid Persia inclined toward giganticism, allowing size to substitute for quality, falling victims to rigidity and repetition of patterns, usually accompanied by a decline of craftsmanship and a loss of environmental sense. The Phoenicians and Corinthians were inclined to respond to market demand, sacrificing craftsmanship and adding elaboration. Such slipped production was not uncommon in the Hellenistic and Roman worlds as well. The quantity produced may have been much greater than we realize, since such baubles were not as likely to be preserved as were the treasures that have survived.

Despite this quantity of dubious art, the peaceful societies of the Ancient World were hospitable to creativity. But they were set in a generally creative environment, and frequently the creative artists came to them from other areas. The term "Silver Age," used of the post-Augustan literature of Pax Romana, perhaps could be applied to the art of peaceful societies in general. It is often good, rarely overwhelming. Usually the artists follow established patterns, patterns that may have developed during periods of previous conflict.

It is probably the case that most of the outstanding art in the peaceful societies comes in the earlier decades. Building is likely to be proceeding most vigorously in those decades. But besides that, artists themselves may have more to say. Vytautas Kavolis argues that one of the most creative periods for artists seems to be the period after a crisis, when there is a strong urge for reinterpretation of a resolved situation. This is certainly true of the Augustan Age which inaugurated the Pax Romana and followed a long period of turmoil. [1]

Exceptions are even supportive of the argument. There is renewed creativity in the Ramessid New Kingdom, but only after a major and disturbing interruption gives cause for new interpretation. The Silver Age itself is followed by a creative phase in philosophy, but this philosophy is given to developing outlooks for a society that is losing its attractiveness. So the Emperor Marcus Aurelius suggests that it doesn't matter to a vessel whether it is whole or in fragments (*Meditations* VIII, 23): ominous thoughts for any imperial philosopher, but more so when he also happens to be the keeper of the vessel.

If artistic vitality is apparent in the early decades of a peaceful society, the signs of reduced or inhibited creativity appear later. The New Kingdom art had grown stale and flat before the Amarna interlude and again in the Ramessid phase toward the end of the peace period. The tendency for art to be massive, uninspired, and poorly executed also was evident in the later periods of the Achaemenid empire and in the later phases of the long Hispanic Peace.

In the crafts, there may be a great flow of art, much of it mass-produced, a small portion of high quality. Moreover, high quality art may inspire cheap imitation. On the other hand, in architecture and sculpture, the waning of the creative impulse is likely to lead to deterioration without compensation, and what is badly imitated is good art of the past, readily available as a model, whereas craftsmen are likely to see only good art of the present.

Aesthetic measures, of course, are not the only guides to creativity. The development of effective government, the management of trade, the formation of laws and the development of defense strategies also involve the creative imagination. But in so far as we can appraise the aesthetic qualities of these societies, what do they tell us about the outlook of the people who lived in them?

We have noted from previous evidence that there was a good deal of pragmatism within these societies and concomitantly a considerable tolerance on the part of the governments and elites. There is little evidence, however, that the atmosphere provided much happiness or freedom. In Egyptian civilization there was increasing rigidity, decreasing freedom, a decline in optimism through the Middle and New Kingdom. If art continued to be vital for much of the time, the subject matter became more melancholy.

The Phoenicians bear some resemblance to the Romans of the Republic. Both seem to have been practical, down-to-earth, focused, and serious. The Greeks of the early city-states may have been more buoyant but they also shared burdens of state that must have created considerable anxiety. The Persians, while tolerant, were harsh in their penalties and elites, at least, must always have been subject to the possibility of treachery, or reversal of fortune, should a *satrap* fail or the brother of a prince bid for power. The Ptolemaic society must always have had its tensions between Greek and Egyptian, not to mention the meddlesomeness of its "big brother" government. Probably the Roman Empire, tolerant as with the Persians but milder and more even-handed in administration of the law, gave the largest percentage of the population the best and freest chance to shape their own lives and deaths. Jesus was a beneficiary of the Roman Peace, a victim of provincial autonomy.

World views varied greatly. We could say that eight of the ten societies placed great emphasis on life in this world. Or we could say that this was the dominant view of people in the Classical eras, the particular view of west Asian societies achieving peace, but not of the New Kingdom Egyptians, whose art focuses more and more on the life to come. When we look at the Egyptian leaders, however, we find pragmatism everywhere:

Amenemhet I compromising with the *nomarchs*, Hatshepsut with the priests (who were also practical and worldly), Haremhab with everyone. On the other hand, Akhenaten, the visionary who attempted to reform his kingdom by lifting it to a higher level, commands our attention and respect but not as a peacemaker.

Values follow from world views and they do not seem to have been of the highest and most lofty sort. Leaders compromised their principles, they were often treacherous in seeking power; merchants were selfish in seeking their own best interests in trade; regional governors were often dishonest and self-seeking; treachery was not uncommon in the annals of Egypt, Greece, Persia and Rome. Saints did not fare well in Egypt or Rome; they do not appear in Phoenicia, Persia or Greece.

If values do not seem to have been lofty in peaceful societies, there were some at any rate that seem to have been middle-range positive to those of us, as Toynbee would say, who are living in the latter half of the 20th century.

Tolerance is the most recurrent and ubiquitous of these positive values. It seems to have been a general characteristic of Classical society and also, of necessity, of imperial governments. It is inferential also in the religious mergers of the Egyptian kingdoms and even the Ptolemies' willingness to tolerate separate systems for native and minority aggregations. It was most notable of all in the Phoenicians, who were not choosy about either religion or nationality; who, in modern rhetoric would have been classified as appeasers, but very successful ones.

Another positive value seems to have been a commitment to justice. This is reflected in the law systems discussed in Chapter 15, Polities. Each of the ancient peaceful societies had a system that provided at least stratified equality: perhaps one system for the elites and another for peasants, or different systems for each ethnic group. The systems may have been harsh or mild and no doubt they were abused to some extent, since bribery appears to have had a status in agrarian societies not much different from tipping in industrial socities. But standards existed and justice was far from arbitrary. Where we can read the cases in Roman law, it appears to be rationally and consistently developed. Whatever the norm, the value of justice appears to have been widely understood and appreciated.

The Classical societies differed from their Egyptian and Mesopotamian predecessors in their emphasis on the value of humans. Greek and Romans religion placed a greater emphasis on man in relationship with the gods. Classical literature testifies to the abilities of people acting within their environment. History was developed to record the achievements of humans in the past so that those in the present and future would better understand their position and could better evaluate the options open to them. Philosophy sought to explain humans and their world through reasoning and contemplation. The values of a humanistic experience are the legacy passed on to the Western world by these societies.

Finally, there seems to have been some appreciation of peace. The idea of Pax Romana was apprehended by visitors and contemporaries as well as by subsequent historians. For the Greeks and Romans, peace became a deity and whether called Eirene or Pax, she symbolized an ideal that was important to her society. The Phoenicians showed themselves willing to make compromises of honor for the sake of peace. The consolidators described in Chapter 14, Leaders, clearly had peace as a central goal, though appreciation may have diminished as the decades went on and memories of a contrasting past faded. The Egyptians, even by the time of the Middle Kingdom, seem to have accepted internal peace under a central pharaoh as normal and that pattern seems to have encouraged the continual recurrence of long periods of peace in the land of the Nile. This perception of a common bond among peoples seems to have been held by the Phoenicians and for a much briefer period among the feisty Greeks. The fourth century Greeks talked of a *koine eirene*, general peace, at a time when warfare was destroying the city-states. They unfortunately could never settle on a method for compromising individual independence for common unity and peace. It is easy to explain why Athens fought Sparta but historians have not given corresponding attention to why, for long periods, Athens did not fight Corinth nor Tyre, Sidon. On the lack of any other evidence, one reason might be that peace was simply taken for granted as a shared value.

20

Foreign Relations

The temper of the ancient peaceful societies tended to be more pragmatic than saintly. Their leaders were not, therefore, seeking to save the world, nor to make it safe for peace. Sometimes their interventions in other territories were purely expansionist, having nothing to do with securing territories necessary for defense or with retaliation against dangerous adversaries. Such was the case with much Roman expansion through the time of Trajan, with the New Kingdom until Akhenaten, and the Achaemenids through the time of Xerxes.

What might be said is that the external policies of the governments of the peaceful societies tended to be prudent. Often their objectives were appropriate to strengthening defense. When they were not, at least they restricted their activities and did not greatly tax the resources of the society. And each time a government miscalculated the effort that would be involved in a conquest, it did not hesitate to liquidate its commitment.

The cases of specific external military missions designed to protect the domestic social order are numerous. The campaigns of Senwosret III in the Middle Kingdom appear to have had the effect of protecting the southern marches as well as trade routes. Ptolemy Soter set out deliberately to control the sea north of the Nile and to do that he needed to conquer and control Cyprus. The Republican Romans of the second century B.C. fought mostly defensive wars, struggling to establish stability in the Greek world and attempting to subdue native tribes in Spain. The Romans of the early Empire were kept busy trying to secure control of areas already won and to establish defensible borders. While there was some unnecessary expansion, as into Britain, the empire was not a dramatically expanding political entity. Nor were any of the peaceful societies, except New Kingdom Egypt.

Limited commitment is less easy to show. There may be some truistic reasoning involved here, since a measure of commitment might be inability to control affairs at home. Since all our societies had domestic peace, their external commitments have been limited by their capacities.

Still, the Roman Republican leaders, on more than one occasion, declined to annex territories that would seem to have fallen to them after military victory, which suggests that such commitments may have involved further conflict. And the Romans of Hadrian's time built walls, which may, as Toynbee suggests, be an early sign of a declining society. But building walls also indicates a long term decision to hold a line, not to expand beyond it, whatever the circumstances may be, whatever political vacuum may emerge in the territory beyond. Both the Romans and Achaemenids had immense power compared to territories around them, but in proportion to their size, neither launched any kind of substantial campaign in any direction. The Middle Kingdom, the Phoenicians and the Greek states seem to have been little interested in annexation, though both Corinth and Phoenicia were involved in colonization.[1]

The liquidation of commitments through prudent withdrawal was demonstrated several times among the peaceful societies. Akhenaten withdrew from Syria during a period of domestic reform; Darius liquidated quagmirish involvements in Scythia and Greece; Augustus withdrew to the Rhine when he found the Elbe too difficult to maintain, and a century later Hadrian withdrew from Armenia, Arabia and Mesopotamia, lands added by Trajan, for the same reasons.

In discussing both Settings (Chapter 13) and Civilizations (Chapter 18), we have indicated that most of the peaceful societies were in favorable situations. The times were generally settled and relatively peaceful. Only the Roman Republic and the Ptolemaic Empire existed in a conflict milieu and they had to give a good deal of attention to foreign affairs. The New Kingdom was also located in an interpower situation, with four other major states. This situation, however, seems to have involved a much lower range of intensity and activity. There was more diplomacy and interchange than battles and when battles were fought, they usually occurred within the territories between the great powers. Kadesh may have been a great battle, but unlike Raphia, it never threatened the survival of either the Hittite or the Egyptian dynasties.

The Greek states and the Phoenicians were in the midst of interpower situations that could have been highly volatile. In these periods the Phoenicians and Greeks do not seem to have worried about attacking or being attacked by one another. We may hypothesize about this in terms of arms or interests, but all the same it is striking that we have no information about their interrelations. They do not seem to have thought much about it. This is often the way with peace. Future historians, for instance, will have an easy time finding data on the more than a century of recurrent war between France and Britain in the 18th and 19th centuries, the so-called Second Hundred Years' War. But they will have a much harder time finding information about the more than a century of peace between the two nations which followed, a period that has acquired no historians' title and which has received very little attention.

The great empires, along with the Middle Kingdom, experienced no substantial external threat and no great attraction for external adventure. Their policies were to attack in areas where they were subject to raids and to domesticate and incorporate these areas if they could — e.g., the Egyptian campaigns in Nubia or the Roman in Spain. But where such campaigns proved difficult, they usually withdrew and established defensive lines. One exception was the Roman Republican campaign in Spain. The Romans caught a tar baby here and seemed unable to let go. The result was that the conflict became ever more vicious without a quick resolution.

The Phoenicians, in addition to having an internal set of relations, were also collectively on the fringe of a larger system. This fringe position and their lack of significant offensive threat left them in a favorable situation vis-à-vis the increasingly violent Assyrians. They were both distant and unthreatening. For a long time they concerned Assyria only as a source of tribute revenue.

Foreign policies were related to situations. There are ten situations to consider, but these do not coincide exactly with our ten cases, since the Roman governors of Spain did not have to worry about foreign policy (unless it was against Rome) while the Phoenicians can be considered in regard to both their collective external relations and their relations with each other.

The Phoenicians, in their external relations, were the only case of a distinctly inferior power. Their general policy seems to have been to make themselves useful to the greater powers, to avoid alliances with others against the great powers, and to make themselves unattractive to attack. By acting as trading middlemen, they benefited the Assyrians, enabling them to increase their wealth. Because of their isolated situation, their walled cities, their strong navy and their lack of dependence on agriculture, they were extremely difficult to attack. By avoiding alliances, they avoided provoking the Assyrians, who could launch a successful attack if they wanted to take the trouble to do so.

Five powers were roughly at military parity with their neighbors: New Kingdom Egypt, the Phoenicians with each other, the Athenians, the Corinthians and the Ptolemies. There is little evidence about the foreign policies of the Phoenicians, Athenians and Corinthians, as we have just observed, beyond active colonization by Phoenicia and Corinth and the relations between various Greek tyrants. New Kingdom Egypt engaged in expansive policies in western Asia and accepted tribute from inferior nations, but never challenged any of the other great powers of the period except in border areas. They engaged in some diplomacy with the Mittani regarding the Hittites but the alliance which developed was never tested and seems to have been of dubious value. The Ptolemaic Empire was also involved in a number of minor conflicts in the Hellenistic world, including one intervention in a Seleucid succession struggle. But, before Raphia, none of these risked any change in the balance of power, except as to which state would control more or less of Syria.

The Achaemenid and Roman empires were obviously great powers compared to their contemporaries—in fact they were the only great powers of their time. The same could be said, oddly enough, about relatively isolated Middle Kingdom Egypt. The Roman Republic, in the second century, was the greatest power in the Mediterranean world, though its beginnings were less imposing than those of other powers.

For the empires and Middle Kingdom Egypt, foreign policy was literally a peripheral problem compared with the maintenance of internal order. The Romans of the Republic were the most active of any of the peaceful societies in external political and military interventions. They sent their citizen soldiers to Spain, Gaul, Macedonia and as far away as the Seleucid Empire to prevent the emergence of any challenging power or to suppress rebellion or imperialism. While New Kingdom Egypt and the Ptolemaic empire were involved in situations they could not control, the Romans in the late Republic acted as a police force for the Ancient World.

There were no important military transformations during any of the periods of peace. Generally the societies used the system of the times. These included both peasant and citizen militias as well as professional or mercenary armies. All of the societies had navies but of course the Ancient World surrounded a great sea.

Often the military was better constituted to defend than attack. The heavily armed forces of the empires could easily stand off the more lightly armed but mobile forces of such areas as Dacia or Scythia. But they were not well constituted to pursue and conquer. The same is true of the Greek *hoplites*. The Phoenician and Greek navies could defend their cities but could not, themselves, easily launch attacks on other lands. This factor could have reinforced the peace among the city-states. The New Kingdom Egyptian army, however, was a highly successful fighting unit revolutionized by the employment of chariotry and Nubian mercenaries that successfully transformed the state into an aggressive military power.

So situations varied; states may have been small, equal, dominant or isolated in relation to others. But the governments of all the peaceful societies seem to have been involved in stable, prudent relations carried on by conservative, predictable techniques. Few risks were taken and conflicts were carried on with limited involvement at a safe distance from home.

21

The Termination of Peace

In the chapter on Leaders (14), we considered that we had 13 situations out of which long periods of peace were created, the New Kingdom, Pax Romana and Hispanic periods each having two phases. It follows that there would be 13 cases of termination, since the same three periods would have had two periods in which peace would have appeared to have come to an end. We designated the later phases of the New Kingdom, Pax Romana and Hispanic periods as the Ramessid Restoration, the Flavian-Antonine Restoration and the Hispanic Revival. The earlier phases of the periods are called the Thutmosid, the Julio-Claudian and the Early Hispanic.

We found three basic ways for a period of peace to begin: by conquest, by the defeat or retreat of the conqueror, and by the conclusion to a succession struggle. For the termination, there seem to be basically two: internal rebellion, whether it be because of a succession struggle or attack by a domestic faction; and external attack, whether it be repelled or not. In the Ancient World the end of peace more often came through external attack.

Precipitating Event Leading to Termination of Peace[1]

Internal	*External*
Middle Kingdom	Ramessid
Thutmosid	Phoenician
Roman Republican	Athenian
Julio-Claudian	Corinthian
	Achaemenid
	Ptolemaic
	Flavian-Antonine
	Early Hispanic
	Hispanic Revival

175

If those cases in which external attack precipitated or was followed by internal rebellion are considered, the balance of cases goes a different way.

Internal Rebellion Ends Peace	External Attack Ends Peace
Middle Kingdom	Phoenician
Thutmosid	Corinthian
Ramessid	Achaemenid
Athenian	Early Hispanic
Ptolemaic	Hispanic Revival
Roman Republican	
Julio-Claudian	
Flavian-Antonine	

When an external attack takes place, one would normally expect internal unity. It would appear, however, that those in which internal rebellion followed were approaching a stage at which the supports for peace had become too fragile.

In those situations, however, in which external attack ends or interrupts domestic peace, one would look for a change in the external situation that had nurtured the peace. And for some this appears to be the case. The Phoenicians were victims of a change in expansiveness and severity of conflict in their own world. The Achaemenids sustained an overwhelming attack coming out of growing conflict in a neighboring situation. The Early Hispanic phase ended in bad luck—or perhaps just a return to normal luck. The Hispanic Revival and the Corinthian periods terminated in external invasions that had their origins within their own larger societies. The Ptolemies and Romans of the Republic had lived in a hostile world to begin with and one of a series of continual dangers finally resulted in the loss of internal peace.

The internal/external classification disguises the variety of precipitating incidents that led to the end of peace in each case. Despite the preponderance of internal problems, however, most of the initial episodes that have been documented have external qualities. Consider the four cases we called purely internal. We do not actually known the details of the Middle Kingdom and Thutmosid breakdowns. The Roman Republic suffered a civil war in which the factions were clearly formed by regions seeking a more important role, so there was a definite quality of state and territorial warfare. The challenge to the Julio-Claudian peace had no such territorial definition but the sources of the sequence of challenges came from outside Italy, mostly from Spain and Germany.

Among the others, the Athenian case involved both defending and challenging factions, each calling for support from external allies, thus converting a civil war into an interstate succession conflict. The Phoenicians, Corinthians, Achaemenids and Ptolemies each were challenged by organized external attacks by other civilized nations. The two Hispanic and the Ramessid peace periods ended with external raids by outlanders, while the Flavian-Antonine phase of the Pax Romana ended in attacks by civilized neighbors and nomadic incursions.

Usually the termination of peace could not be attributed to weak leadership. Commodus, it is true, was unusually bad and Darius III appears weak and disorganized. But Darius had to face Alexander the Great, who overcame all adversaries he encountered, while the collapse of peace Commodus ignored had begun under the leadership of Marcus Aurelius, generally perceived to have been the last of a series of competent emperors.

The crises that emerged during these periods were frequently met by determined and energetic leaders. Akhenaten's measures proved unsuccessful, but he was not wanting in energy and imagination. Merenptah and Ramesses III did what anyone could to stem attacks on New Kingdom Egypt. Ptolemy IV Philopator showed energy and organizational capacity and the unsuccessful Roman *tribune* M. Livius Drusus showed considerable insight.

Senwosret III in the Middle Kingdom may have erred in attempting to control too much personally, so that succeeding rulers were left to face rebellious elites. Hippias of Athens may have lost some of his capacity through personal misfortune and Persia may have had a better chance against Alexander if Ochus had not been assassinated, but in all these cases events seemed to be moving beyond the shortcomings of particular leaders.

A hundred years is a long time in political history. The political balance that brings about peace changes over time until one element or another appears to gain too much power and causes others to react strongly. It was the increased power of the *nomarchs* in the Middle Kingdom that led to such a conflict, while in the New Kingdom it was the threat of or to the priesthood of Amun. The military played a peace-disrupting role in both phases of the *Pax Romana,* the Julio-Claudian disruption complicated by the efforts of the Roman Senate. In Athens it was the exacerbation of a tyranny that was losing its control; in Persia, harem intrigue and the growing power of eunuch ministers around the king.

In the Roman Republic and Ptolemaic Egypt there were changes in sociopolitical balance of a different kind. In each case there was a privileged ethnic group relating to an ethnic majority. In the case of the Italian peninsula an earlier openness to the extension of the privileges of citizenship or other rights gradually closed, creating social dissatisfaction. In the case of Egypt it was a matter of closed privilege creating dissatisfaction over a period of time as the native majority recovered from the devastations of war and new generations arose that had not been humiliated and defeated. When precipitating factors arose that brought about war, there was sufficient fuel of dissatisfaction to prolong it beyond its original cause.

A political phenomenon noted above in the chapter on polities needs only brief repetition here. The peaceful societies tended to be politically decentralized. A tendency to centralization in the Roman Republic, Athens, the Thutmosid New Kingdom and the Hispanic Revival was followed by an end to peace. The Ptolemaic Empire was an exception in that it was always centralized but then its period of peace was among the shorter and more precarious. Corinth was the one exception in gravitating from tyranny to oligarchy.

Among the societies that suffered a termination of peace through external invasion, the Achaemenid has already been discussed as having suffered a change in the balance of its elites. The Corinthians also experienced a change from tyranny to oligarchy. This change does not seem to have been significant in terms of internal support, though it could have contributed to less rapid and less imaginative responses to external challenges. The Hispanic Revival period ended in a deluge of external invasions. Since the empire could not cope with these any-where else, it is difficult to consider them a local problem. But in one sense they may have been. Imperial forces had the capacity to withstand assaults by outlanders. That they failed everywhere was a problem of organization and will. The fifth century Roman governors could hardly have perceived their positions in the same sense as those of the first and second centuries had. The latter-day positions were sinecures and their primary purpose was peculation. Peculation occurred in the earlier period but more as compensation for astute management, which brought the possibility of promotion and was sustained by pride of position in imperial management.

It is not easy to perceive a radical change in social situations at the end of peaceful periods. Changes in perceptions of relationships seem to have been more important. One factor in the change of perception could have been peace itself. In the early decades of peace, older people can remember and compare favorably the present with the past. By the end of a century of peace, no one can remember what conflict in home territory was like. If there is a militia or a professional army, it has never had to defend its homeland. Social inequalities, which once may have had a reason, now become cause for resentment.

With the exception of the ending of the Thutmosid period, there seems to have been no change in religious situations. Clearly, conflict between two strong religious groups can be cause for war, but absence of religious conflict is only one of many factors supporting peace.

We have observed a recurrent flagging of creativity in later decades of peace. There does not seem to have been much resurgence of art preceding periods of resumed conflict. Whether the decline of creative impulse reflects a general decline of creative ability in the societies is difficult to assess. It may be that it was an indication of satiation. If peace had not become quite a bore still it was no longer central to perceptive sensibilities.[2]

In the cases in which external attacks were the principal cause for the ending of peace, it does not seem that there is much evidence of change in foreign policy. Neither the raids on Spain nor Alexander's attack on Persia were brought on by changes in foreign policy. The Phoenicians had dabbled a bit in alliances against the Assyrians but the tide of Assyrian expansion was moving in their direction anyway.

In the earlier Hispanic period, the raids seem fortuitous. They were coped with successfully; the balance of administration seems to have remained intact. Of the internal nature of Phoenician relations we know very little. On the evidence we have, the Phoenicians seem to have been overwhelmed by external forces that were devastating in power and unaffected by negotiation or logic.

Two political categories that seemed to be factors during the peace periods appear to have remained constant in the periods of termination. The governments of peaceful societies were generally not oppressive and generally they provided an acceptable system of justice. While these factors continued to be operative as the periods of peace were ending, perceptions were changing. The Romans of the Republic continued to provide the same standards of justice while perceptions of injustice in land distribution and citizenship were expanding. The Ptolemies continued to provide separate systems of justice for Egyptian and Greek when Egyptians were no longer satisfied with separation.

We have already observed, in Chapter 16 on Economies, that although economic prosperity tended to follow the establishment of peace, economic decline preceded the termination of peace periods. In the Ancient World, political factors seem to have been more important than economic in success or failure in maintaining peace. Political policies, of course, had economic consequences: increase in taxation to support a faltering or fattening government caused dissatisfaction when the present was compared to the past; failure to protect domestic farmers and craftsmen would be injurious to trade; failure to protect trade routes would be injurious to production.

Corinthian policies toward Corcyra may have brought on the Peloponnesian Wars more quickly. But the Corinthians were responding defensively to Athenian expansion, and their more involved foreign policy had been in effect for more than three decades.

In the cases in which there were external factors as well, there is a mixed picture. The external attacks on Ramessid Egypt and those at the end of the Flavian-Antonine Imperial period were both partly attributable to a decline in the defensive energies of the empires. In the case of Athens, there was a decision by both rebels and government to bring in outside support, a decision that clearly places victory over peace as a priority. In the Ptolemaic case, Raphia was an episode of the times. There had been other attacks during the peace which had not gotten so far. It was Raphia that revealed internal weakness in the Ptolemaic structure and not the weakness that brought on the attack.

Generally, then, there had been no precipitous change in policy. Rather, changes in balances led to the termination of peace. Either external powers had grown greater, beyond the control of the government of the peaceful society, or an internal situation had deteriorated so that defensive policies were no longer effective. Only in the Athenian case is it possible to second guess policy choices within the society.

In all cases, however, governments were on the defensive. In none were they actively engaged in expansion. In the Amarna phase of the Thutmosid New Kingdom, the government failed to send adequate military support to tribute states and allowed external control to lapse. So if avoidance of "overreaching" was a factor in ancient peace, the opposition policy does not seem to have been a factor in any of the terminations.

We have noticed, in the foreign relations chapter 20, that there were no important changes in military techniques during the peaceful periods. Such changes play a part in two of the terminations. The Corinthians failed to defend their homeland from invasion because they lost a naval battle in which their older board-and-grapple techniques were defeated by newer ramming techniques. The Persians lost out where their arrow volley techniques fell before the cavalry-phalanx combinations of Alexander.

From those two cases we might conclude that a peaceful society can become complacent from previous success. Why alter techniques that have brought more than a century of peace? The Ptolemies at Raphia, however, did match a new technique — elephants — with elephants of their own. Though they won the battle, their elephants lost, indication that late adoption of a new technique may be riskier than staying with the techniques previously successful.

Considering the terminations together, it would appear that a system that once satisfied perceived needs is likely to grow inadequate over a period of time. It must change as perceptions change, and as the system changes, its subsystems must change appropriately. That such changes rarely occur peacefully for a period as long as a century is indicated by the difficulty in finding cases. In a sense, the ways in which the many causes of conflict were avoided for a long period of time are more important than isolating the cause or combination of causes that finally terminated the peace. Analogously, when we applaud the cricket batsman who has made a century, we are less concerned that he was finally caught at long leg than we are about his careful placements, his wise grasp of opportunities, his sage avoidance of action where action would have been dangerous.

22

Recapitulation

Centuries of peace do seem to have occurred in the Ancient World. Great political areas, larger than most contemporary states, were able to maintain peace as were very small states that would seem not to have the population to defend against any sustained attack.

Physical conflict, however, was normal, in that in most areas there is at least one major conflict a century. In another sense peace was normal, in that it prevailed in most places at most times. If one were to hurtle randomly into the Mediterranean world between the A.D. 500's and the 2500's B.C., one would probably land in a society that was at peace.

Most areas were subject to recurrent war, but one — Egypt — seems to have had recurring periods of peace for nearly three millennia.

Environments in which peace existed were variable. Some of the peaceful societies were isolated, some involved with neighboring powers. Most were autonomous but they had varying weights in the political systems in which they existed. Most existed in generally favorable environments, not undergoing periods of political crisis or turmoil. Most were protected by at least some supportive physical barriers. Climate does not seem to have been a distinguishing factor, except perhaps indirectly through its environmental effect on molding a society.

The most important political leaders in the Ancient World seem to have been not the founders of societies but the consolidators who established the resulting political structures. These consolidators seem to have a character resemblance: pragmatism, tolerance, persistence. That reconsolidation takes place less frequently suggests that the odds are against any particular leader's putting together the combinations that will maintain peace for a long time. Overall, the most important quality such leaders had seems to have been the ability to understand the particular situation they confronted. Another important common factor is that the objective of peace seems to have been very much a part of their planning. Once peace is established, quality of leadership seems to be less important.

In an age generally dominated by monarchy, the peaceful societies seem to have had a surprising variety of governmental forms. Besides monarchies there were to be found monarchal federations, republics, tyrannies, empires, oligarchies and a provincial governorship. Contrary to expectation, there was a great deal of instability to be found in systems of succession.

It does appear, however, that there was a recurring tendency toward political decentralization among the peaceful societies, sometimes geographically, sometimes in division of power among political interest groups.

While law codes were developed in a few cases, the more important factor in the peaceful societies seems to be the establishment of a system that gave a reasonable expectation of justice, at least within classes. The governments administering this law were, if not popular, at least tolerant and relatively mild for the standards of the day.

Peace encourages economic prosperity. Most of the ancient peaceful societies were exceptionally prosperous, the prosperity becoming apparent some decades after peace had commenced. This prosperity, however, often showed signs of waning before peace itself came to an end. Government intervention in the economy had positive effects where it widened economic distribution.

The peaceful societies were generally active in trade, but this was true of many of their neighbors who were not peaceful. Most of them developed some areas of specialization which provided them with a surplus for trade.

We do not know much about the kind of life people lived in ancient peaceful societies. To some extent it must have had the limitations that peasant society has anywhere. But there are some indications that several of them encouraged a wider range of citizen participation, that governments were generally mild and tolerant. There was a great deal of ethnic intermixture, travel was frequently undertaken, and there was considerable social mobility at all levels from slave to nobleman.

Though classifications differ, the peaceful societies could be said to exist in three different civilizations. Interaction of the civilizations did not prevent peace, but it does appear that there was a better chance for peace if the civilization in which the society was situated was in a normal, untroubled phase. Where a civilization was in a conflict stage, long periods of peace were unlikely. Peace periods, if they reached a century, did not last much longer during conflict phases of civilization.

Religious tolerance was characteristic of most of the peaceful societies. Governments were likely to be tolerant where religious patterns were weak and a diversity of religions existed. In Egypt, where the patterns were strong, government absorbed them and promoted them. Nevertheless, Egypt was as open to foreign deities and their cults as to the foreigners who worshiped them and wished to settle in the country.

Peaceful societies seem to have been creative. They produced a considerable quantity of architecture, sculpture, painting, crafts, music, literature, philosophy, science and law. If they did not represent the strongest periods in their respective histories, at least their output was respectable. They were, moreover, often centers attracting creative talents from other areas.

On the other hand, they produced a great quantity of second rate crafts, and more than once endured periods of boorish architecture and sculpture. The second rate crafts often overwhelmed a smaller stream of fine work. The stilted and gigantic sculpture and architecture often followed earlier, more creative periods. On the whole it can be said that peaceful societies, particularly in their earlier decades, have been productively creative. Certainly peaceful societies cannot be characterized as dull.

While it is risky to extract attitudes and outlooks from art, literature and scattered writings, there is evidence to indicate that within the peaceful societies there was generally tolerance, a willingness to accept a variety of views and styles, an inclination toward pragmatic rather than visionary outlooks, a willingness to compromise, often selfishness, and sometimes treachery. There seems to have been a general commitment to justice and a widespread appreciation of the blessings of peace.

In foreign policy the governments of peaceful societies tended to be prudent. Often, when their policies were expansive, they were related to securing areas important for defense. If that was not the case, at least they did not commit themselves beyond their capacities, and were willing to withdraw where they had underestimated resistance. Several of the peaceful socities had no neighbors of comparable power to worry them. When there were such neighbors, relations were usually cautious on both sides, and encounters limited. Where a common ethnic bond was perceived, there were often no military encounters at all.

There were likely no major military transformations during any of the periods of peace. Thus, generally the governments of the societies had reasonable intelligence about the military capacities of their neighbors. Usually the military organizations of the societies were better constituted to defend than to attack.

Both in policy and technique, then, there was a tendency for general stability, cautious expansion, limited commitment and general predictability.

Peace came to an end because of internal rebellion or external invasion or some combination of the two. In more than half the cases, primarily external invasion was involved, and in more than half the cases, internal rebellion was an additional factor. Where external attack was involved, often the external situation had changed from that which existed when peace began. The initial precipitating episode was generally external.

The termination of peace could not be attributable solely to weak leadership. The various crises that accompanied termination were often met by determined, energetic and capable measures.

The basic cause of termination was likely to be a gradual alteration of balances, either among internal elites, between governors and subjects, or between the societies and the powers surrounding them. One frequent internal change was a tendency toward the centralization of power.

Political factors seem to have been more important than economic in periods of termination. Economic decline toward the end of peace periods was generally a sign of changing political or social balances.

There was usually little change in government approaches to justice or in religious tolerance in periods of termination. But there may have been a decline in appreciation of peace, and clearly there was generally a decline in creativity.

There were no marked changes in foreign policy before peace came to an end in any of the cases. Rather the changes were in the situations with which governments had to deal. In two cases there were external changes in military techniques which governments of peaceful societies tried to meet with techniques that had been successful previously. It does appear that the governments of peaceful societies tended to become committed to policies and techniques that had been successful for a long period of time and they failed in part because new situations called for changes in such policies and techniques.

On the other hand, shifts in balances occur over decades, not centuries. Though ultimately they failed, governments of the peaceful societies had shown a capacity to maintain flexibility and make adjustments for long periods of time. An examination of the terminations only illuminates the complex arrangement of situation and policy by which governments of ancient peaceful societies managed to maintain peace for as long as they did.

Societies remained peaceful for a long time because leadership assessed situations correctly, and established structures appropriate to those situations. Such a generalization can be meaningful only if one reviews the variety of specific responses which, in varying situations, led to the creation of long periods of peace.

Notes to Part I

1. The Criteria for Peace

1. Among the many books on war and/or the military in the Ancient World are:

Frank E. Adcock, *The Greek and Macedonian Art of War,* Berkeley, 1957.

_____, *The Roman Art of War under the Republic,* rev. ed., New York, 1963.

M. Amit, *Athens and the Sea: A Study in Athenian Sea Power,* Brussels, 1975.

John Anderson, *Military Theory and Practice in the Age of Xenophon,* Berkeley, 1970.

E. Badian, *Roman Imperialism in the Late Republic,* Ithaca, 1968.

Bazalel Bar-Kochva, *The Seleucid Army: Organization and Tactics in the Great Campaigns,* New York, 1976.

Andrew R. Burn, *Persia and the Greeks: The Defense of the West, 546-478 B.C.,* New York, 1962.

F. W. Clark, *The Influence of Sea Power in the History of the Roman Republic,* Menasha, Wis., 1915.

Theodore A. Dodge, *Ceasar: A History of the Art of War Among the Romans Down to the End of the Roman Empire,* New York, 1892.

_____, *Hannibal: A History of the Art of War Among the Carthaginians and Romans Down to the Battle of Pydna, 168 B.C.,* New York, 1891.

Richard Duphy, *The Encyclopedia of Military History: From 3500 B.C. to the Present,* New York, 1977.

John F.C. Fuller, *The Generalship of Alexander the Great,* New York, 1968.

Yvon Garlan, *War in the Ancient World: A Social History,* New York, 1975 (tr. from French, 1972).

Michael Grant, *The Army of the Caesars,* New York, 1974.

P. Greenhalgh, *Early Greek Warfare: Horsemen and Chariots in the Homeric and Archaic Ages,* Cambridge, 1973.

G. T. Griffith, *The Mercenaries of the Hellenistic World,* Cambridge, 1935.

William V. Harris, *War and Imperialism in Republican Rome, 327-70 B.C.,* New York, 1979.

Bernard W. Henderson, *The Great War Between Athens and Sparta,* London, 1927.

Charles Hignett, *Xerxes' Invasion of Greece,* Oxford, 1963.

Edward N. Luttwak, *The Grand Strategy of the Roman Empire From the First Century A.D. to the Third,* Baltimore, 1976.

Ramsay MacMullen, *Soldier and Civilian in the Later Roman Empire,* Cambridge, Mass., 1963.

Eric William Marsden, *Greek and Roman Artillery,* Oxford, 1969.

E. Ewart Oakeshott, *The Archaeology of Weapons: Arms and Armour from Pre-History to the Age of Chivalry,* New York, 1960.

Herbert Williams Parke, *Greek Mercenary Soldiers,* Oxford, 1933.

H. M. D. Parker, *The Roman Legions,* 2d ed., New York, 1958.

William Pritchett, *The Greek State at War,* Berkeley, 1974.

William L. Rogers, *Greek and Roman Naval Warfare,* Annapolis, 1937.

Anthony M. Snodgrass, *Arms and Armour of the Greeks,* Ithaca, 1967.

Sir William Woodthrope Tarn, *Hellenistic Military and Naval Developments,* Cambridge, 1930.

Arnold J. Toynbee, *Hannibal's Legacy: The Hannibalic War's Effect on Roman Life,* London, 1965.

Flavius Vegetius Renatus, *The Military Institutions of the Romans,* tr. by J. Clark, Harrisburg, 1944.

George Ronald Watson, *The Roman Soldier,* Ithaca, 1969.

Graham Webster, *The Roman Imperial Army,* New York, 1974.

2. On the lethargy of imperial peace, see—in the Selected Bibliography—Toynbee (1939-54, V-VII); Quigley (1961, p. 87-88 *passim*); and Wesson (1967).

3. For one of the earliest and most extensive appeals for studying peace as we study war, see Richard Coudenhove-Kalergi, *From War to Peace* (1959). Coudenhove-Kalergi is right about the rarity of the plural of the word peace. It does occur, however, in Shakespeare, when Leontes, subjected to a collective upbraiding from his advisors, orders them to "Hold your peaces" *(Winter's Tale,* II:i).

4. The development of these criteria is described by Melko (1972, 1973b, 1975).

5. Morgenthau's book was published in 1948, with many subsequent editions; Kissinger, 1957 (both New york). David Fabbro (1978, p. 67) is one scholar who suggests additional qualitative criteria besides the negative absence of physical conflict. In his own preliminary study of primitive societies he includes absence of standing military police and absence of interpersonal violence. He would also like to include, in future studies, absence of structural violence and a capacity for peaceful change.

6. Centers of Peace Research include the Conference on Peace Research, the Consortium for Peace Research, Education and Development, the Canadian Peace Research Institute, the International Peace Research Institute at Oslo, and many others.

7. Wight's observation appears in Melko (1973a, p. 81).

8. Leitenberg (1975). Fabbro also rejects this criterion in his study of primitive societies (1978, p. 67).

2. The Definition of Periods of Peace

1. Cases considered but not included were Old Kingdom Egypt (2494-2181 B.C.); Kassite Babylonia c. 16th-13th centuries B.C.; Saite Egypt (664-525 B.C.); Sparta c. 7th-5th centuries B.C.; and the Sassanian Empire A.D. 300's to 500's. Kassite Babylonia and the Sassanian Empire have been rejected on further investigation. The two Egyptian cases and Sparta were considered possible or even likely, but insufficiently verified.

2. The observation on the absence of major periods of Judaic history from the records of neighboring peoples is made by Mark Zborowski and Elizabeth Herzog in *Life Is with People*, New York, 1952, p. 29.

Notes to Part II

3. The Middle Kingdom Peace

1. For the assassination of Amenemhet I, see the *Instruction of Amenemhet I* as translated in Miriam Lichtheim, *Ancient Egyptian Literature*, vol. 1 *The Old and Middle Kingdoms*, Berkeley, 1973, pp. 135ff.; William Kelley Simpson, ed., *The Literature of Ancient Egypt: An Anthology of Stories, Instructions, and Poetry*, New Haven, 1972, pp. 193ff.; Adolf Erman, ed. (tr. by Aylward M. Blackman), *The Ancient Egyptians: A Sourcebook of Their Writings*, New York, 1966, pp. xxvii, 72ff.

2. John A. Wilson, *The Intellectual Adventure of Ancient Man: An Essay on Speculative Thought in the Ancient Near East*, Chicago, 1946, p. 84. For translation of P. Sallier, Ricardo A. Caminos, *Late Egyptian Miscellanies*, *Brown Egyptological Studies I*, London, 1954, p. 323f.

3. For translation of *The Eloquent Peasant* see Miriam Lichtheim, p. 169ff.; Simpson, p. 31 ff.; Erman, pp. xxx-xxxi, 116ff.; Gustave Lefèbvre, *Romans et contes égyptiens de l'époque pharaonique*, Paris, 1949, pp. 41ff. For translation of *Merikare* see Lichtheim, pp. 97ff.; Simpson, pp. 180ff.; Erman, pp. xxviii, 75ff.

4. For translation of *Ipuwer* see Lichtheim, pp. 149ff.; Simpson, pp. 210ff.; Erman, pp. xxix-xxx, 92ff. For translation of *Sinuhe* see Lichtheim, pp. 222ff.; Simpson, pp. 57ff; Lefèbvre, p. 1ff.; Erman pp. xxiii, 14ff. For translation of *Trades* see Lichtheim, pp. 184ff.; Erman, pp. xxvii, 67ff. For translation of *The Shipwrecked Sailor* see Lichtheim, pp. 211ff.; Simpson, pp. 50ff.; Erman, pp. xxiii-xxiv, 29ff.; Lefèbvre, pp. 29ff.

5. For medical treatises see James Henry Breasted. *The Edwin Smith Surgical Papyrus, Oriental Institute Publications*, vols. II−IV, Chicago, 1930; Georg Ebers, *Papyros Ebers: Das hermetische Buch über die Arzeneimittel der alten Ägypter in hieratischer Schrift*, 2 vols., Leipzig, 1875; George Andrew Reisner, *The Hearst Medical Papyrus, University of California: Egyptian Archaeology I*, Leipzig, 1905; and Walter Wreszinski, *Der grosse medizinische Papyrus des Berliner Museums*, Leipzig, 1909. On mathematics, A. B. Chace, H. P. Manning, and L. Bull, *The Rhind Mathematical Papyrus; British Museum 10057 and 10058*, 2 vols., Oberlin, 1927, 1929.

6. Kurt Sethe, *Die Ächtung feindlicher Fürsten, Volker and Dinge auf altägyptischen Tongefässcherben des mittleren Reiches, Abhandlungen Berlin,* 1926, No. 5, Berlin, 1926. Also, Georges Posener, *Princes et pays d'Asie et de Nubie: Textes hiératiques sur les figurines d'envoûtement du Moyen Empire,* Brussels, 1940.

7. William Foxwell Albright, "An Indirect Synchronism between Egypt and Mesopotamia ca. 1730 B.C.," *Bulletin of the American Schools of Oriental Research* vol. 99 (1945), pp. 11ff. See also Bertha Porter and Rosalind L.B. Moss, *Topographical Bibliography of Ancient Egyptian Hieroglyphic Texts, Reliefs and Paintings,* vol. VII (Oxford, 1951), p. 389.

8. The inscription from the reign of Neferhotpe III comes from Stela Cairo 20799 (J. 59635), unpublished. See Raymond Weill, "Sekhemre-Souaztaoui Sebkhotepa Elkab: Un Nouveau roi, Sekhemre-Sankhaui Neferhotep, à Elkab et à Karnak," *Revue d'Égyptologie* 4 (1940), 218ff. On the problem of determining the dating of the termination of the Middle Kingdom Peace, see the following discussions of Egyptian chronology for the period: Hans Stock, *Studien zur Geschichte und Archäologie der 13. Bis 17. Dynastie Ägyptens...,* *Ägyptologische Forschungen* 12, Glückstadt, 1942, p. 63; Herbert E. Winlock, *The Rise and Fall of the Middle Kingdom in Thebes,* New York, 1947, p. 96; Torgny Säve-Söderbergh, "The Hyksos Rule in Egypt," *Journal of Egyptian Archaeology* 37 (1951), 62.

9. Although sources for the period are very scanty, it appears that the Old Kingdom also may have produced a long period of peace, from about 2494 to 2181 B.C. The peaceful pattern that would characterize several later Egyptian periods was therefore probably established during the Old Kingdom.

4. The New Kingdom Peace

1. The date of the commencement of the New Kingdom Peace is based upon a consideration of the troublesome chronology of the Eighteenth Dynasty. The most recent reconsideration of New Kingdom chronology is that of Edward F. Wente and Charles C. Van Siclen III, "A Chronology of the New Kingdom," *Studies in Honor of George R. Hughes, Studies in Ancient Oriental Civilization,* no. 39 (Chicago: Oriental Institute, 1976), pp. 217ff. The chronology suggested by Wente and Van Siclen starts out similarly to that of the *Cambridge Ancient History* but diverges considerably with far earlier dates soon thereafter. Significant changes in the dating of the reigns of Amenhotpe II and Thutmose IV set back Amarna dating by some thirty years, thus affecting seriously the chronology of the Nineteenth and Twentieth dynasties. For convenience, the readily available CAH dating is followed here. Although the commencement of the New Kingdom is customarily dated to the beginning of the reign of Ahmose I (1570), the New Kingdom Peace probably should be dated some years following. Allowing for the final expulsion of the Hyksos and restoration of nation-wide peace, the New Kingdom Peace may be dated to ca. 1560. See too John Van Seters, *The Hyksos: A New Investigation* (New Haven, 1966, p. 160.

2. On Amenhotpe III see Alan H. Gardiner, *Egypt of the Pharaohs,* Oxford, 1961, p. 208.

3. Cyril Aldred, *Akhenaten Pharaoh of Egypt: A New Study, New As-*

pects of Archaeology, ed. by Sir Mortimer Wheeler, New York, 1968.

4. For fragment of Sety I's Kadesh stela see M. Pézard, in *Syria* III (1922), pp. 108ff., and G. Loukianoff in *Ancient Egypt,* 1924, pp. 101ff. On the Hittite-Egyptian treaty see Samuel Langdon and Alan H. Gardiner, "The Treaty of Alliance between Hattusili, King of the Hittites, and the Pharaoh Ramesses II of Egypt," *Journal of Egyptian Archaeology* 6 (1920), pp. 179ff., and M. B. Rowton, "The Background of the Treaty between Ramesses II of Egypt and Hattusillis III," *Journal of Cuneiform Studies* 13 (1959) pp. 1ff. Translations of both treaties are readily available in James B. Pritchard, ed., *Ancient Near Eastern Texts Relating to the Old Testament,* 3rd ed., Princeton, 1969, pp. 199-203.

5. While this peace is conservatively terminated at 1231, with the defense of Egypt against the Sea Peoples, there is no substantial evidence that peace was not in fact maintained for another century, perhaps until the Suppression of Amenhotpe.

6. For *P. Harris I* see translation in James Henry Breasted, *Ancient Records of Egypt: Historical Documents,* vol. IV, Chicago, 1906, Sections 151-412. See also Herbert D. Schädel, *Die Listen des grossen Papyrus Harris* (Leipziger Ägyptologische Studien 6), Glückstadt, 1936. On possible hostilities before the Twentieth Dynasty, see *P. Salt 124* in Jaroslav Cerny, "Papyrus Salt 124" (Brit. Mus. 10055); *Journal of Egyptian Archaeology* 15 (1929), pp. 243ff.

7. On the Suppression of Amenhotpe see Hermann Kees, *Die Hohenpriester des Amun von Karnak von Herihor bis zum Ende der Äthiopenzeit,* Leiden, 1964, pp. 2-6. Note that Kees dates these events between the 12th and 15th years of Ramesses XI. Contemporary opinion is well summed up in Wente, Edward F., "The Suppression of the High Priest Amenhotpe," *Journal of Near Eastern Studies* 25 (1966), pp. 73ff. Amenhotpe is last attested in the Office of High Priest of Amun in years 16 and 17 of Ramesses IX in the tomb robbery papyri where he occurs as a member of the high court. Thereafter is a long gap in documentation concerning the High Priest of Amun. In year 3 of Ramesses X, the High Priest is referred to but not mentioned by name. In year 19 of Ramesses XI the High Priest is again mentioned in tomb robbery papyri, although also not by name. In this case, however, it is certain that the incumbent High Priest was no longer Amenhotpe, his tenure clearly a thing of the past. *P. British Museum 10053* verso suggests that the suppression may have taken place somewhat before year 9 of Ramesses XI. See Wente, *op. cit.,* pp. 85ff.

8. On the Second Intermediate Period neurosis, see John A. Wilson in Henri Frankfort et al., *The Intellectual Adventure of Ancient Man,* Chicago, 1946, p. 111. Wilson describes the Egyptian mental state during the New Kingdom and later as characterized by a "psychosis for security, a neuropathic awareness of danger similar to that which has characterized Europe in modern times." It may be preferable, however, to distinguish between the Egyptian psyche during the early New Kingdom (the better part of the Eighteenth Dynasty) and later years since a gradual change may certainly be detected. The early New Kingdom could be said to be characterized by a neurotic preoccupation with security while the later New Kingdom could be said to be characterized by a deepening neurosis bordering upon psychotic preoccupation with safeguarding the frontiers.

9. Even the great Saite Revival of the Twenty-Sixth Dynasty failed to turn

the tide; the best the Saite leaders could produce apparently was just such a revival of past glories as often occurs in an historical period which has nothing innovative or unique of its own to offer.

10. Nina M. Davies, *Ancient Egyptian Paintings,* vol. 2, Chicago, 1936, plates 91ff.; Arpag Mekhitarian, *Egyptian Painting,* Geneva, 1954, pp. 140, 142-3.

11. For translations of the expansive literature of the New Kingdom, see Lichtheim, *op. cit.,* vol. 2, *The New Kingdom,* 1976; Erman, *op. cit.,* and Simpson, *op. cit.*

12. It should be mentioned that the Saite Period (664-525) is a good candidate for yet another Egyptian Peace Period. Only the relative lack of documentation about a coup d'état that brought Amasis (570-526) to the throne has prevented its inclusion in the present study. If the peace was interrupted by that process, the total length of the Saite Peace would have been about 94 years. If it were not considered to be interrupted, it would have lasted nearly 150 years.

5. The Phoenician Peace

1. The dating of the peace at 1150 is conservative. As in the case of the New Kingdom Peace, it presumes the possibility of armed conflict during an interim period, without evidence that such conflict took place. The peace could well have begun as early as 1190 B.C.

2. The Phoenicians, sharing the tendencies of most peoples of the day (the Jews being a significant exception) were polytheistic. Their pantheon worship bore many similarities to others in the area, though in antiquity they seem to have been universally condemned for certain excesses, the most notorious being the practice of infant sacrifices — a practice archaelogical finds appear to confirm at least among their Western descendants.

3. The image of the Phoenicians as Philistines may be unjust. Little material has survived. There are some indications that they may have produced architecture of significance, e.g. the Temple of Melqart at Tyre, and they appear to have given considerable assistance to the building of Solomon's temple and palace at Jerusalem as well as to other major edifices in Israel. Their architectural style is believed to have contributed to the Greek Ionic capitol. Pomponius Mela commented on the excellence of Phoenician writing, literature and other arts, but samples have not yet been discovered (Moscati, 42; Harden, 14; Landay, 153-162).

4. After Sennacherib, Tyre was beseiged several times, by Assurbanipal in 668, Nebuchadnezzer in 574, and in the fourth century by Alexander and then by Antigonas (for 13 months).

6. The Athenian Peace

1. The peace, if it existed, would have been dated from about 631-464 B.C. The image of the Spartans as a warlike people who preserved their homeland from conflict is reinforced by a well-known exchange in Plutarch (*Agesilaus,* XXXI) in which an Argive says to a Spartan: "Many of you lie buried in the lands of Argos." The Spartan retorts: "But not a man of you in the

lands of Laconia." Plutarch, in the same chapter, states that Laconia at an earlier period had been free from invasion for six centuries.

2. On the relation between religion and polities, see Nilsson, 240-242, 253-262.

3. On the relation between technology of warfare and social structures, see Andrewes, 31-38.

4. There was one other possible interruption to the Athenian Peace besides Pallene. Plutarch (*Solon* 8-9) records a possible earlier break in the peace of Attica around 600 when Athens was fighting Megara over possession of Salamis. He describes one account of a battle at Cape Colias, but then goes on to give an alternative version, to which he lends greater credence, which would not have threatened Attica's peace.

8. The Achaemenid Peace

1. In the Egyptian chapters, Egyptian names were used, with Greek alternatives listed in the notes. In this chapter, Greek names have been used. The italicized Persian alternatives follow the Greek: Cyrus *Kurush,* Cambyses *Kambujiya,* Darius *Darayavaush,* Xerxes *Khshayarsha,* and Artaxerxes *Artakhshathra.*

2. Darius fought 19 battles in less than two years, probably the most violent of all introductions to a peace period. Huart, an earlier authority, saw the 19 battles as taking seven years, which, if correct, would move the beginning of the peace period up to 515.

3. Interpretations differ on the temperament and attitudes of Achaemenid authorities. What has been described here as brutally imaginative tortures and executions can be interpreted as a swift and necessary response to corruption and treachery. What has been described as harsh government may be perceived as vigorous restoration of order. What has been described as expediency may also be described as decisiveness.

4. The story of Megabyzus and the lion is related in Olmstead, 344. Ctesias was at the Persian court several decades after the episode is supposed to have occurred.

5. On the King's Eyes, see Bausani, 22, and Frye, 97. There seems to be some disagreement among translators about whether the inspectors were perceived as eyes, ears or both.

6. Herodotus describes the postal system in terms familiar to the modern postal service consumer: "Nothing mortal travels so fast as these Persian messengers ... and these men will not be hindered from accomplishing at their best speed the distance which they have to go, either by snow, or rain, or heat, or by the darkness of night" (Herod. 8.98, Rawlinson translation).

7. On the economic policies of Darius, see Olmstead, 185-194.

8. On Achaemenid Zoroastrianism, see Olmstead, 94-106, 197-199, 232-234, and 471-479.

9. The Ptolemaic Peace

1. Ptolemy Soter thrice conquered the area of Syria, Phoenicia and Pales-

tine in 318, 312, and 301. In 276 Ptolemy Philadelphus captured Damascus from a preoccupied Antiochus, who later regained it and drove the Ptolemaic forces back toward Egypt. In 246 Ptolemy III Euergetes initiated his reign with a march into Syria as far as the Tigris, but Ptolemaic forces were driven out two years later.

Fighting also occurred extensively in the Aegean and Ionia during the reigns of Ptolemy II and III. Cyrene attempted to rebel more than once since its 323 annexation by Ptolemy, following the outbreak of a civil war there.

2. On Ptolemaic "state nationalism" see Tarn, 207-208.

3. Wheat exports to the Mediterranean by way of Rhodes brought in an appreciable revenue. A more efficient organization and the advantages of Greek technology which improved the irrigation system, placing more land under cultivation, allowed for incrased yield. Greek presence resulted in the introduction of a new strain of wheat, sheep raising and much greater emphasis in olive growing, and use of iron farming implements.

4. For Rostovtzeff's analysis of Raphia's consequences, see *Cambridge Ancient History*, 1928, VII:151.

10. *The Roman Republican Peace*

1. On the social decline of the second century, see Heitland, II, 219-225.

Notes to Part III

14. *Leaders*

1. Solon and Peisistratus also could be considered reformers. Solon fits the personality type, but Peisistratus certainly does not.

16. *Economies*

1. See Braudel (1972, pp. 355-374).

17. *Societies*

1. Quigley introduces the concept of the recurrent quartet in his introduction to the paperback edition of *The World Since 1939*, pp. xiv ff.

18. *Religion and Civilization*

1. Toynbee's characterization of civilizations as institutions that "comprehend without being comprehended" is to be found in his *Study of History* I:455 n.1. Please note that the term "Mesopotamian" is used in this chapter in Toynbee's sense, not in the more restricted meaning of the Tigris-Euphrates Valley.

2. The cycle of civilizations from growth through the disintegration of empires is described in Toynbee, III-IV.

3. A brief summary of civilizationists' views of the relation between religion and civilization is to be found in Melko (1969) 27-29.

4. Mesopotamian Civilization. There is general agreement among civilizationists that there has been a distinct civilization or group of civilizations originating in ancient Sumeria and continuing through the Sassanian Empire, if not until the present day. There is considerable disagreement, however, about the number of civilizations occupying this area. We used the term Mesopotamian to cover the entire period. Toynbee's Syriac, which he saw as a separate civilization, would have been a subsystem of this Mesopotamian Civilization. If we compare the work of another civilizationist, Carroll Quigley (1961, pp. 152-156), we find the Phoenicians part of a Canaanite Civilization, and the Achaemenid Empire part of a Mesopotamian Civilization (but a more restricted Mesopotamian than we have used here). Still, the Phoenicians occupy a growth phase in Quigley's conception, while the Achaemenid Society forms an imperial phase.

5. It could be argued, since Zoroastrianism called for religious tolerance, that the Achaemenids were closer to the ideal than were the Sassanids.

19. Creativity and Outlook

1. For Kavolis's theory of post-crisis creativity see *History on Art's Side,* Chapter 9.

20. Foreign Relations

1. For Toynbee on the significance of walls, see *A Study of History* VIII:2.

21. The Termination of Peace

1. Precipitating event: the term is borrowed from the Kerner Report (1967).

2. Art before conflict: it was noted in Chapter 19 above that the theory of Vytautas Kavolis (1972) regarding the relation between social conflict and art was well supported by the cases of peace in the Ancient World. Periods of high creativity did follow the cessation of conflict. But Kavolis's view that artistic creativity also surges before conflict takes place is not as well supported by the cases. Certainly creativity accompanied conflict in the Amarna period, and may well have preceded, even caused it. The Julio-Claudian period reflects a burst of literary activity in the reign of Nero. But in most of the cases, there is no special burst of aesthetic creativity preceding conflict. It would appear, in the Ancient World, that artists responded more frequently to the resolution of conflict than to its imminence.

Selected Bibliography

General References

Braudel, Fernand. *The Mediterranean and the Mediterranean World in the Age of Philip II,* tr. by Sian Reynolds. New York, 1972-1973, 2 vols.

Coudenhove-Kalergi, Richard. *From War to Peace.* London, 1959.

Fabbro, David. "Peaceful Societies: An Introduction," *Journal of Peace Research* 15 (1978) 1.

Kavolis, Vytautas. *History on Art's Side.* Ithaca, 1972.

Leitenberg, Milton. "Obscene Definition," *Bulletin of the Atomic Scientists,* September 1975, p. 2.

Melko, Matthew. "Discovering Peace," "The Government of Peaceful Societies," "The Qualities of Peaceful Societies," "The Termination of Peace," and "The Termination of Peace as a Consequence of Institutionalization," *Peace Research,* December 1971, January 1972, March 1972, April 1973(b).

_____. *52 Peaceful Societies,* Oakville, Ont., 1973.

_____. *The Nature of Civilizations,* Boston, 1969.

_____. "Peace: A Subject Worth Studying," *The Bulletin of the Atomic Scientists,* April 1975.

Quigley, Carroll. *The Evolution of Civilizations.* New York, 1961.

_____. *The World Since 1939.* New York, 1966.

The Report of the National Advisory Commission on Civil Disorders, New York, 1967 (Kerner Report).

Toynbee, Arnold. *A Study of History.* London, 1934-1961.

_____. *A Study of History,* abridgement of vols. I-VI by D.C. Somervell. London, 1946.

Wesson, Robert. *The Imperial Order.* Berkeley, 1967.

Zborowski, Mark, and Elizabeth Herzog. *Life Is with People.* New York, 1952.

The Middle Kingdom Peace

Aldred, Cyril. *The Development of Ancient Egyptian Art, from 3200 to 1315 B.C.,* London, 1962.

Badawy, Alexander. *A History of Egyptian Architecture: The First Intermediate Period, the Middle Kingdom, and the Second Intermediate Period.* Berkeley, 1966.

Cambridge Ancient History, Vol. 1, part 2, Cambridge, 1971; vol. 2, part 1, 1973.

Clère, J. J. "Histoire des XIe et XIIe dynasties égyptiennes," *Journal of World History* 1 (1954) 643-668.

Drioton, Étienne, and Jacques Vandier. *L'Egypte,* 4th rev. ed. Paris, 1962.

Erman, Adolf, ed. *The Ancient Egyptians: A Sourcebook of Their Writings,* tr. by Aylward M. Blackman. New York, 1966.

Emery, Walter B. *Archaic Egypt.* Baltimore, 1963.

Gardiner, Alan. *Egypt of the Pharaohs.* Oxford, 1961.

Hallo, William, and William K. Simpson. *The Ancient Near East.* New York, 1971.

Hayes, William C. *The Scepter of Egypt,* Vol. I. New York, 1953.

Kees, Herman N. *Ancient Egypt.* Chicago, 1961.

Lefèbvre, Gustave. *Romans et contes égyptiens de l'époque pharaonique.* Paris, 1949.

Lichtheim, Miriam. *Ancient Egyptian Literature,* Vol. I, *The Old and Middle Kingdoms.* Berkeley, 1973.

Nims, Charles F. *Thebes of the Pharaohs.* New York, 1965.

Posener, Georges G. *Littérature et politique dans l'Égypte de la XIIe dynastie.* Paris, 1956.

Simpson, William K. *The Literature of Ancient Egypt.* New Haven, 1972.

Smith, William Stevenson. *The Art and Architecture of Ancient Egypt.* Harmondsworth, 1965.

Westendorf, Wolfgang. *Painting, Sculpture, and Architecture of Ancient Egypt.* New York, 1968.

Wilson, John A. *Burden of Egypt: An Interpretation of Ancient Egyptian Culture.* Chicago, 1951.

Winlock, Herbert E. *Models of Daily Life in Ancient Egypt,* Cambridge, Mass., 1955.

————. *The Rise and Fall of the Middle Kingdom in Thebes.* New York, 1947.

The New Kingdom Peace

In addition to the general works on Egypt listed above, see:

Aldred, Cyril. *Akhenaten, Pharaoh of Egypt: A New Study.* London, 1968.

Badawy, Alexander. *A History of Egyptian Architecture: The Empire.* Berkeley, 1968.

Cambridge Ancient History, vol. 2, part 2. Cambridge, 1975.

Davies, Nina M. *Ancient Egyptian Paintings.* Chicago, 1936, 3 vols.

Desroches-Noblecourt, Christiane. *Tutankhamen: Life and Death of a Pharaoh.* Boston, 1963.

Frankfort, Henri, et al. *The Intellectual Adventure of Ancient Man.* Chicago, 1946.

Hayes, William C. *The Scepter of Egypt,* vol. 2. New York, 1959.

Kitchen, Kenneth A. *The Egyptian Nineteenth Dynasty.* Warminster, 1980.
Mekhitarian, Arpag. *Egyptian Painting.* Geneva, 1954.
Otto, Eberhard. *Ägypten: Der Weg des Pharaonenreiches.* Stuttgart, 1953.
Pritchard, James B., ed. *Ancient Near Eastern Texts Relating to the Old Testament,* 3d ed. Princeton, 1969.
Redford, Donald B. *History and Chronology of the Eighteenth Dynasty of Egypt: Seven Studies.* Toronto, 1967.
_____. "On the Chronology of the Egyptian Eighteenth Dynasty," *Journal of Near Eastern Studies* 25 (1966) 112-124.
Steindorff, George, and Keith C. Seele. *When Egypt Ruled the East,* 2d ed. Chicago, 1957.
Van Seters, John. *The Hyksos: A New Investigation.* New Haven, 1966.
Wente, Edward F., and Charles C. Van Siclen III. "A Chronology of the New Kingdom," *Studies in Honor of George R. Hughes* (Studies in Ancient Oriental Civilizations no. 39), Chicago, 1976, pp. 217ff.

The Phoenician Peace

Cambridge Ancient History, vol. 2. Cambridge, 1971, 1977.
Fleming, Wallace B. *The History of Tyre.* New York, 1915.
Harden, Donald. *The Phoenicians.* New York, 1963.
Herm, Gerhard. *The Phoenicians.* New York, 1975.
Moscati, Sabatino. *The World of the Phoenicians.* New York, 1968.
Rawlinson, George. *History of Phoenicia.* London, 1889.

The Athenian Peace

Andrewes, Antony. *The Greek Tyrants.* London, 1956.
Berve, Helmut. *Die Tyrannis bei den Griechen.* Munich, 1967, 2 vols.
Burn, Andrew. *The Lyric Age of Greece.* New York, 1960.
Bury, J. B., and Russell Meiggs. *A History of Greece,* 3d ed. New York, 1967.
Cook, Robert M. *The Greeks until Alexander.* New York, 1962.
Ehrenburg, Victor. *From Solon to Socrates.* London, 1968.
Freeman, Kathleen. *The Work and Life of Solon.* New York, 1926.
_____. *Greek City-States.* New York, 1950.
Hignett, Charles. *History of the Athenian Constitution.* Oxford, 1952.
Lehmann-Haupt, C. F. *Solon of Athens.* Liverpool, 1912.
Linforth, Ivan M. *Solon the Athenian.* Berkeley, 1919.
Nilsson, Martin P. *A History of Greek Religion,* 2d ed. Oxford, 1952.
Wilcoxon, George D. *Athens Ascendant.* Ames, Iowa, 1979.
Woodhouse, William J. *Solon the Liberator.* Oxford, 1938.
Zimmern, Alfred. *Solon and Croesus.* London, 1928.

The Corinthian Peace

Andrewes, Antony. *The Greek Tyrants.* New York, 1956.

Freeman, Kathleen. *Greek City-States.* New York, 1950.
Graham, A. J. *Colony and Mother City in Ancient Greece.* Manchester, 1964.
Payne, Humfry. *Necrocorinthia: A Study of Corinthian Art in the Archaic Period.* Oxford, 1931.
_____. *Protokorinthische Vasenmalerei.* Berlin, 1933.
Sealey, Raphael. *A History of the Greek City-States ca. 700-338 B.C.* Berkeley, 1976.
Ure, P. N. *The Origin of Tyranny.* New York, 1962.
Will, Edouard. *Korinthiaka.* Paris, 1955.
Wiseman, James. *The Land of the Ancient Corinthians.* Göteberg, 1978.

The Achaemenid Peace

Bausani, Alessandro. *The Persians,* tr. by J. B. Donne. New York, 1971.
Cambridge Ancient History, vols. 4 to 6. Cambridge, 1926-1927.
Culican, William. *The Medes and the Persians.* New York, 1965.
Dandamayer, M. A. "Social Stratification in Babylonia (7th-4th Centuries B.C.)," in *Acta Antiqua 22,* Budapest, 1974, 433-444.
Frye, Richard N. *The Heritage of Persia.* Cleveland, 1963.
Ghirshman, R. *Persia from the Origins to Alexander the Great.* London, 1964.
Olmstead, Arthur T. *History of the Persian Empire.* Chicago, 1948.
Pope, Arthur U., ed. *A Survey of Persian Art from Prehistoric Times to the Present,* vols. I and IV. London, 1938.
Zaehner, Robert C. *The Dawn and Twilight of Zoroastrianism.* London, 1961.

The Ptolemaic Peace

Bell, Harold I. *Egypt from Alexander the Great to the Arab Conquest.* London, 1948.
Bevan, Edwyn R. *A History of Egypt under the Ptolemaic Dynasty.* London, 1927.
_____. *The House of Seleucus.* London, 1902, 2 vols.
Botsford, George W., and C. A. Robinson, Jr. *Hellenistic History.* London, 1956.
Bury, J. B., et al. *The Hellenistic Age.* London, 1970.
Cambridge Ancient History, vols. 6 and 7. Cambridge, 1927-1939.
Cary, Max. *A History of the Greek World from 323 to 146 B.C.* London, 1932.
Farrington, Benjamin. *Greek Science.* London, 1961.
Hadas, Moses. *Hellenistic Culture: Fusion and Diffusion.* New York, 1959.
Mahaffy, John P. *History of Egypt under the Ptolemaic Dynasty.* London, 1915.
Peters, Francis E. *The Harvest of Hellenism.* New York, 1970.
Rostovtzeff, Mikhail I. *The Social and Economic History of the Hellenistic World.* Oxford, 1941, 3 vols.
Tarn, Sir William Woodthrope. *Hellenistic Civilisation.* London, 1952.
Walbank, Frank William. *A Historical Commentary on Polybius.* Oxford, 1957.

Welles, Charles Bradford. *Royal Correspondence in the Hellenistic Period.* London, 1934.

The Roman Republican Peace

Badian, E. *Foreign Clientelae.* Oxford, 1958.
Beare, W. *The Roman Stage.* London, 1968.
Botsford, George W. *The Roman Assemblies.* New York, 1909.
Broughton, T. R. S. *The Magistrates of the Roman Republic.* New York, 1952-1960, 2 vols. and supplement.
Frank, Tenney. *An Economic Survey of Ancient Rome,* vol. 1. Baltimore, 1933.
_____. *Life and Literature in the Roman Republic.* Berkeley, 1930.
Gruen, Erich S. *Roman Politics and the Criminal Courts, 149-78 B.C.* Cambridge, Mass., 1968.
Heitland, William E. *The Roman Republic.* Cambridge, 1909, 3 vols.
Marsh, Frank B. *A History of the Roman World, 146-30 B.C.* London, 1953.
Münzer, F. *Römische Adelsparteien und Adelsfamilien.* Stuttgart, 1920.
Salmon, E. T. *Roman Colonization under the Republic.* Ithaca, 1970.
Scullard, Howard H. *A History of the Roman World, 753-146 B.C.* London, 1951.
_____. *Roman Politics, 220-150 B.C.* Oxford, 1951.
Suolahti, Jaakko. *The Roman Censors.* Helsinki, 1963.
Walbank, Frank W. *Philip V of Macedon.* Cambridge, 1940.
Wissowa, Georg. *Religion und Kultus der Römer.* Munich, 1902.

The Pax Romana

Abbott, Frank F. and Allan C. Johnson. *Municipal Administration in the Roman Empire.* Princeton, 1926.
Brilliant, Richard. *Roman Art.* London, 1974.
Clarke, Martin L. *The Roman Mind.* London, 1956.
Cambridge Ancient History, vols. 10 and 11. Cambridge, 1934, 1936.
Crook, John A. *Consilium Principis.* Cambridge, 1955.
De Laet, Siegfried J. *Aspects de la vie sociale et économique sous Auguste et Tibère.* Brussels, 1944.
Dessau, Hermann. *Geschichte der römischen Kaiserzeit.* Berlin, 1924-1930, 2 vols.
Dill, S. *Roman Society from Nero to Marcus Aurelius.* New York, 1957.
Duff, J. Wight. *A Literary History of Rome from the Origins to the Close of the Golden Age,* 3d ed. New York, 1960.
_____. *A Literary History of Rome in the Silver Age,* 2d ed. New York, 1960.
Frank, Tenney, ed. *An Economic Survey of Ancient Rome.* Baltimore, 1936-1940, 6 vols.

Garnsey, Peter. *Social Status and Legal Privilege in the Roman Empire.* Oxford, 1970.
Garzetti, Albino. *From Tiberius to the Antonines,* tr. by J. R. Foster. London, 1974.
Hammond, Mason. *The Antonine Monarchy.* Rome, 1959.
————. *The Augustan Principate.* Cambridge, Mass., 1933.
Heatley, N. R. *The Cult of Pax and the Templum Pacis,* dissertation, Austin, Texas, 1976.
Henderson, Bernard W. *Five Roman Emperors.* Cambridge, 1927.
Holmes, Thomas R. *The Architect of the Roman Empire.* Oxford, 1928, 1931, 2 vols.
Moretti, G. *Ara Pacis Augustae.* Rome, 1948.
Parker, Henry D. *The Roman Legions,* 2d ed. Cambridge, 1958.
Petit, Paul. *Pax Romana,* 2d ed., tr. by James Willis. Berkeley, 1976.
Rostovtzeff, Mikhail. *The Social and Economic History of the Roman Empire,* 2d ed. Oxford, 1957, 2 vols.
Scullard, H. H. *From the Gracchi to Nero.* London, 1959.
Sherwin-White, Adrian. *The Roman Citizenship.* Oxford, 1939.
Starr, Chester G. *The Roman Imperial Navy,* 2d ed. Cambridge, 1960.
Stevenson, George H. *Roman Provincial Administration,* 2d ed. Oxford, 1949.
Taylor, Lily R. *The Divinity of the Roman Emperor.* Middleton, Conn., 1931.
Waddy, Lawrence. *Pax Romana and World Peace.* London, 1950.
Zampaglione, Gerado. *The Idea of Peace in Antiquity.* North Bend, Ind., 1973.

The Hispanic-Roman Peace

Albertini, E. "The Latin West," in *Cambridge Ancient History,* vol. 11. Cambridge, 1936.
Altamira, Rafael. *A History of Spain,* tr. by Muna Lee. New York, 1949.
Bouchier, Edmund S. *Spain under the Roman Empire.* Oxford, 1914.
Blazquez, J. M. "Hispania desde el año 138 al 235," *Hispania,* 132 (1976) 5-87.
Chapman, Charles E. *A History of Spain.* Glencoe, Ill., 1918.
Jones, A. H. M. *The Later Roman Empire.* Norman, Okla., 1964, 2 vols.
Jones, R. F. J. "The Roman Military Occupation of Northwest Spain," *Journal of Roman Studies* 66 (1976) 45-66.
Livermore, Harold. *A History of Spain.* London, 1958.
McElderry, R. Knox. "Vespasian's Reconstruction of Spain," *Journal of Roman Studies* 8 (1918) 53-102.
Parker, H. M. D. *A History of the Roman World from A.D. 138 to 337.* London, 1935.
Payne, Stanley G. *A History of Spain and Portugal.* Madison, Wis., 1973.
Schulten, Adolf. "Hispania," in Pauly-Wissowa, *Realencyclopädie der klassischen Altertumswissenschaft.* Stuttgart, 1894.
Sutherland, C. H. V. *The Romans in Spain.* London, 1939.
West, Louis C. *Imperial Roman Spain: The Objects of Trade.* Oxford, 1929.
Wiseman, F. J. *Roman Spain.* London, 1956.

Index

abdication 83, 92
accountability 111
Achaea 94, 108
Achaean League 93
Achaemenes 72
Achaemenid Empire 9-11, 72-82, 120, 131, 136, 140, 142, 159, 166; *see also* Achaemenids
Achaemenid Peace 9-11, 72-82, 142; *see also* Achaemenid Empire; Achaemenids
Achaemenids 83, 110, 118-20, 123, 137, 144, 145, 160-5, 170, 171, 177; *see also* Achaemenid Empire
Acropolis 59, 61
Actium 108, 109, 122, 135
Adadnirari III 5
administration 70, 76, 78, 82, 85, 86, 89, 90, 97, 107, 110-14, 118-21, 125, 126, 138, 144-7, 167, 180, 184
"Admonitions of Impuwer" 23
Adonis 50
Adriatic 116
advancement 126, 179
Aegean Sea 56
Aegina 56, 69
aesthetics 167; *see also* art
affluence 70, 130, 149
Africa 8, 23, 50, 86, 90, 110, 128
after-life 42; *see also* immortality
aggression 95
agora 1
agrarian societies 131, 160
agriculture 1, 15, 77, 113, 117, 123, 126, 139, 149, 152, 173; *see also* farming
Agrippa 123, 135
Ahmose I 29-30, 92, 135, 136, 156
Ahura Mazda 79
Akhenaten 33-4, 41, 43-4, 47, 137, 139-40, 156, 161, 168, 170-1, 177
Akhetaton 14, 33, 34
Akkadian Empire 72
Alans 122, 129
Alcmaeonids 59, 64
Alexander III (the Great) 73, 79, 83, 87, 92, 149, 177, 179, 181
Alexandria 84, 86, 87, 88, 92, 108, 155, 164, 165
alienation 11, 163
aliens 137, 146, 153
alimenta 120
allegories 41
alliances 52, 53, 61, 69, 71, 72, 92, 95-6, 103-6, 173, 177, 179
alphabets 51-2, 164, 165
Alps 97
amalgamation 49
ambition 156, 157
Amenemhet I 16, 17, 27, 28, 30, 37, 136, 141, 145, 168
Amenemhet III 18-9, 24, 25, 139
Amenemhet IV 24
Amenhotpe I 30, 33, 34, 37, 42, 136, 141
Amenhotpe III 81, 138
Ammenemes *see* Amenemhet
Amorites 18
Amosis *see* Ahmose
amphitheaters 115

205

Amun Herihor 37
Amun Re 22, 32, 33, 39, 43, 161
Amyntas 83
anarchy 23, 29, 43, 109, 111, 116, 117, 128, 140
Anatolia see Asia Minor
ancient societies 168, 170, 184
Ancient World 1, 2, 6, 8-9, 129, 131, 133, 135, 137, 139, 145, 146, 148, 151, 153, 155, 156, 164, 165, 174, 175-80, 183, 187
Andronicus Livius 98
anger 3
annexation 95, 171
anthropomorphism 160
Antigonus I 83, 89
Antigonus Gonatas 89
Antioch 48
Antiochus III 89, 93, 96
Antonines 109, 111, 119, 120, 139; see also Hadrian; Trajan; Antoninus Pius; Marcus Aurelius
Antonius, Marcus (Mark Antony) 109, 135
Antoninus Pius 112, 113, 119
Apollonius of Perga 88
Apollonius Rhodius 87
Apophis I 24
appeasement 119, 168
appointments 21, 75
appreciation 187
Apulia 94, 102
aqueducts 98, 102, 115, 126, 139, 149
Aquileia 116
Ara Pacis 115
Arabia 14, 84, 86, 94, 108, 112, 171
Aradus 48, 49, 51
Arcadia 56
archaeological evidence 9
archery 3, 78, 80
arches 98, 115
Archimedes 88
architects 165
architecture 15, 40, 41, 68, 79, 98, 115, 116, 120, 121, 127, 163, 166, 185
archon 58, 59, 60, 147
areas 2, 4, 6, 10, 11, 13, 70, 72, 73, 75, 90, 91, 95, 109, 110, 118, 133, 137, 146, 151, 153, 183
Areopagus 143

Argos 56, 69
Arion of Lesbos 68
Aristarchus of Samos 88
aristocracy 27, 28, 30, 58, 59, 62, 97, 105
Armenia 108, 109, 112, 116, 171
armies 31, 34, 44, 45, 46, 54, 78, 81, 82, 89, 91, 96, 98, 100, 105, 106, 109-12, 116-22, 128, 129, 174
armor 18, 31, 59, 174
Arrian 92
arrogance 38
arrow volley techniques 181
art 1, 15, 22, 37, 38, 39, 50, 51, 55, 63, 68, 79, 87, 88, 92, 98, 115, 116, 127, 154, 163, 179, 185
Artaxerxes I 76
Artaxerxes II 78
artifacts 154, 164
artisans 154, 155; see also craftsmen
artists 164
Asia 18, 23, 25, 32, 33, 34, 35, 44, 65, 72, 77, 83, 92, 94, 96, 108, 122, 173
Asia Minor 9, 19, 32, 73, 110, 116
assassination 17, 63, 78, 80, 103, 116, 138, 139, 143, 177
assemblies 60, 61, 97, 100-3, 110
Assurnasirpal 51, 53
Assyria 51, 52, 53, 74, 76, 81
Assyrians 9, 49, 52, 54, 80, 131, 132, 158, 172, 173, 180
Astarte 50
astronomy 88
Astyages 73, 135
Aswan 14, 19, 26
Aten 33, 34
Athena 59, 61, 62, 160
Athenian Peace 9, 55-65; see also Athenians
Athenians 70, 106, 138, 143, 144, 146, 150, 151, 154, 155, 159, 164, 173, 175, 177
Athens 56, 57, 61, 62, 64, 69, 88, 132, 136, 140, 142, 143, 147, 148, 149, 156, 169, 178, 181
Atlantic Ocean 8, 94, 124
atmosphere 3, 11, 115, 163, 167
attack 92, 97, 174, 183
Attica 9, 56, 58, 71
attitudes 38, 105

Augustus 98, 107, 109, 110, 112, 118, 119, 123, 128, 135, 136, 141, 145, 166, 171
austerity 41, 101
authority 15, 17, 26, 27, 39, 71, 76, 130, 145, 147
autonomy 49, 53, 106, 132, 153, 183
auxiliary soldiers 112, 113
Avaris 14, 26
Ay 35

Baal 50, 53
Baalat 50
Babylon 25, 52, 74, 75
Babylonia 14, 25, 73, 76, 81, 154; *see also* Babylon
Bacchiads 135
backwaters 163
Baetica 74, 124, 125, 128
Bagoas 79
balance 22, 41, 71, 110, 130, 165, 173, 178, 180, 186
balance of power 71, 173
Balearic Island 124
Baltic Sea 8, 105
banishment 157
banks 86
barbarians 117, 120, 122, 177
barriers 57, 133, 183; *see also* mountains; deserts
barter 50
baths 115
battles 1, 47, 53, 69, 77-9, 89, 90, 109, 129, 143, 158, 172, 181
bawdy tales 41
beauty 41
Berber language 23
Bithynia 108
Black Sea 74, 78
"Blinding of Truth" 41
board and grapple techniques 70, 181
Boeotia 56
boorishness 165, 185
borders 29, 30, 47, 49, 58, 109, 112, 125, 132, 170
botany 88
boundaries 97, 131, 133
Braudel, Fernand 151
bread and circuses 101, 114, 120

bribery 168
bridges 98, 102, 114, 115, 126, 149
Britain 6, 109, 128, 170, 172
bronze 19, 55
brutality 75
Bruttium 94
buffer states 112
building 87, 92, 115, 125, 136, 138, 165, 166
buildings 31, 33, 41, 42, 44, 62, 98, 164
bureaucracy 30, 33, 34, 43, 76, 80, 85, 90, 110, 117
business 77, 161
Byblos 18, 26, 48, 49, 51
Byzantine Empire 129

Cadusia 75
Cadusians 74, 78-123
Caesar, Julius 109, 122, 123
Caesar, Octavian *see* Augustus
calendars 24
Callimachus 87
Cambyses II 73, 78
campaigns 116, 133, 170, 172
camps 167
Canaanites 47, 49
canals 19, 31, 77, 85, 87, 149
Cantabrians 122
capability 139
capitalization 148
Cappadocia 94
Caracalla 116
careers 110, 126
Caria 56
Carthage 1, 50, 93, 94, 96, 98, 108
Carthaginians 93, 127
Cases of Peace 9-130, 137, 144, 153, 158
cash crop farming 126
Caspian Sea 74, 78
casualties 59
Cato the Elder 98
cattle 31, 100
Caucasus Mountains 25, 74
caution 92, 186
cavalry 59, 77, 78, 100
"cedars of Lebanon" 50
censors 112
census 86, 111

centers 3, 87, 88, 130, 164, 185
central government 76, 81, 130
centralization 17, 18, 25, 30, 62, 70,
  71, 95, 107, 126, 129, 136, 144-7,
  178, 186
century 2, 4, 10
ceramics 127
Chalcidice 64
Chaldean Babylonia 52, 73, 153; see
  also Babylonia
challenge 163
change 64, 65, 82, 97, 100, 140, 145,
  147, 154, 175, 178, 180, 182, 186,
  187
character 123, 136, 137, 158, 183
Characterization of Peace 10, 16-24,
  30-6, 47-52, 67, 68, 75-9, 85-9, 96-
  101, 110-6, 123, 125-8
charisma 42, 91, 136
charm 156
checks 111
cheerfulness 154
children 114, 120
Christianity 114, 127, 161, 162
Cilicia 84, 108
Cimbri 105
cinnabar 127
Cisalpine Gaul 94, 96, 97
cities 49, 50, 53, 54, 57, 59, 86, 89,
  95, 100, 110, 113, 117, 123, 125,
  126, 127, 130, 144, 160, 173, 174
citizenship 50, 51, 57, 60, 62, 70,
  100, 103, 112, 125, 154, 155, 178,
  180, 185
city-states 70, 92, 104, 132, 153, 157,
  160, 174
civil service 30, 88, 111, 118
civil war 104, 106, 107, 109, 111,
  116, 117, 122, 137, 177
civility 117
civilization 8, 38, 55, 57, 65, 155,
  158, 159, 171, 185
class 58, 60-3, 88-91, 101, 110, 154,
  157, 184; \see also stratification
classical civilization 158-60, 162,
  167-9
classification 137, 159, 165, 176, 185
Claudius 111
clay 58
Cleisthenes 64
Cleomenes 64, 65

Cleopatra 1, 109
clergy 21, 28, 30-3, 43, 82, 86, 88, 99,
  155, 161, 168, 178
climate 11, 13, 58, 133, 183
coast 49, 61, 85, 89, 91, 97, 110, 125
codification 60, 114, 120, 139, 146
coherence 153
coinage 60, 77, 98, 101
collusion 76
colonies 50, 60, 65, 69, 102, 160, 171,
  173
colossalism 41, 115, 165, 185
Colosseum 115
Columella 127
combinations 184
comedy 98
commerce 15, 47, 50-4, 62, 68, 86,
  98, 101, 102, 109, 113, 118, 151,
  152; see also trade
commitment 171, 186, 187
Commodus 116, 119, 128, 177
common touch 136
communications 52, 81, 82, 102, 118,
  120, 140, 148, 151
competition 160
complacency 20, 181
complexity 187
compromise 168, 169, 185
concentration 101
conciliation 75, 80
confederacy 49
confederation 104
confidence 44, 155
confiscation 79
conflict 2, 3, 7, 10, 23, 58, 65, 75, 82,
  90-3, 97, 99, 112, 117, 118, 129,
  132, 134, 138, 140, 150, 152, 153,
  158-66, 171-6, 179, 183, 185
conformity 123
conjecture 154
conquerors 90, 91, 134, 135, 137,
  138, 146; see also conquest
conquest 53, 83, 100, 102, 138, 170,
  174, 175-82; see also conquerors
consciousness 140
conscription 18, 86, 100, 103
consistency 168
consolidators 28, 42, 64, 80, 83, 91,
  92, 95, 118, 135-41, 169, 183
conspiracy 78
Constantine 121, 128

constitutions 61, 97, 109
construction 31, 79, 102, 139, 149
consuls 96-8, 147
contemplation 169
"Contendings of Horus and Seth" 41
contiguous areas 2, 5, 11; *see also* areas
controversy 3, 6, 7
cooperation 58, 91
copper 19, 86, 127
Corcyra 48, 180
Córdoba 124
co-regency 17, 24, 27
Corinth 9, 56, 61, 66-71, 132, 133, 135, 140, 142, 144, 145, 147, 149, 150, 154, 156, 165, 169, 171, 178; *see also* Corinthians
Corinthian Peace 9, 66-71; *see also* Corinth
Corinthians 70, 71, 106, 138, 143, 151, 153, 159, 164, 173, 177, 180, 181; *see also* Corinth
Coriolanus 1
corruption 35, 75, 99, 168
Corsica 94, 108
cosmopolitanism 54, 92, 117, 120, 155, 159-61
cotton 86
Coudenhove-Kalergi, Richard 2
councils 49, 60
coups 61, 143
courage 79, 139
court 92
crafts 15, 22, 41, 51, 61, 68, 101, 128, 139, 154, 155, 164, 166, 185
creativity 1, 22, 41, 127, 163-9, 179, 185, 187
Crete 14, 19, 55, 84, 94, 108
crisis 102, 139, 166, 177, 183
criteria for peace 1-7, 10, 11, 121
criticism 87
Croesus 73
Ctesias 76
cults 75, 160
culture 9, 18, 40, 63, 68, 70, 82, 87, 88, 100, 102, 115, 120, 130, 153, 158
Cunaxa 74, 75
currencies 86, 117, 118
custom 88, 91, 105, 125-7
Cyaxares 73

Cyprus 9, 14, 19, 32, 48, 50, 52, 59, 84, 85, 108, 170
Cyrus II 73, 75, 80, 134, 135, 140

Dacia 6, 94, 108, 109, 112, 174
Dalmatia 94, 108
Damascus 14, 48, 74, 84
dams 85
danger 151
Danube River 74, 94, 108-12, 116
Darius I 73, 76, 82, 136, 141, 171
Darius III 79, 83, 139, 177
data 9
David 9, 51
Dead Sea 48
debt 60
decentralization 15, 17, 24, 25, 27, 43, 53, 65, 71, 122, 137, 139, 144-6, 156, 178, 184
decline 15, 16, 99, 113, 117, 128, 130, 148, 152, 165, 171, 180, 181, 186, 187
decorating 51
defeat 175-82
defense 18, 26, 45, 54, 69, 71, 80, 85, 89-92, 95, 98, 106, 112, 117, 118, 130, 167, 170, 174, 180, 181, 183, 186
deities 160
Delian League 69
delicacy 22, 25, 163
Delphi 56
Delphic oracle 64, 65
Demetrius 89
democracy 15, 21, 63, 97, 145
deportation 75
descriptive models 3
desert 13, 91, 133
destruction 169
deterioration 166
determination 177, 186
development 148
dexterity 64
didactic literature 23
Diocletian 121, 127, 137
Dionysius 68
diplomacy 18, 42, 49, 171, 173
discontent 91, 102
discouragement 113
discovering peace 1-7

disease 130
disintegration 21, 23, 25, 38, 103,
    129, 139, 140, 144, 156, 159, 181
display 149
dissatisfaction 103, 178, 180
distance 172, 174
distortion 41
distribution 91, 101, 126, 147-50,
    154, 157, 184
dithyramb 68
diversity 114, 161, 185
divine monarchs 15, 21, 22, 27, 32,
    87, 161
divorce 99
documentation 153
Domitian 112, 126
Dor 48
Dorians 55
Draco 59, 60, 146, 147
drainage 115, 139
drama 115, 164
drought 133
Drusus, M. Livius 104, 177
Duero River 124
dullness 165, 185
duration 4, 8-10, 58, 64, 73, 83,
    121, 129, 131, 185, 187
duty 99
dye 47, 50
dynamism 22, 24
dynasties 17, 146, 155, 172

Early Hispanic Phase 175-82
earthenware 127
Ebro River 124
Ecbatana 74
economies 9, 11, 21, 27-8, 44, 57, 59,
    77, 80, 85, 86, 91, 100, 101, 113,
    114, 117, 118, 123, 125, 127,
    130, 136, 148-52, 155, 180, 184,
    186
edicts 114, 120, 147
education 125
efficiency 82
Egypt 9, 13-5, 23, 36, 45, 47, 53, 74,
    82, 92, 94, 110, 108, 119, 133, 146,
    149, 150, 158, 160, 167, 168, 169,
    183, 185; see also Middle King-
    dom Peace; New Kingdom Peace;
    Ptolemaic Peace

Egyptian 75, 85, 88, 90, 91, 142, 143,
    147, 148, 155, 156, 158, 161, 163,
    172
Eighteenth Dynasty 29, 30, 41
Eirene 169
El 50
elaboration 115, 164, 165
Elam 72, 74, 75, 98
Elbe River 108, 112
elections 97, 100, 105, 110
elegance 41, 125
elephants 1, 89, 90, 181
elites 15, 27, 71, 78, 88, 101, 119,
    126, 129, 130, 144, 145, 146, 147,
    149, 154, 156, 161, 167, 168, 177,
    184, 186
el-Lisht 14, 16, 25-6, 28, 41
Emerita Augusta 124
emotion 23
emperors 79, 107, 109-11, 114, 118-
    20, 126, 127, 139, 160-1, 177
empires 4, 25, 52, 54, 72, 77, 82, 106,
    110-1, 118, 120, 126-9, 132, 133,
    144-5, 151, 153, 156, 159, 164, 168-
    74, 184
endowments 114
energy 177, 181, 186
enfranchisement 100, 104
engineering 98, 114, 115, 164
England 1, 7
engraving 79
Ennius 98
environment 11, 132, 155, 165, 169,
    183
epics 23, 164
Epicureanism 99
epigrams 115
Epirus 56
equality 3, 21, 90, 150, 154, 168
equestrian class 110-3, 130
Eratosthenes 88
Eshmun 50
essays 115
ethnicity 100, 155, 168, 178, 186
Etruria 94, 102
Etruscan 95
Eubaea 56
Euclid 88
euhemerization 134
eunuchs 79, 178
Euphrates River 8, 14, 18, 33, 73, 84

Europe 8-9, 109, 110, 122
Execration Texts 25
executions 75, 116
exile 64
expanding peace 2, 5
expansion 79, 141, 170, 180, 181, 186; *see also* expansive policies
expansive policies 6, 18, 32, 39, 43, 44, 52, 85, 92, 101, 102, 105, 112, 139, 170
expedience 76
export 113, 126
external conditions 7, 85, 89, 104, 109, 128, 131, 140, 170-4, 176, 180-1
external invasion 96, 132, 137, 175-82, 186

factions 61, 135, 175-82
families 97, 99, 110-3, 126, 143, 145, 160, 161
famine 130
fanaticism 52
fantasy 23
farmers 62, 100, 106, 147, 156, 180
farming 103, 113, 117, 120, 123, 126, 130-1, 150; *see also* agriculture
fear 1, 3, 41
federation 142, 144, 184
fellahin 86, 88, 89
festivals 59, 62, 101, 160
feudalism 26-7
finances 31, 42, 85, 109-12, 117
First Intermediate Period in Egypt 16, 20, 23, 28, 38, 41, 46
fishing 61, 86
Flaccus, Fulvius 104
Flavian 109, 115
Flavian-Antonine phase 137-8, 175-82
flax 86, 126
fleet 89, 91
flexibility 96, 114, 141, 147, 157, 187
floods 133
florescence 72
food 97, 100
forcefulness 24, 27, 81
foreboding 42
foreign 26, 33, 34, 45, 51, 58, 61-4, 68-9, 92-3, 132, 170-5, 179, 185,

187
foresight 136
formalism 22
forms 147
fortifications 26
fortresses 18
Forum of Augustus 115
foundation 80
founder 27, 42, 80, 91, 92, 118, 134-7, 140, 183
fragmentation *see* disintegration
France 172
franchise 104
Franco-British Peace 172
Franks 11, 128
freedmen 101, 110, 113, 117, 156
freedom 40, 53, 69, 95, 154, 167
Fregellae 94, 104
frontiers 45, 109, 112, 116, 117, 129, 132, 156, 172
fruits 86
funerary cults 21, 39, 40
future 141, 145

Gades 50, 124
Galba 125
Galicians 122
garrisons 76, 81, 109, 112, 120, 123, 125
Gaugamela 79
Gaul 94, 108, 110, 112, 113, 116, 123, 124, 128, 129, 174
Gaza 83, 84
generals 79, 83, 104, 109, 123, 128
generosity 123
geography 88, 89, 90, 97, 118, 123, 131, 133
Germania 94, 108, 112
Germanic tribes 105, 112, 116, 129
glory 141
goals 169
gods 127, 160
gold 19, 31, 86, 127
golden age 115
good will 3
government intervention 149, 152
governments 3, 5-6, 9-11, 20, 25, 27, 30-1, 42, 59, 62, 71, 72, 76-7, 82, 87, 97, 106, 107, 110, 111, 113, 142, 143, 147, 149, 150, 155, 161,

166, 168, 170, 174, 180, 181, 184-87
governors 122, 128, 129, 142, 146, 156, 173, 184
Gracchi 139, 145, 147
Gracchus, Gaius 104
Gracchus, Tiberius 102, 103
grace 41
grain 10, 31, 51, 86, 100, 101, 104, 113, 126, 130, 151, 155
grandeur 79
grandioseness 22, 33
grapes 58, 155
Great Mother 99
Greece 55, 58, 59, 72, 83, 96, 110, 130, 151, 171
Greeks 1, 55, 57, 59, 72, 80, 83, 85, 88-93, 98, 101, 114, 118, 127, 132, 145, 147, 153, 155, 156, 158, 160-1, 165, 167, 168, 170, 172, 173
growth 113, 117, 152, 159
Guadiana River 124
Guaganiela 74
guerrilla campaign 80, 123
Gulf of Corinth 69
Guti 72

Hadrian 6, 112, 114, 171, 188
Halys River 74
Hammurabi 18, 25, 76, 81
Hannibal 93, 95, 96, 103, 136
happiness 27, 42, 167
harbors 89, 91, 97
harem intrigue 79, 178
Haremhab 35, 39, 44, 64, 81, 137, 156, 161, 168
harmony 43, 105
harshness 63, 147, 154, 167, 168
Hatshepsut 31, 32, 34, 39, 156, 168
Hatti see Hittites
Health 115, 154
hegemony 49, 93, 96
Heliaea 60
Heliopolis 14, 21-2, 155
Hellenic culture 83, 115, 117, 159
Hellenistic culture 72, 86-8, 91, 97, 152, 164-5, 173
Heracleopolis 14, 16-7, 135
herders 77
hereditary offices 76, 111

Herodotus 68, 72
heroes 134, 135, 145
heterogeneity 161
hinterlands 5, 11
Hipparchus 88
Hippias 63, 64, 66, 177
Hiram the Great 51, 138
Hispanic Revival 137, 138, 175-82
Hispanic-Roman Peace 9-11, 122-30, 131-2, 137-8, 153, 159, 161, 166, 175-82; see also Roman Spain
Hispatis 124
historians 72, 92, 153, 167, 172
history 2, 8, 23, 43, 55, 64, 72, 98, 115, 118, 134, 140, 141, 153, 154, 164, 177
Hittites 14, 25, 32, 33, 34, 35, 42, 45, 47, 53, 172-3
homogeneity 70, 120, 145
honesty 50, 75, 118
honey 86
honor 65
hoplites 1, 59, 62, 119, 174
Horace 115
Hortensian Law 99
horticulture 131, 150
hospitals 115
hostages 62
housing 101
human 23
humanitarianism 20, 114, 154, 169
humanity 22, 76
humiliation 38
hunger 154
Hyksos 1, 24-5, 29-31, 135, 41-2

Iberall, Arthur 4
Iberian Peninsula 9, 125, 126, 127, 129, 122-3
ideals 51
ideas 161
ideologies 129
image 87
imagination 70, 154, 163, 167, 177
imitation 166
immortality 15, 21, 40, 154, 160, 167
immortals 78
imperialism 96
incompetence 25, 78, 111, 116, 119
incorporation 160

independence 47, 49, 53, 95, 160, 169
India 8, 73, 86
Indian Ocean 74
indifference 160
individualism 42, 57, 99, 134
Indus 74
industrial societies 8, 50, 139
industry 86, 101, 113, 126, 136
inequality 70, 91, 117, 149-50, 179;
  see also equality
infant sacrifice 50
infantry 59, 78
inflation 86, 117, 126
influence 65, 105, 132
inheritance 27, 86, 138, 145
initiative 76
innovation 40
inns 76
insight 177
instability 184
institutionalization 140
institutions 27-8, 62, 102
Instruction for Merikare 21, 23
integrity 63, 82
intelligence 63, 76, 81, 186
intensity 171
intention 141
interaction 148, 158, 185
interest rates 86
interior decoration 116
internal factors 11, 131, 180-1
internal rebellion 175-82, 186
interpower situations 171-4
interpretation 163
interrupted peace 2-5, 10-11, 109,
  111-2, 119, 123, 128
intervention 170, 174, 184
intransigence 103
intrigue 78-9, 143, 178
intrusiveness 147, 155
invasion 36, 49, 51, 52, 54, 69, 79,
  80, 83, 85, 89, 90, 92, 97, 109, 116,
  117, 122, 125, 128, 129, 137, 159,
  177, 181
investment 139, 149
involved societies 132
involvement 174, 183
Ionia 56
Ionian Sea 56
Iran 9, 72, 74; *see also* Persia
iron 77, 127

irrigation 11, 19, 76, 92, 139
Isagoras 64
Isin-Larsa Dynasty 18
island 47, 60
isolation 13, 26, 38, 54, 64, 65, 72,
  123, 131, 132, 133, 151, 173, 174,
  183, 186
Israel 9, 48, 51
Isthmian Games 68
Isthmus 68, 71, 133
Isthmus of Corinth 68
Italy 9, 93, 94, 96, 98, 101-4, 106,
  108, 110, 112, 128, 130, 133, 178
ivory 86
iwntyw 29

Jaxartes 74
jealousy 63
Jerusalem 14, 48, 74, 84, 112
Jesus 164, 167
jewelry 22, 79
Jews 47, 51, 89, 114, 147
Jordan River 48
journeys 151
Judah 48, 51
Judea 94, 108, 109
judgment 40, 136
judges *see* judiciary
judicial review 114
judiciary 17, 27-8, 31, 35, 60, 77, 89,
  136, 147
Julianus, Salvius 114
Julio-Claudian Phrase 111, 113, 175-
  82
jungle 133
justice 17, 20-1, 35, 61, 62, 81, 82,
  89, 147, 154, 168, 180, 184, 186,
  187
Juvenal 115

Kadesh 14, 32, 35, 48, 172
Karnak Stela 34
Kassites 25, 72
Kavolis Vytautas 166
kingship *see* monarchy
Kissinger, Henry 3
Kition 48, 50
knights 110
knowledge 146

koine eirene 169

labor 51, 88, 101, 126, 147, 156
Lake Moeris 14, 87
Lake Urnia 74
land 13, 19, 27-8, 30, 49, 57, 58, 60-
  2, 68, 86-92, 99-103, 106, 110, 113,
  117, 118, 148, 149, 150, 154-5, 156-
  7, 180
land reform 103, 156
landed gentry 27-8, 30, 86, 110, 154-
  5
landowners 100, 103, 106; *see also*
  landed gentry
language 2, 22-3, 41, 59, 88, 98, 118,
  125
Latin 98, 102-3, 118
Latin Confederation 95, 97, 99, 106
Latium 94, 95
law 60, 76, 81, 82, 98, 102-4, 114,
  120, 121, 126, 139, 146, 147, 168,
  184, 185
law code 80, 184; *see also* law
lead 127
leadership 25, 28, 37, 42, 43, 44, 49,
  61, 62, 63, 71, 75, 79, 81, 83, 85,
  87, 90-2, 100, 104, 109, 118, 134-
  48, 154, 165-71, 175-87
legions 1, 6, 96, 100, 112, 119, 123,
  125
legislation 110
leisure 136
levant 9, 18, 151
libraries 15, 87, 92, 114
Libya 15, 17, 29-30, 36-7, 45, 73-4,
  94, 108
life 9, 39, 101, 131, 144, 153, 154,
  155, 156, 167, 184
Lili 52
Linear A and B Scripts 55
Linen 19
liquidation 171
literature 20-4, 38-42, 51, 59, 92, 115,
  120, 121, 127, 163-5, 169, 185
litigation 89
Livy 115
location 131, 132, 151, 152
loftiness 168
logic 180
love 3

loyalty 27, 30, 76, 95, 106, 110, 113,
  130, 156
Lucan 115, 127
luck 64, 156, 176
Lullubi 72
Luristan Mountains 72, 74
Lusitania 124-5, 128
luxuries 60, 62, 67, 119, 136
Lydia 56, 75

ma'at 20-1, 154
Macedonia 74, 85, 87, 89, 91, 93-4,
  108, 174
Macedonian phalanx 1, 80, 181; *see
  also* Phalanx
Macedonian Wars 93
Magabyzus 76
Magas 89
magistrates 97, 98, 105, 110, 111; *see
  also* judiciary
magnificence 79
magnificent monarch 81, 92, 118,
  138, 139
Magnus Maxiumus 127
managers 135
mannerism 163
manufacturing 60, 62, 113, 152
Marathon 56, 62
marble 58
Marcus Aurelius 116, 117, 118, 139,
  166, 177
maritime societies 150, 154, 155
Marius 104, 105
markets 50, 101, 165
Marsic War 104
Martial 115, 127
martyrs 127
mass production 164
massiveness 41, 163, 166; *see also*
  colossalism
materialism 115
Maternus 128
mathematics 24, 87, 88
Mauretania 94, 108, 124
Mazaces 83, 135
measurement 11, 77, 155
meddlesomeness 147, 155
Medes 73, 76
medicine 24, 88
Medinet el Fayyum 14, 18, 87

meditations 166
Mediterranean Sea 8, 13, 14, 25, 36, 48, 55, 58, 66, 67, 71, 83, 84, 85, 89, 91, 93, 96, 109, 124, 125, 133, 151, 183
Medjay 44
Megacles 59, 69
Megalomania 41
Megara 56, 59, 69
Megiddo 14, 32
Mela 127
melancholy 23, 167
Melquart 50
memory 154
Memphis 14, 15-6, 26, 74, 83, 84, 87
Mentuhotpe II 16, 28, 42, 65, 135
mercantile 160
mercenaries 51, 61, 63, 83, 85, 86, 88-90, 104-6, 119, 174
merchants 54, 60, 67, 69, 77, 82, 90, 139, 155, 168
mercury 127
Merenptah 36, 39, 139, 177
mergers 162, 168
merit 76
Mesopotamia 8, 9, 14, 18, 22, 47, 59, 72, 73, 79, 84, 108, 109, 112, 129, 158, 160, 161, 164, 167, 169, 171
Messenia 56-7, 71
metals 19, 77, 127; *see also* copper; iron; tin; gold; etc.
metalware 127
middle class 110, 113, 114, 117; *see also* stratification
Middle Kingdom Peace 9-10, 13-30, 38-42, 92, 131-2, 136-9, 143-6, 149-50, 154-5, 156, 159, 167-72, 175-8
middlemen 62, 173
migration 67, 100-1
mildness 154, 167, 168, 184, 185
Miletus 68
military affairs 17-9, 27-32, 69, 75, 85, 90, 95, 96, 100, 102, 105, 109-10, 112, 119, 120, 126, 130, 133-5, 138-40, 143, 144, 151, 159, 163, 163-70, 173, 178, 181, 186-7
militias 17-8, 100, 103, 117, 174, 179
mining 19, 86, 126, 127
Minoans 55
misfortune 177
Mitanni 14, 32, 33, 34

mobility 113, 156, 157, 174
models 3, 26-7, 107, 121, 166
moderation 61, 149
modification 147
Moeris, Lake 14, 18
momentum 78
monarchy 15, 20, 22-3, 25, 27-8, 30, 33-5, 38, 39, 40-2, 45, 49-50, 57, 75-7, 81, 85, 86, 97, 118, 142-4, 160, 168, 184; *see* emperors
money 86
monopolies 86
monotheism 75
Mont of Hermonthis 21
monuments 118
Moors 128
mopping-up 134
moralities 3
mosaics 127, 164
Moses 9
Moslems 122
mountains 57, 58, 59, 65, 97, 125, 133
multipower situation 64
municipal spirit 126-30
municipia 123
museums 87
music 185
Mycenaean Society 47, 55
Mysia 56
mystery cults 114
mythology 23, 160

Nabonidus 73
Naenius 98
Narbonensis 108
nationalism 19-20, 28, 40, 113
nationalities 76, 168
naturalism 22, 41, 163
navies 51, 54, 68, 71, 85, 89, 173, 174, 181
Neferhopte I 26
Neferhopte III 26
Nefertari 41
negotiation 180
neighbors 186
nepotism 76
neurosis 39, 147
New Carthage 124
New Kingdom Peace 9-11, 24, 29-45,

76, 92, 120, 137, 138, 139, 140,
143, 144, 145, 148, 151, 152, 154,
155, 156, 158, 159, 163, 164,
165, 173, 174, 175-82
Nile River 8-9, 13-9, 25, 29, 77, 83-5,
87, 91, 133, 151, 169, 170
Nineteenth Dynasty 35, 40
nobility 59, 60, 61, 63, 64, 70, 78,
185; *see* landed gentry
nomads 18, 25, 29, 77, 177
nomarchs 15-7, 25, 28
nomes 16-7
nonviolence 64
Noricum 116
norm 168
normality 131, 183, 185
normative models 3
nuances 141
Nubia 29, 32, 37, 174
Numantia 124
Numidia 94, 108

obedience 81, 91
obscurity 64
obstacles 90
Ochus 80, 81, 139, 177
Octavius, Marcus 103
offense 45, 54, 106
offices 97, 110
officials 76, 85, 155
oil 19, 51, 60, 86, 113
Old Kingdom 15-9, 22-8, 31, 38, 39,
47, 144, 163
oligarchies 49, 54, 57, 67, 97, 101,
142, 143, 144, 149, 178, 184
olives 58, 100, 126
Olympia 67
openness 178
opportunities 140, 148, 154-56
opposition 126
oppression 147, 154, 180
optimism 38, 91, 155
oracles 160
oratory 98
order 79, 174
organization 80, 95, 118, 123, 130,
135, 137, 177
Origins of Peace 10, 16-8, 27, 29-30,
57-8, 66-7, 70, 73-5, 83, 85, 93, 95-
6, 107, 109-11, 122-3, 134, 137,

175-82
Oróntes River 14, 35, 48
Orosius 128
Osiris 21
ostentation 101
outlook 160, 163-9, 185
overreaching 92, 181, 186
Ovid 115
Oxus River 74

pacification 123
painting 22, 27, 40, 115, 127, 165,
185, 198
palaces 78-9
Palestine 9, 14, 18-9, 26, 32, 35, 53,
73
Pallene 62
Panaetius 99
Panathenaic festival 62
Pa Nene 56
Panhellenic festivals 68
Pannonia 94, 108, 116
pantheon 99
papyrus 19, 24, 86
parables 164
Paraetonium 84
paranoin 25, 63
parcel post 87
Parsa 72, 73
Parthian Empire 6, 74, 108-9, 116,
153
particularism 58
parties 61
patrician 99
patron 92
patterns 65, 71, 91, 92, 131, 138, 155,
158, 161, 165-6, 169, 185
Pax Romana 1, 4, 9-11, 90, 108-21,
122, 136, 137, 138, 142, 146, 164,
166, 169, 175-82; *see also* Roman
Empire
Peace
(and) agriculture 1
(and) anger 3
appreciation of 186-7
area of 2, 4, 6, 10
(and) art 1, 164
(and) atmosphere 3
awareness of 107
(as) background 2

(*peace, cont.*)

(as) cause of war 179

causes of 7

(and) commerce 66

(and) conflict 2-3, 7

(in) contiguous areas 2-3, 4-5, 11

controversy about criteria 3, 6-7

(as) creation 1

(and) creativity 1

Cretan 55

(and) culture 9

data on 9

dating 8-9

(and) decentralization 144

definition of 2-3

(as) deity 169

disagreement about 2

discovering 1-7

duration of 66, 183

(and) economies 11

(and) environment 11

(and) equality 3

expanding 2, 5

(and) expansive policies 6

expectation of 152

external 128

(and) external conflict 7, 11

(as) firmament 2

(on) frequency curve 4

(and) government 3, 5-6, 9

(and) hinterlands 5, 11

(as) human achievement 8

interpower 75, 172

interrupted 2-3, 4-5, 10-11, 34

(and) language 2

(and) law 81, 146

(and) literature 1

(and) love 3

maintenance of 26, 31, 54, 61, 92, 96, 98, 138, 139

measurement of 11

(and) memory 179

normality of 131, 151, 169, 183

perception of 1

periods of 8-11

phases of 159

(and) philosophy 1

physical conflict 2

plural for 2

(as) policy 141, 184

(*peace, cont.*)

(as) priority 181

(and) quality of life 9

recurrence of 169

(and) religion 39

(and) space 2

study of 3, 7

(and) succession 17, 81

(and) threats 3

(and) time 2

(and) trade 1

types 63

ubiquity of 131

universals 8

peace: *see also* characterizations of peace; origins of peace; terminations of peace; reflections on peace

peaceful societies 3, 5-6, 9-10, 131, 170, 174

peacemakers 7, 147

pearls 86

peasants 59-77, 88-91, 131, 139, 150, 154-6, 168, 174, 184

peculation 179

pediment 68

Peisistratus 61, 62, 64, 67, 147, 149, 156, 160, 164

Peloponnesian Wars 66, 69, 180; *see also* Peloponnesus

Peloponnesus 56, 66, 69, 71, 180

Pelusium 83, 84

penalties 167

peninsula 122, 133, 178

people 111

perception 141, 149, 153, 154, 163, 179, 180, 182

Perdiddas 89

Periander 67, 68, 69, 70, 136, 164

Pericles 64

peripheral locations 129, 132, 172

Persepolis 74, 79, 80, 82

Persia 1, 11, 52, 59, 63, 68, 71-2, 74-5, 83, 119, 136, 138, 140, 143, 145, 146, 148, 149, 158-61, 168, 177, 179; *see also* Achaememid Peace; Achaememid Empire

Persian Gulf 73-4

Persians 71, 76, 91, 112, 118, 122

Persis (Fars) 72

persistance 183

Persius 115
pessimism 23, 167
Petronius 115
phalanx 1, 80
pharaohs 15, 30, 31, 45, 85, 88, 91,
    144, 147, 161
phases 175-82, 185
philanthropy 114
Philip V of Macedon 80, 96
Philistines 47, 48, 51
philosophy and peace 23, 40, 44, 87,
    88, 99, 115, 164, 165, 166, 169, 185
Phoenicia 82, 136, 140, 142, 143,
    149, 161, 168; see Phoenician
    Peace
Phoenician Peace 9-11, 47-54, 65,
    128, 131, 133, 137-8, 144, 147, 150,
    153-9, 165, 167, 172, 173, 175, 180
Phoenicians 47, 49, 51, 65, 92, 106,
    127, 128, 137, 151, 164, 169, 177,
    179; see also Phoenicia; Phoe-
    nician Peace
Phrygian goddess 99
physics 88
pictures 163
piracy 50, 152
planning 141, 148, 184
Plautus 98
pleasantness 154, 155
plebeian 99
Pliny 115
poetry 68, 87, 98, 115, 164
police 31, 44, 76, 93, 174
policies 181, 186, 187
polis 57
politics 30, 33, 41, 42, 57, 59-60, 64,
    153, 180, 186
polities 59, 60, 102, 126, 130, 139,
    147, 152, 165, 168, 183
Polybius 97, 98, 99
polytheism 75, 79, 160-1
Pompeii 116
Pomponius 127
Pontus 108
popularity 63, 67, 145, 147, 184
population 13, 76, 86, 100, 101, 103,
    109, 113, 117, 128, 130, 150, 167,
    183
portraiture 98
Portus Cale 124
Poseidon 68

postal service 76, 85, 87
potboilers 165
pottery 19, 50, 61, 63, 68, 164
poverty 60, 61, 63, 68, 70, 89, 91,
    101-3, 114, 150, 151, 156
power 15-7, 22, 27, 30, 32, 33, 42-3,
    54, 60-1, 63, 65-6, 69-71, 82, 97,
    100, 104, 109, 117-8, 129-33, 138,
    141, 143-5, 147, 156, 167, 172-3,
    178, 180
Praetorian Guard 111, 112, 116
praetors 96, 98, 100, 102, 104, 147
pragmatism 50, 51, 114-5, 137, 139,
    160-1, 167, 168, 170, 183, 185
prayers 23
precipitating incidents 176, 178, 186
predictability 186
preemptive defense 6, 39, 92, 106,
    170, 174
preservation 23-4
prestige 32, 33, 65, 97, 141, 145, 147
prices 77
priests see clergy
princeps 145
principate 109, 111
principles 168
Priscillian 127
privileges 88, 95, 126, 178
procurators 111
production 100, 101, 103, 117, 126,
    127, 130, 148-9, 151, 152, 180
professions 23
propaganda 23
Propertius 115
property 21, 155, 157
prosperity 20, 27-28, 32, 34, 38, 43,
    49, 63, 66, 67, 86, 109, 113, 114,
    116, 123, 125, 126, 148, 152, 154,
    164, 180, 184
protection 95
provinces 76, 105, 110, 111, 112,
    113, 114, 116, 118, 122, 125, 129-
    30, 145
provincial autonomy 15, 17, 27, 52-
    3, 81, 95, 109, 118, 120, 126, 129,
    142, 144, 147-50, 156, 167-8, 184
prudence 136, 137, 170, 171, 174,
    186
Psammetichus 67
psyche 40
Ptolemaic Dynasty 86, 87, 88, 91,
    141

Ptolemaic Empire 132, 135, 140, 142, 147, 154, 156, 173, 178
Ptolemaic Peace 82-92, 137, 144, 148, 149, 150, 151, 159, 171, 174, 175, 181
Ptolemies 119, 145, 160, 168, 173
Ptolemy I Soter 83, 85, 87, 92, 136, 170
Ptolemy II Philadelphus 85, 87
Ptolemy III Euergetes 85
Ptolemy IV Philopator 89-90, 92, 139, 177
public welfare 120
public works 43, 87, 109, 114-5
Punic Wars 90, 93, 95-100, 125
punishment 21, 81, 157
pursuit 174
Pyrenees Mountains 123-4

quagmire 171
quality 163, 166
quantity 165
quartet 155
Quigley, Carroll 155
Quintilian 127, 155

races 155
Raetia 94
raids 125, 128, 130, 180
Ramesses I 35
Ramesses II 35, 41, 42, 139
Ramesses III 36, 37, 42, 45, 139, 177
Ramessid Period 35-7, 40-2, 44, 45, 137-8, 163, 166, 175-82
Ramessid Restoration 175-82
ramming techniques 70, 181
Raphia 84, 89, 90, 156, 172, 181
ratification 110
rationalists 3
rationality 168
raw materials 50, 113
Re 21-2, 161
realism 3, 19, 22, 41, 98, 115, 141, 164
reason 169
rebellion 35, 47, 57, 58, 64, 70, 75, 76, 81, 88, 90, 92, 95, 96, 102, 104, 109, 111, 112, 113, 122, 125, 129, 130, 159, 170, 174, 177, 181

Recapitulation 183-7
reconstitution 27, 137, 183
recruitment 89
recurrence 168, 169
Red Sea 14, 84, 86, 87, 94
reevaluation 134
reflections on peace 10, 26-8, 37-46, 53-4, 64-5, 70-1, 80-2, 105-6, 190-2, 118-21, 129-30
reform 34, 39, 42, 61, 64, 81-2, 104, 110, 112, 118, 137, 139, 140, 147, 156, 168, 171
regional control *see* provincial autonomy
relationships 106, 153, 169, 179
relief work 79
reliefs 164
religion 15, 21-2, 38, 41, 44, 50, 52, 53, 54, 57, 58, 59, 62, 65, 67, 70, 75, 79, 87, 88, 99, 105, 114, 115, 121, 122, 127, 154, 158-62, 168, 179, 185, 187
remoteness 65, 129, 131, 132
reorganization 140
repression 63
republics 110, 113, 142, 145, 184
requisitions 113, 130
resistance 97
resources 117, 151, 170
responsibility 99
restorations 35, 64, 112, 137, 161
retaliation 170
retirement 44
revenue 110
rhetoric 21
Rhind Papyrus 24
Rhine River 94, 109, 110, 111, 112, 171
rights 90, 95, 154
rigidity 155, 157, 165, 167
rigor 81
risk 174
rituals 99, 127
rivers 97, 126
roads 76, 77, 85, 87, 102, 114, 115, 123, 126, 138, 149, 151
roles 134
Roman 1, 6, 93, 96, 98, 117, 125, 126, 127, 128, 131, 144, 146, 147, 148, 149, 153, 155, 159, 165, 170, 171, 178

Roman Empire 72, 118, 137, 139, 140, 143, 149, 159, 179; *see also* Pax Romana
Roman Republic 6, 9, 132, 138-40, 142, 143, 145, 149, 150, 151, 156, 160, 171, 174-5, 180; *see also* Roman Republican Peace
Roman Republican Peace 9, 10, 89, 93-107, 136, 144
romance 23
romanization 97, 102, 117, 125, 126, 127, 129, 153
Romans 118, 120, 130, 158, 160, 161, 170, 179
Rome 1, 93, 95, 101, 108, 114, 128, 130, 155, 168
Rostovtzeff, Mikhail 90
Rubicon 1
rural 89, 99, 100, 117, 154

Saigon 6
saintliness 168, 170
Saite, Egypt 11
Salamis 1, 48, 56, 60, 78
Salmantica 124
salt 86
sanctuary 91
Sardes 74
Sardinia 94, 108
Sarmatia 108
Sassanid Empire 153, 161
satire 23, 41, 42, 115, 164
satraps 76, 77, 83, 145, 149, 156, 167
Scipio Aemilianus 103
Scipio Africanus 6-7, 96, 135
scribes 23-4
sculpture 22, 24, 27, 98, 115, 127, 165-6, 185
Scythians 78, 61, 123, 171, 174
sea 65, 89, 97, 125, 129, 133, 151, 170, 174
Sea Peoples 30, 37, 49, 55
Second Intermediate Period in Egypt 25, 29-30, 38, 46
secularization 115
security 39, 47, 89, 95, 123, 170
segregation 88, 156, 168, 180
Seleucid Empire 84-5, 89, 93-6, 173-4
Seleucus 83
self-confidence 40

self-control 23
self-interest 105
selfishness 99, 168, 185
self-sufficiency 60
Semitic 23, 25, 47, 50
Senate, Roman 97, 103, 104, 105, 109, 110, 111, 112, 118, 125, 130, 136, 143, 145
Seneca 115, 127
Sennacherib 52
sense of the situation 136, 140, 141, 142, 187
Senwosret I 17, 45, 136, 139
Senwosret III 17-8, 24, 25, 27, 81, 139, 170, 177
Serapis 88
serfs 86, 150
seriousness 23, 61, 67
serpents 23
servants 18
Sesostris *see* Senwosret
settings 87, 131, 132, 171
Sety I 35, 42, 47
Sety II 36
severity 123
Severus, Alexander 116
Severus, Septimus 116-8, 120
Shakespeare, William vii, 7
Shalmaneser III 51
Shalmaneser V 52
Sharuhen 14
sheep 100
shepherd 61
shipping 67, 139
Sibylline Books 99
Sicily 50, 98, 100, 102, 108
Sidon 48-50, 52, 53, 84, 169
sieges 52, 53, 56, 69
silver 19, 31, 58, 127
Silver Age 127, 115, 164, 166
simplicity 163
Sinai Desert 13, 15, 19, 89
situations 136-7, 140, 144, 146, 165, 169, 171-5, 179, 184, 186-7
Siwa 84
size 71, 131, 142, 160, 164, 165, 174, 183
slaves 67, 68, 70, 77-86, 88, 100, 101, 102, 105-6, 117, 150, 154, 155, 156, 185
Sobekhopte IV 26

Sobeknefur 24
Sobriety 136
social change 41, 62; *see also* change
social concern 99
social mobility 113, 145, 156, 185;
    see also mobility
social spirit 114
Sogdinan 74, 75, 79
soldiers 97, 101, 109, 117, 120, 174;
    see also armies
Solomon 9, 51
Solon 60, 61, 62, 63, 64, 119, 146-7,
    149, 156, 164
Somali Coast 14, 19
sources 49, 163
sovereignty 69, 144-5; *see also*
    authority
space *see* area
Spain 50, 93, 94, 96, 108, 110, 113,
    122, 125, 127-30, 133, 136, 137,
    142, 143, 150, 151, 152, 153, 170,
    172, 173, 174
Sparta 57, 64, 65, 68, 69, 71, 169
Spartacus 102
spears 59
specialization 151, 184
spices 86
spirit 114, 154
spoils 95
stability 20, 31, 36, 38, 49, 72, 78, 80,
    96, 98, 101, 102, 106, 107, 109,
    112, 113, 120, 125, 129, 131, 136,
    138, 142, 144, 147, 149, 174, 186
stagnation 40
standardization 77
standing army 78, 112
state ownership 85
state spending 139
states 157, 169, 171, 172
status quo 100
stewards 155
Stilicho 128
Stoicism 99, 114
stone 19, 50
stories 23, 41-2
storms 133, 151
strategy 80
stratification 62, 77, 85, 88, 91, 99,
    144, 145, 155, 156, 157, 168
strikes 2, 88, 91
structure 88, 110, 126, 135, 141, 142,

157, 183, 187
style 18, 22, 51, 87, 123, 126, 127,
    185
stylization 163
subcultures 158
subjects 186
subtlety 42, 140
success 139, 187
succession 17, 27, 31, 35, 50, 63, 75,
    78, 81, 85, 88, 90, 92, 109, 110,
    111, 116, 117, 118, 119, 122, 137-9,
    143, 145, 147, 173, 175, 184
Suevi 122, 128-9
Suppililiumas 33
supplier 78
suppression 174
Suppression of Amenhotpe 37, 40
Susa 74, 79, 155
suzerainty 54, 57
Switzerland 4
syllabary 51
symbol 107
synoikismos 58
Syracuse 67
Syria 9, 11, 14, 15, 18, 19, 26, 32, 34,
    35, 36, 47, 52, 53, 73-4, 82, 85, 89,
    92, 94, 108, 109, 110, 116, 129,
    171, 173
Syriac Civilization 159
systems 95, 110, 114, 117, 126, 138,
    139, 143, 147, 153, 168, 174

Tacitus 115
tactics 31, 59, 140
Tagus River 124
Tanasses 48, 50
tar baby 172
Tarn, W.W. 85
Tarrace 124, 128
Tarraconesis 124, 125, 128
taxation 17, 31, 42, 61, 62, 63, 81,
    82, 86, 88, 101, 111, 117, 118, 127-
    8, 139, 148-50, 180
techniques 22, 31, 70, 80, 181, 186
Tell el-Amarna 33
temperament 54, 118
temperance 82
temple of Janus 107
temples 50, 87-8, 91, 98, 115, 160

temporizing 141
tenants 113-4, 116-7, 149
Terence 98
terminations 24-6, 27, 36-7, 43, 52-3, 58, 63-4, 69-70, 79-80, 89-90, 102-5, 116-7, 128-9, 139, 144, 148-9
Teutones 105
textiles 31
Theagenes 59
theaters 115
Thebes (Egypt) 14, 16-7, 22, 23, 29, 33, 36, 37, 84, 92, 135
Thebes (Greece) 56, 63, 64
Theocritus 87
Theodosius I 121
Thessaly 56, 64-5
thetes 60
Thirteenth Dynasty 18, 24, 25
Thrace 80, 94
Threats 3, 89, 172
Thutmose I 42
Thutmose II 31
Thutmose III 31-2, 42
Thutmose IV 33, 41
Thutmosid phase 30-5, 40-1, 138-9, 175, 177, 181
Thutmosis see Thutmose
Tiglath Pileser III 52
Tigris River 8, 14, 18, 74, 84
Timber 19, 32, 47, 50, 51, 86
time 2, 4, 8-9, 10; see also duration
"times of troubles" 159
tin 19, 127
Tingis 124
tolerance 3, 52, 54, 75-6, 79, 81, 99, 154, 159-61, 167-8, 183-7
Toletum 124
tortures 75
totalitarianism 155
toughness 139
touring 132
towns 47, 54, 95, 125, 127, 128, 130
Toynbee, Arnold J. 158-9, 168, 171
trade 1, 18-9, 25, 32, 33, 47, 50, 52, 54, 60, 61, 62, 66, 67, 68, 69, 77, 85-7, 90, 95, 101, 113, 118, 125, 129, 130, 132, 149-51, 156-7, 161, 167, 170, 173, 180, 184; see also commerce
trade routes 87, 170, 180
traditions 98, 103, 105-6

tragedy 62, 98
traitors 75
Trajan 6-7, 115, 139, 170, 171
transformations 147, 174, 186; see also change
transportation 76, 81, 118, 123, 151
travel 76, 80, 102, 148, 151, 154, 158, 185
treachery 167, 168, 185
treasure 79
tribes 99
tribune 102, 103, 104
tribute 32, 51, 52, 53, 54, 95, 173
trigonometry 88
Troy 1
trust 58
tunnels 114
Tura 14, 19
Tutankhamun 34, 35
Twelfth Dynasty 16-26, 161
Twentieth Dynasty 30, 36, 43
types 136, 137
tyrants 58, 59, 61, 62, 63, 64, 66, 67, 68, 70, 142-5, 173, 178, 184
Tyre 14, 49, 51, 52, 53, 84, 138, 169

ubiquitousness 168
Ugarit 48
understanding 169, 184
unemployment 100, 109, 114, 150; see also employment
unification 58, 65, 97, 102, 107, 147
uniformity 147
United Nations 163
United States 6-7
unity 79, 82, 90, 95, 96, 106, 113-4, 126, 130, 163, 169, 175
universals 8, 139
urban migration 67, 100-1
urban poor 68, 101-3, 106
urbanites 154, 160
urbanization 117, 149
Utica 50

Valentia 124
values 99, 105, 163, 168, 169
vandals 122-3, 128-9
variety 139, 176, 187
vase painting 68

vengefulness 75
Vergil 115
Vespasian 109, 111, 115, 117-8, 120, 125, 137
vested interests 80, 106
Vesuvius 116
victory 181
Vietnam 6-7
vigor 166
villages 85, 126
violence 2, 91, 102-6, 137, 146
virtuosity 22
Visigoths 122, 128
visionary 185
visions 139
vitality 1, 22, 27, 43, 69-70, 128, 144, 163, 166
viziers 17, 25-8, 31-2, 144, 178

wages 88
walls 6, 57, 69, 171, 173
war 1-3, 8-9, 11, 57-9, 65, 69, 71-3, 83, 85, 93, 95, 98, 104, 107, 109, 114, 116, 122, 129, 131-2, 152, 169, 177-8, 183
warriors 23, 134
waterways 149, 151; *see also* canals; rivers; seas
weakness 181, 186
wealth 43, 50, 53, 54, 60, 61, 67, 77, 86, 91, 100-1, 113, 118, 125-30, 145 148-51, 155-6, 161, 173
weapons 18, 40, 59, 77, 97
weights 77
Wesson, Robert G. 1
Western civilization 8, 72, 107, 129, 146, 163, 169
wheat 58, 60, 86
Wight, Martin 3, 6
Wilson, John 20
wine 19, 86, 113, 126
withdrawal 92, 141, 170, 171, 181, 186
women 76, 79
working class 62
World Federalists 3
world views 40, 163, 167, 168
worldliness 167, 168
worldsaving 170
writers 164

Xenophon 75
Xerxes 78, 118, 138, 170
Xois 26

yeoman 101

Zagros Mountains 72, 74
Zama 93-4, 135
zoology 88
Zoroastrians 79, 161